HANDBOOKS

DALLAS & FORT WORTH

JONANNA WIDNER

Contents

Maps

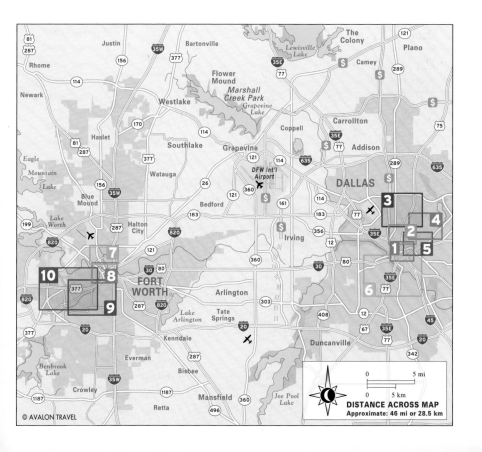

DISTANCE ACROSS MAP
Approximate: 46 mi or 28.5 km

© AVALON TRAVEL

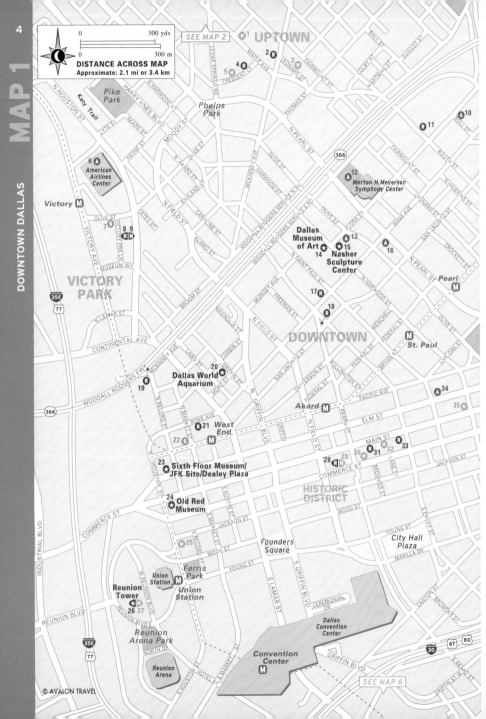

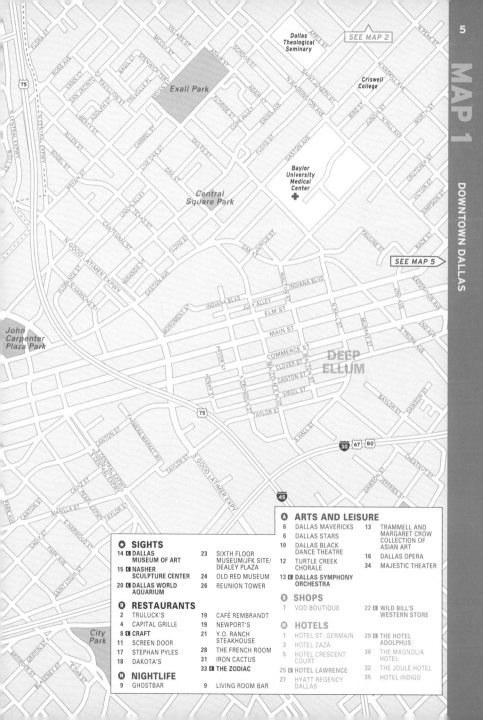

SEE MAP 2

SEE MAP 5

☉ SIGHTS

14 ℂ DALLAS MUSEUM OF ART
15 ℂ NASHER SCULPTURE CENTER
20 ℂ DALLAS WORLD AQUARIUM
23 SIXTH FLOOR MUSEUM/JFK SITE/ DEALEY PLAZA
24 OLD RED MUSEUM
26 REUNION TOWER

ℝ RESTAURANTS

2 TRULUCK'S
4 CAPITAL GRILLE
8 ℂ CRAFT
11 SCREEN DOOR
17 STEPHAN PYLES
18 DAKOTA'S
19 CAFÉ REMBRANDT
19 NEWPORT'S
21 Y.O. RANCH STEAKHOUSE
28 THE FRENCH ROOM
31 IRON CACTUS
33 ℂ THE ZODIAC

ℕ NIGHTLIFE

9 GHOSTBAR
9 LIVING ROOM BAR

◭ ARTS AND LEISURE

6 DALLAS MAVERICKS
6 DALLAS STARS
10 DALLAS BLACK DANCE THEATRE
12 TURTLE CREEK CHORALE
13 ℂ DALLAS SYMPHONY ORCHESTRA
13 TRAMMELL AND MARGARET CROW COLLECTION OF ASIAN ART
16 DALLAS OPERA
34 MAJESTIC THEATER

Ⓢ SHOPS

7 VOD BOUTIQUE
22 ℂ WILD BILL'S WESTERN STORE

Ⓗ HOTELS

1 HOTEL ST. GERMAIN
3 HOTEL ZAZA
5 HOTEL CRESCENT COURT
25 ℂ HOTEL LAWRENCE
27 HYATT REGENCY DALLAS
29 ℂ THE HOTEL ADOLPHUS
30 THE MAGNOLIA HOTEL
32 THE JOULE HOTEL
35 HOTEL INDIGO

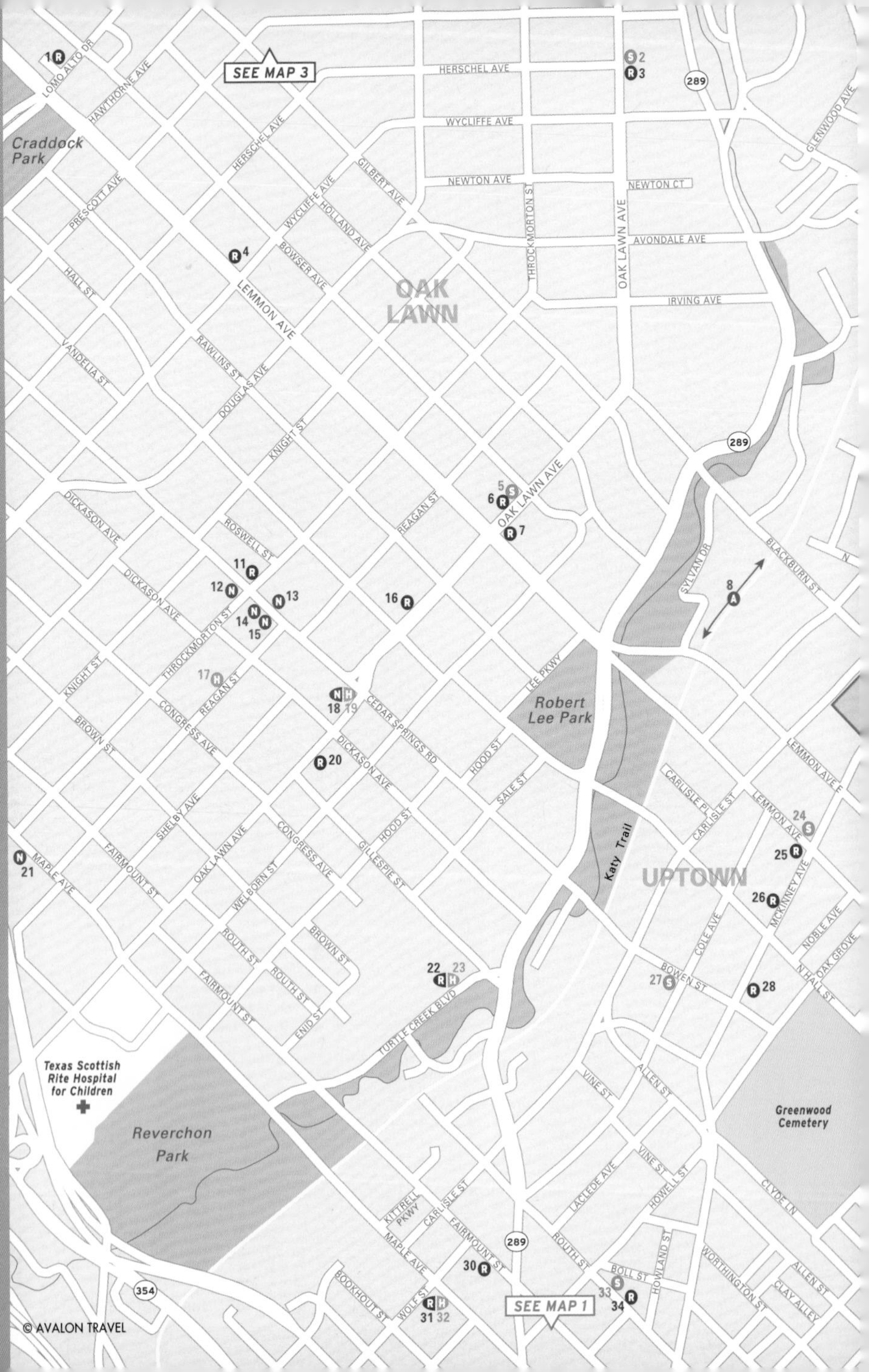

SEE MAP 3

Craddock
Park

OAK
LAWN

UPTOWN

Robert
Lee Park

Katy Trail

Texas Scottish
Rite Hospital
for Children

Reverchon
Park

Greenwood
Cemetery

SEE MAP 1

© AVALON TRAVEL

SEE MAP 3

SEE MAP 4

SEE MAP 5

Katy Trail

Cole Park

Cochran Park

KNOX-HENDERSON

West Village

Cityplace

Freedman's Memorial 29 ✪

Emanu-El Cemetery

Griggs Park

SEE MAP 5

✪ SIGHTS
29   FREEDMAN'S MEMORIAL

Ⓡ RESTAURANTS
1	NONNA	22	THE MANSION RESTAURANT
3	AURORA		
4 Ⓒ	BOB'S STEAK AND CHOPHOUSE	25	HOOK, LINE, & SINKER
6	LUCKY'S	26	BREADWINNERS
7	EATZI'S	28	CAFÉ EXPRESS
11	HUNKY'S	30	LOLA
16	PARIGI	31	BOLLA MODERN ITALIAN
20	COSMIC CAFÉ		
		34	ARCODORO & POMODORO

Ⓝ NIGHTLIFE
12	SUE ELLEN'S	15	STATION 4
13 Ⓒ	THE ROUND-UP SALOON	18 Ⓒ	THE LIBRARY BAR
14	JR'S BAR AND GRILL	21	BUDDIES II

Ⓐ ARTS AND LEISURE
8	KATY TRAIL	9	MAGNOLIA THEATER

Ⓢ SHOPS
2	SARTEL	24	FORTY FIVE TEN
5	LUKE'S LOCKER	27	KRIMSON & KLOVER
10	COWBOY COOL	33	KACKY & CARL
10	WEST VILLAGE	35	EMERALDS TO COCONUTS

Ⓗ HOTELS
17	DAISY POLK INN	23	ROSEWOOD MANSION ON TURTLE CREEK
19	WARWICK MELROSE HOTEL		
		32	THE STONELEIGH

0		300 yds
0		300 m

DISTANCE ACROSS MAP
Approximate: 2.1 mi or 3.4 km

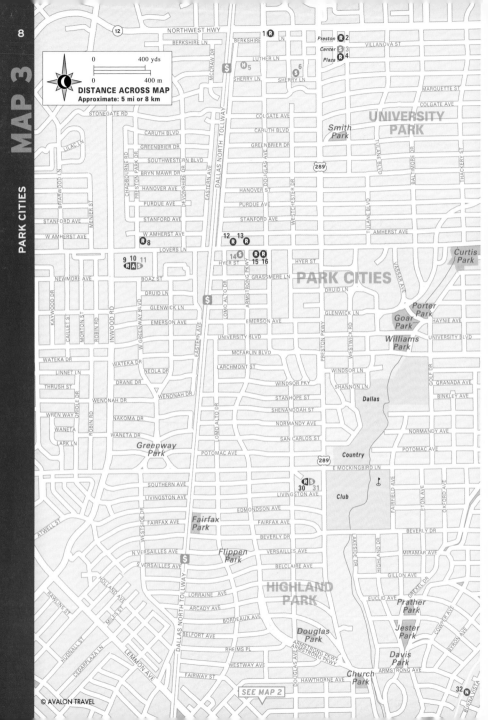

SIGHTS

28 SOUTHERN METHODIST UNIVERSITY

RESTAURANTS

1 SOUTH PAW'S ORGANIC CAFÉ, SUPPLEMENTS, AND SMOOTHIES
2 SPRINKLES CUPCAKES
4 THE CULTURED CUP
8 DUNSTON'S
9 CAFÉ ISTANBUL
9 RISE NO. 1
9 BIJOUX
12 MANGO THAI
13 KATHLEEN'S SKY DINER
15 DRIP

16 YUMMY DONUTS
17 DUPRE'S SHORT STOP
21 PEGGY SUE BBQ
22 AUSTINUTS
23 BUBBA'S
25 GOFF'S HAMBURGERS
30 CAFÉ PACIFIC
30 MI COCINA
33 LITTLE KATANA
37 FADI'S
38 HECTOR'S ON HENDERSON
39 HIBISCUS

NIGHTLIFE

29 ACROSS THE STREET BAR

32 BILL'S HIDEAWAY
34 SUITE

ARTS AND LEISURE

10 INWOOD THEATER

10 TEXAS ART GALLERY

SHOPS

3 LUCKY DOG BARKERY
6 CLOTHES CIRCUIT
7 NORTHPARK CENTER
11 COLLECTOR'S COVEY
11 HAUTE BABY
11 RAGAN BURNS
11 RICH HIPPIE
14 MINE

18 SNIDER PLAZA
19 ALLIE-COOSH
20 NEST
24 CD SOURCE
26 CULLWELL & SON
31 HIGHLAND PARK VILLAGE
31 ANGIE AMADI
35 FROGGIE'S 5&10
36 CARLA MARTINENGO BOUTIQUE

HOTELS

5 HILTON DALLAS PARK CITIES

27 HOTEL LUMEN

SEE MAP 4

MAP 4

GREENVILLE

E MOCKINGBIRD LN

WINTON ST

ANITA ST

ELLSWORTH AVE

Glencoe
Park

KENWOOD AVE

MATALEE AVE

PENROSE AVE

MARTEL AVE

LONGVIEW ST

SEE MAP 3

McCOMMAS BLVD

MORNINGSIDE AVE

MERCEDES AVE

MERRIMAC AVE

MONTICELLO AVE

RIDGEDALE DR

VANDERBILT AVE

GOODWIN AVE

VICKERY BLVD

MILLER AVE

WILLIS AVE

RICHARD AVE

BONITA AVE

GREENVILLE

SEE MAP 2

RICHMOND AVE

MELROSE AVE

BELL AVE

SEARS ST

ORAM ST

LA VISTA DR

LEWIS ST

ROSS AVE

HUDSON ST

INDELL AVE

Garrett
Park

BRYAN ST

WINTON ST

ELLSWORTH AVE

KENWOOD AVE

PENROSE AVE

MARTEL AVE

REVERE PL

MARTEL AVE

MALCOLM DR

McCOMMAS BLVD

"M" STREETS

MORNINGSIDE AVE

MERCEDES AVE

MONTICELLO AVE

MARQUITA AVE

MARQUITA AVE

VANDERBILT AVE

VANDERBILT AVE

Tietze
Park

GOODWIN AVE

VICKERY BLVD

VICKERY BLVD

WESTLAKE AVE

LLANO AVE

VELASCO AVE

VELASCO AVE

GLENROSE CT

PALO PINTO AVE

PALO PINTO AVE

LAKESHORE DR

GOLIAD AVE

GOLIAD AVE

BELMONT AVE

BELMONT AVE

RICHMOND AVE

PROSPECT AVE

PROSPECT AVE

Harrell
Park

LA VISTA DR

LEWIS ST

ROSS AVE

Swiss
Avenue

GASTON AVE

BRYAN ST

DISTANCE ACROSS MAP
Approximate: 3 mi or 4.8 km

0   400 yds
0   400 m

SEE MAP 5

Randall
Park

⊛ SIGHTS
27 SWISS AVENUE

ℝ RESTAURANTS
4   CAMPISI'S
5   CAFÉ IZMIR
6   AW, SHUCKS
9   THE GRAPE
11 THE LIBERTINE
14 NANDINA
21 LA CALLE DOCE
22 GOLD RUSH CAFÉ
23 ◖ YORK STREET
25 LAKEWOOD LANDING
29 THE COCK AND BULL

ℕ NIGHTLIFE
7   THE GRANADA THEATER
12 ZUBAR
13 GEZELLIG
15 BILLIARD BAR
16 THE CAVERN
18 SLIP INN
19 BARCADIA
20 ◖ SHIPS
26 COSMO RESTAURANT AND BAR
30 BALCONY CLUB

🅐 ARTS AND LEISURE
3   ANGELIKA THEATER

Ⓢ SHOPS
2   MOCKINGBIRD STATION
8   HD'S CLOTHING COMPANY
10 GREENVILLE AVENUE
17 ◖ GOOD RECORDS
24 PAPERBACKS PLUS
28 CURIOSITIES

Ⓗ HOTELS
1   HOTEL PALOMAR

© AVALON TRAVEL

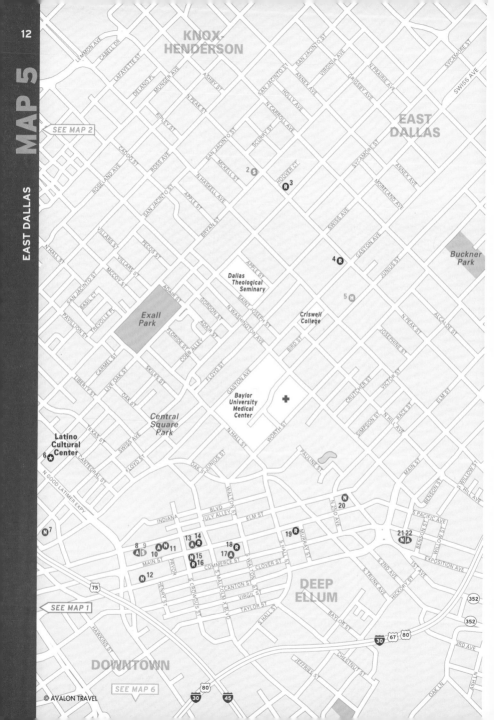

MAP 5

EAST DALLAS

KNOX-HENDERSON

EAST DALLAS

Buckner Park

SEE MAP 2

Dallas Theological Seminary

Exall Park

Criswell College

Baylor University Medical Center

Central Square Park

Latino Cultural Center

DEEP ELLUM

SEE MAP 1

DOWNTOWN

SEE MAP 6

© AVALON TRAVEL

SIGHTS
6 LATINO CULTURAL CENTER
24 FAIR PARK

RESTAURANTS
1 GARDEN CAFÉ
3 CIVELLO'S RAVIOLISMO
4 THE TACO JOINT
14 MONICA'S ACA Y ALLA
16 COWBOY CHOW
18 ALLGOOD CAFE
19 MURRAY STREET COFFEE

NIGHTLIFE
7 LIZARD LOUNGE
11 CLUB DADA
12 ADAIR'S SALOON
15 CURTAIN CLUB
20 SONS OF HERMANN HALL
21 THE DOUBLE-WIDE

ARTS AND LEISURE
8 DEEP ELLUM ARTS FESTIVAL
10 KETTLE ART
13 SPACE
17 THE PUBLIC TRUST
22 500X GALLERY
23 DALLAS FIREFIGHTERS MUSEUM
25 TEXAS BLACK RODEO

SHOPS
2 HOUSE OF DANG!
9 DEEP ELLUM

HOTELS
5 CORINTHIAN BED & BREAKFAST

0   300 yds
0   300 m
DISTANCE ACROSS MAP
Approximate: 2.5 mi or 4.1 km

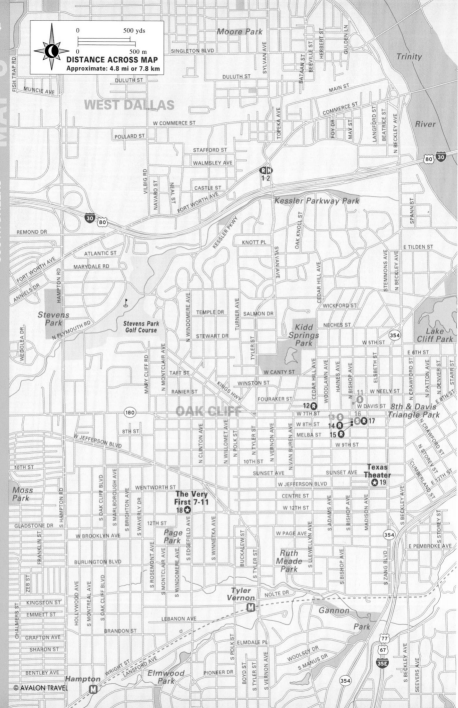

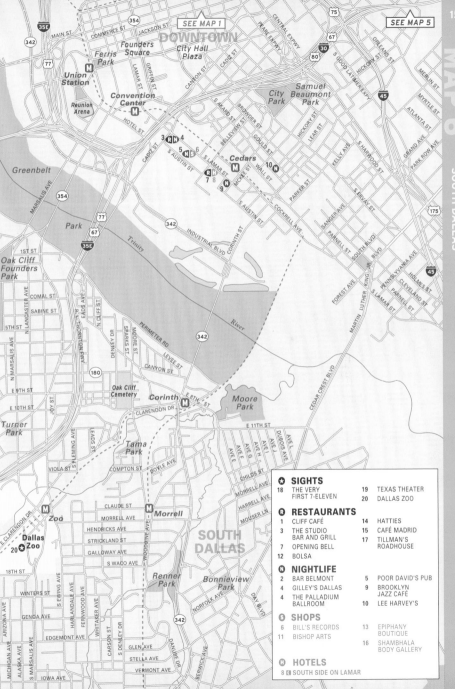

SIGHTS
18 THE VERY FIRST 7-ELEVEN
19 TEXAS THEATER
20 DALLAS ZOO

RESTAURANTS
1 CLIFF CAFÉ
3 THE STUDIO BAR AND GRILL
7 OPENING BELL
12 BOLSA
14 HATTIES
15 CAFÉ MADRID
17 TILLMAN'S ROADHOUSE

NIGHTLIFE
2 BAR BELMONT
4 GILLEY'S DALLAS
4 THE PALLADIUM BALLROOM
5 POOR DAVID'S PUB
9 BROOKLYN JAZZ CAFÉ
10 LEE HARVEY'S

SHOPS
6 BILL'S RECORDS
11 BISHOP ARTS
13 EPIPHANY BOUTIQUE
16 SHAMBHALA BODY GALLERY

HOTELS
8 SOUTH SIDE ON LAMAR

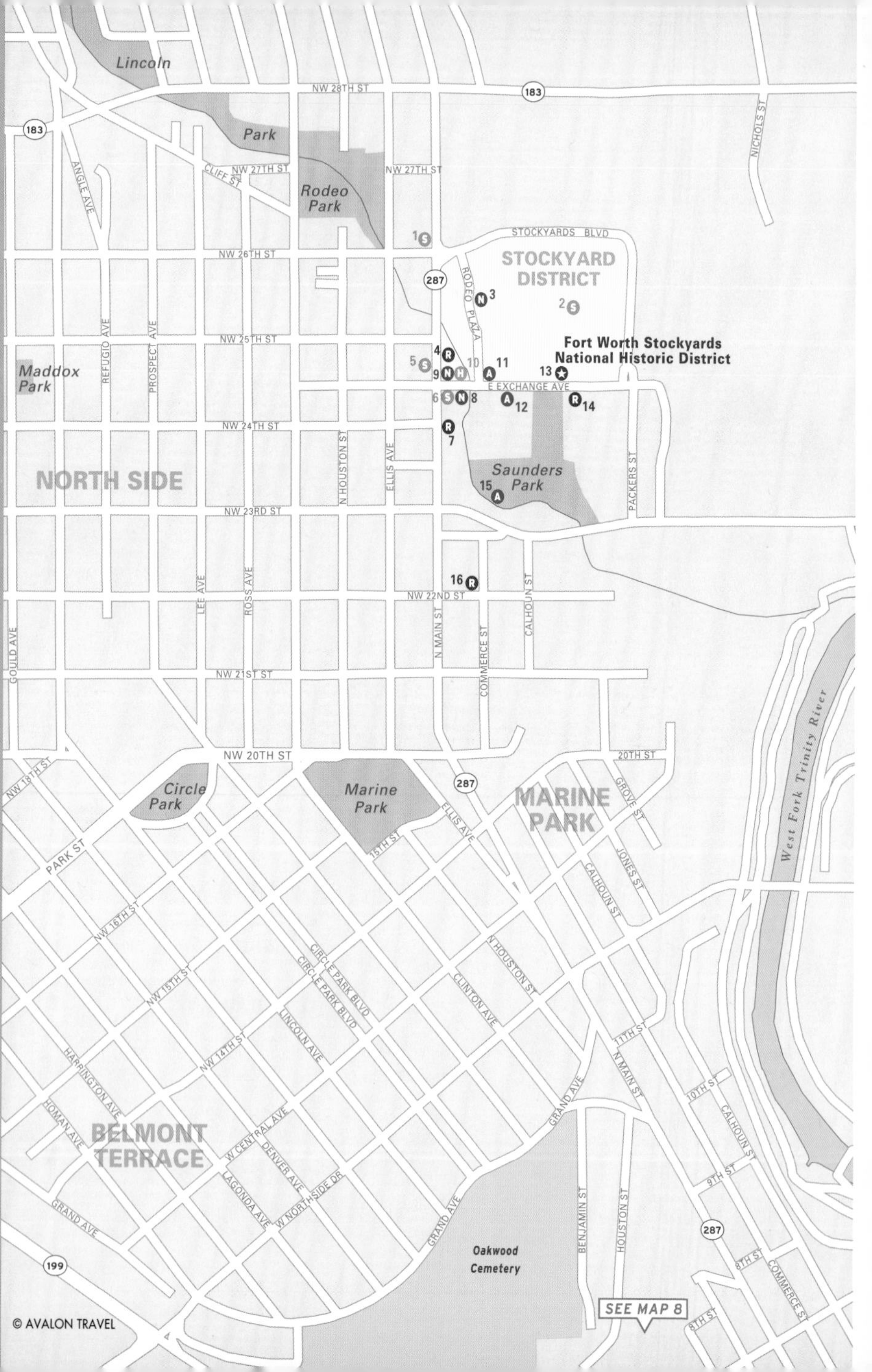

MAP 7

Lincoln

Park

Rodeo
Park

NW 28TH ST

NW 27TH ST

NW 27TH ST

CLIFF ST

ANGLE AVE

183

183

STOCKYARDS BLVD

NW 26TH ST

1 S

STOCKYARD
DISTRICT

287

3 N

2 S

Fort Worth Stockyards
National Historic District

NW 25TH ST

REFUGIO AVE

PROSPECT AVE

RODEO PLAZA

Maddox
Park

5 S

4 N

9 N H

10

11

13

NW 24TH ST

6 S N

8

E EXCHANGE AVE

12 A

14 R

7

NORTH SIDE

N HOUSTON ST

ELLIS AVE

Saunders
Park

15 A

NW 23RD ST

LEE AVE

ROSS AVE

PACKERS ST

16 R

NW 22ND ST

N MAIN ST

COMMERCE ST

CALHOUN ST

NW 21ST ST

GOULD AVE

NW 20TH ST

20TH ST

Circle
Park

Marine
Park

287

MARINE
PARK

West Fork Trinity River

NW 19TH ST

PARK ST

ELLIS AVE

15TH ST

CALHOUN ST

GROVE ST

JONES ST

NW 18TH ST

NW 15TH ST

CIRCLE PARK BLVD

CIRCLE PARK BLVD

CLINTON AVE

N HOUSTON ST

N MAIN ST

11TH ST

10TH ST

CALHOUN ST

9TH ST

NW 14TH ST

LINCOLN AVE

HARRINGTON AVE

HOMAN AVE

BELMONT
TERRACE

N CENTRAL AVE

DENVER AVE

CAGONDA AVE

N NORTHSIDE DR

GRAND AVE

BENJAMIN ST

HOUSTON ST

8TH ST

COMMERCE ST

GRAND AVE

287

199

Oakwood
Cemetery

SEE MAP 8

© AVALON TRAVEL

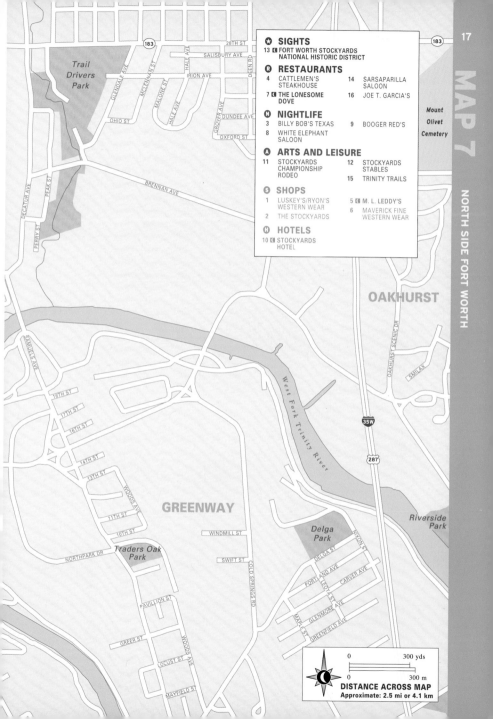

☆ SIGHTS
13 ◀ FORT WORTH STOCKYARDS NATIONAL HISTORIC DISTRICT

® RESTAURANTS
4 CATTLEMEN'S STEAKHOUSE
7 ◀ THE LONESOME DOVE
14 SARSAPARILLA SALOON
16 JOE T. GARCIA'S

☾ NIGHTLIFE
3 BILLY BOB'S TEXAS
8 WHITE ELEPHANT SALOON
9 BOOGER RED'S

☺ ARTS AND LEISURE
11 STOCKYARDS CHAMPIONSHIP RODEO
12 STOCKYARDS STABLES
15 TRINITY TRAILS

⑤ SHOPS
1 LUSKEY'S/RYON'S WESTERN WEAR
2 THE STOCKYARDS
5 ◀ M. L. LEDDY'S
6 MAVERICK FINE WESTERN WEAR

ⓗ HOTELS
10 ◀ STOCKYARDS HOTEL

DISTANCE ACROSS MAP
Approximate: 2.5 mi or 4.1 km

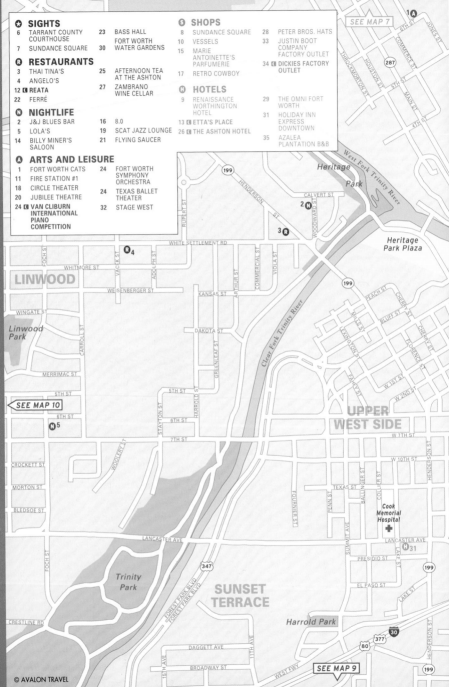

SEE MAP 7

SIGHTS
6 TARRANT COUNTY COURTHOUSE
7 SUNDANCE SQUARE
23 BASS HALL
30 FORT WORTH WATER GARDENS

RESTAURANTS
3 THAI TINA'S
4 ANGELO'S
12 REATA
22 FERRÉ
25 AFTERNOON TEA AT THE ASHTON
27 ZAMBRANO WINE CELLAR

NIGHTLIFE
2 J&J BLUES BAR
5 LOLA'S
14 BILLY MINER'S SALOON
16 8.0
19 SCAT JAZZ LOUNGE
21 FLYING SAUCER

ARTS AND LEISURE
1 FORT WORTH CATS
11 FIRE STATION #1
18 CIRCLE THEATER
20 JUBILEE THEATRE
24 VAN CLIBURN INTERNATIONAL PIANO COMPETITION
24 FORT WORTH SYMPHONY ORCHESTRA
24 TEXAS BALLET THEATER
32 STAGE WEST

SHOPS
8 SUNDANCE SQUARE
10 VESSELS
15 MARIE ANTOINETTE'S PARFUMERIE
17 RETRO COWBOY
28 PETER BROS. HATS
33 JUSTIN BOOT COMPANY FACTORY OUTLET
34 DICKIES FACTORY OUTLET

HOTELS
9 RENAISSANCE WORTHINGTON HOTEL
13 ETTA'S PLACE
26 THE ASHTON HOTEL
29 THE OMNI FORT WORTH
31 HOLIDAY INN EXPRESS DOWNTOWN
35 AZALEA PLANTATION B&B

SEE MAP 10

LINWOOD

Linwood Park

UPPER WEST SIDE

Cook Memorial Hospital

Trinity Park

SUNSET TERRACE

Harrold Park

Heritage Park

Heritage Park Plaza

SEE MAP 9

© AVALON TRAVEL

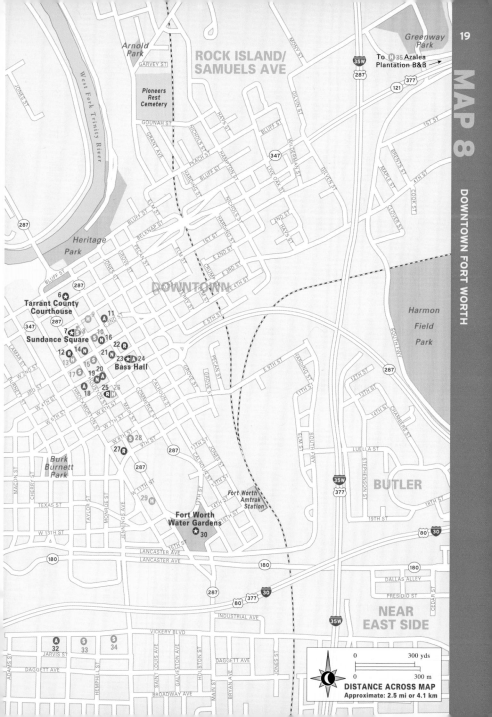

Greenway
Park

To ⓗ 35 Azalea
Plantation B&B →

35W
287

377

121

347

Arnold
Park

GARVEY ST

ROCK ISLAND/
SAMUELS AVE

Pioneers
Rest
Cemetery

GOUNAH ST

West Fork Trinity River

287

Heritage
Park

Harmon
Field
Park

287

DOWNTOWN

6 ★
**Tarrant County
Courthouse**

347
287

7 ⓡ ★ 8
9 ⓐ 11
10
12 ⓡ 14 ⓝ 16
13 ⓡ 15
17 ⓡ ★ 20
19 ⓝ 18 ⓐ ⓝ
22 ⓡ
21 ⓝ
23 24 ⓗ ⓐ
Bass Hall
25 ⓡ 26

Sundance Square

Burk
Burnett
Park

27 ⓡ

28 ⓢ

287

29 ⓗ

★
**Fort Worth
Water Gardens**
★ 30

Fort Worth
Amtrak
Station

BUTLER

35W
377

80 30

180

LANCASTER AVE
LANCASTER AVE

180

180

287
80 377 30

35 ⓗ

**NEAR
EAST SIDE**

DALLAS ALLEY

PRESIDIO ST

ⓐ
32 ⓢ 33 ⓢ 34

INDUSTRIAL AVE

VICKERY BLVD

JARVIS ST

DAGGETT AVE

0   300 yds
0   300 m

DISTANCE ACROSS MAP
Approximate: 2.5 mi or 4.1 km

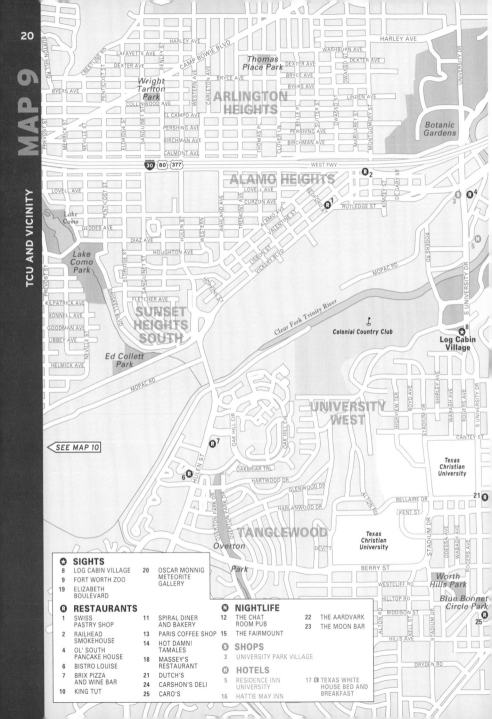

HARLEY AVE

Thomas
Place Park

ARLINGTON
HEIGHTS

Botanic
Gardens

ALAMO HEIGHTS

WEST FWY

Lake
Como

Lake
Como
Park

SUNSET
HEIGHTS
SOUTH

Clear Fork Trinity River

Colonial Country Club

Log Cabin
Village

Ed Collett
Park

SEE MAP 10

UNIVERSITY
WEST

Texas
Christian
University

TANGLEWOOD

Overton

Texas
Christian
University

Park

Worth
Hills Park

Blue Bonnet
Circle Park

SIGHTS
- 8 LOG CABIN VILLAGE
- 9 FORT WORTH ZOO
- 19 ELIZABETH BOULEVARD
- 20 OSCAR MONNIG METEORITE GALLERY

RESTAURANTS
- 1 SWISS PASTRY SHOP
- 2 RAILHEAD SMOKEHOUSE
- 4 OL' SOUTH PANCAKE HOUSE
- 6 BISTRO LOUISE
- 7 BRIX PIZZA AND WINE BAR
- 10 KING TUT
- 11 SPIRAL DINER AND BAKERY
- 13 PARIS COFFEE SHOP
- 14 HOT DAMN! TAMALES
- 18 MASSEY'S RESTAURANT
- 21 DUTCH'S
- 24 CARSHON'S DELI
- 25 CARO'S

NIGHTLIFE
- 12 THE CHAT ROOM PUB
- 15 THE FAIRMOUNT
- 22 THE AARDVARK
- 23 THE MOON BAR

SHOPS
- 3 UNIVERSITY PARK VILLAGE

HOTELS
- 5 RESIDENCE INN UNIVERSITY
- 16 HATTIE MAY INN
- 17 TEXAS WHITE HOUSE BED AND BREAKFAST

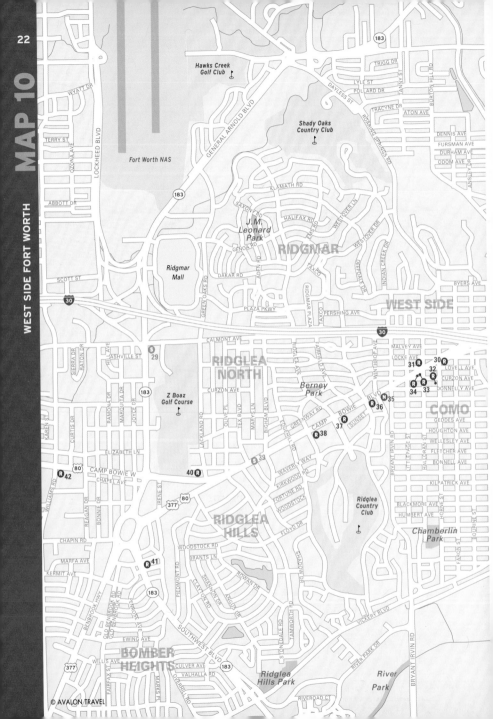

RIVERBEND

Greenwood Memorial
Park Cemetary

Monticello
Park

MONTICELLO

LINWOOD

Linwood
Park

Modern
Art Museum
of Fort Worth

Amon
Carter
Museum

The Kimball
Art Museum

Fort Worth Museum
of Science and History

Will Rogers
Memorial Center

River Crest
Country Club

CRESTLINE

The National
Cowgirl Museum
and
Hall of Fame

Trinity
Park

Thomas
Place
Park

Wright
Tarlton
Park

ARLINGTON
HEIGHTS

Fort Worth
Botanic Gardens

SEE MAP 9

SEE MAP 8

ALAMO
HEIGHTS

Forest
Park

Lake
S Como

Lake
Como
Park

SUNSET
HEIGHTS
SOUTH

Ed Collett
Park

Overton
Park

DISTANCE ACROSS MAP
Approximate: 5.3 mi or 8.6 km

0   500 yds

0   500 m

★ SIGHTS

10	MODERN ART MUSEUM OF FORT WORTH
11	THE KIMBELL ART MUSEUM
12	AMON CARTER MUSEUM
13	WILL ROGERS MEMORIAL CENTER
17	THE NATIONAL COWGIRL MUSEUM AND HALL OF FAME
18	FORT WORTH BOTANIC GARDENS
20	FORT WORTH MUSEUM OF SCIENCE AND HISTORY

® RESTAURANTS

1	LAMBERT'S
3	SAINT-EMILION
5	J&J OYSTER BAR
6	SARDINE'S RISTORANTE ITALIANO
7	FRED'S TEXAS CAFÉ
19	MONTGOMERY ST. CAFÉ
21	CURLY'S CUSTARD
23	THE ORIGINAL MEXICAN EATS CAFÉ
25	KINCAID'S
28	ROY POPE GROCERY
30	SZECHUAN
31	MAMA'S PIZZA
32	DREW'S PLACE
33	GALLIGASKIN'S SUBMARINE SANDWICH
34	FORTUNA ITALIAN RESTAURANT
36	OVATION
37	ITALIAN INN RIDGLEA
39	EL FENIX
40	JOE'S
41	EDELWEISS
42	JAPANESE PALACE

ℕ NIGHTLIFE

9	POUR HOUSE
35	RIDGLEA THEATER

Ⓐ ARTS AND LEISURE

14	FORT WORTH STOCK SHOW AND RODEO
16	CASA MAÑANA
43	FOREST PARK

Ⓢ SHOPS

2	7TH STREET	
4	NAMASTE	
8	DEAN-KINGSTON	
22	J. SAUNDERS	
24	SPOILED PINK	
26	A. HOOPER'S & CO.	
27	PS THE LETTER	
29	WESTERN WEAR EXCHANGE	
39	CAMP BOWIE	

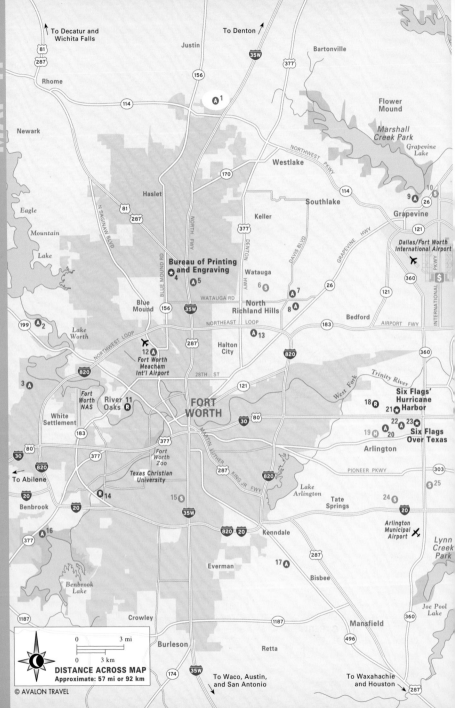

To Decatur and Wichita Falls

To Denton

Justin

Bartonville

Rhome

Newark

Flower Mound

Marshall Creek Park

Grapevine Lake

Westlake

Haslet

Southlake

Keller

Grapevine

Eagle Mountain Lake

Dallas/Fort Worth International Airport

Bureau of Printing and Engraving

Watauga

Blue Mound

WATAUGA RD

North Richland Hills

Bedford

Lake Worth

NORTHEAST LOOP

Halton City

Fort Worth Meacham Int'l Airport

NORTHWEST LOOP

Fort Worth NAS

River Oaks

FORT WORTH

28TH ST

Trinity River

Six Flags' Hurricane Harbor

White Settlement

Six Flags Over Texas

To Abilene

Fort Worth Zoo

Texas Christian University

Arlington

PIONEER PKWY

Benbrook

Lake Arlington

Tate Springs

Arlington Municipal Airport

Kenndale

Lynn Creek Park

Benbrook Lake

Everman

Bisbee

Joe Pool Lake

Crowley

Mansfield

Burleson

Retta

To Waco, Austin, and San Antonio

To Waxahachie and Houston

DISTANCE ACROSS MAP
Approximate: 57 mi or 92 km

0   3 mi
0   3 km

© AVALON TRAVEL

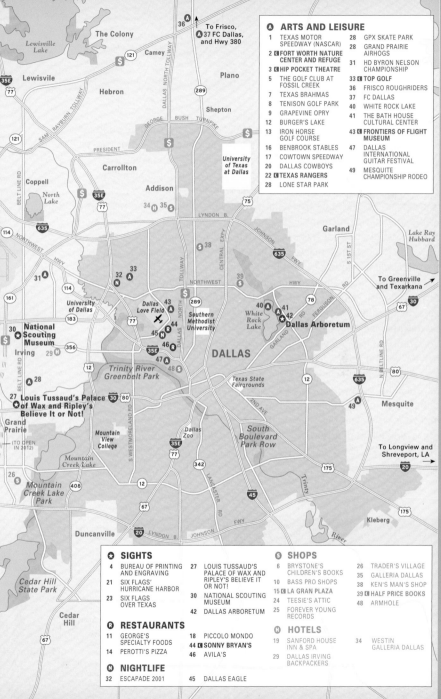

Discover
Dallas & Fort Worth

Recently, the folks at NASA released a satellite photo of Dallas-Fort Worth. From the height of outer space, DFW looks like a colossal nebula. From ground level, that's what DFW is, too: Grandly sprawling but anchored by distinct communities, DFW is made up of several individual stars that shine brightly on their own; yet, taken as a whole, they form one giant light. Considering the grandness of the region and the variety of what it has to offer, such a metaphor is necessary. How else to describe a place large enough to make room for its cowpoke tradition *and* its globalist future?

In Dallas, for example, you'll find honky-tonks right next door to alternative music venues. Just to the west, denizens of Fort Worth might dine on a humble chicken-fried steak in the old Stockyards, then hustle downtown afterward to see the opera at the resplendent Bass Hall. You want rodeos? We've got them. You want shopping worthy of Rodeo Drive? We've got that, too.

Both towns overflow with variety, and such symbiotic fusing of disparate cultures is what sets DFW apart. What this means for a visitor is to be ready for tradition and surprise – you'd better bring your blue jeans *and* your little black dress. No matter where you choose to wear that dress, you'll find things in DFW are bright indeed.

Planning Your Trip

▶ WHERE TO GO

Downtown Dallas

Anchored by a cluster of skyscrapers, the central part of Dallas is where you'll find all the perks of the big city, along with a number of historical sights. Downtown Dallas also encompasses the Arts District, home of world-class visual and performing arts, alongside the more laid-back, historic West End.

Uptown Dallas

The denizens of Uptown tend to fall into three categories: gay, upwardly mobile, or some combination of the two. This is a part of town where you're most likely to find the trendiest food, clothes, drinks, and entertainment. Some of it is quite charming, especially the older high- and mid-rise apartments you'll find flanking lush Turtle Creek and the bars and clubs that make up the "gayborhood" off Oak Lawn Avenue. Other parts are a bit plastic, though with all the amenities and the high concentration of fancy joints, it's hard to complain.

The downtowns of both Dallas and Fort Worth combine classic and modern architecture.

Park Cities

Butting up against the busy concrete bustle of Uptown and the vibrant Oak Lawn party scene, Park Cities is an opulent oasis of giant houses, Lexus SUVs, and exclusive shopping centers (and the home of former president George W. Bush). This is the best place to go if you need the latest Chanel bag or a unique (and probably expensive) gift.

Greenville

Lower Greenville Avenue is the central artery that connects the patchwork of neighborhoods and aesthetics that make up this area. On the southeastern end of the street, you'll find the outer edges of Lakewood, which is populated by an improbable combination of yuppies and hipsters, lured by beautiful older houses and bungalows. They are also lured by their proximity to the heart of Lower Greenville, long a raucous, popular destination for nightlife, dining, and shopping.

East Dallas

East Dallas has almost always been the bastion of Dallas's funky, edgy population. Shaded by tons of old oak trees, the neighborhoods here are charming and old-school, though there are definitely some rough edges. Deep Ellum—long the epicenter of Dallas's music scene—is perhaps the most well-known neighborhood here, with its low-slung red brick clubs, restaurants, and shops, but hipster Expo Park and the more family-oriented Lakewood have plenty of shopping, food, and entertainment to offer.

South Dallas

Long a troubled, blight-ridden area, South Dallas has experienced quite a renaissance lately. Fine-dining establishments now stand where crumbling warehouses once did, and a number of old hotels and structures have been rehabbed into new, hip watering holes and down-home restaurants, with stunning views of the downtown skyline and the surrounding refurbished homes. The Bishop Arts area is particularly hopping, especially on weekend nights when young revelers, queer folks, and hip families stroll the streets and peer into the cute, unique boutiques before grabbing dinner.

Greater Dallas

Irving, Grand Prairie, Plano, Frisco—the greater Dallas area contains many a suburb and "mid-city," as the towns between Fort Worth and Dallas are known. Usually rivals,

Sundance Square, in downtown Fort Worth

citizens of both Dallas and Fort Worth used to agree on one thing: their mutual disdain for the greater Dallas area and its "boring" suburban feel. Nowadays, however, as these small cities continue to grow and make a name for themselves, city dwellers actually view them as sports, food, recreation, and shopping destinations.

North Side Fort Worth

No other part of town reflects Fort Worth's history more genuinely than this area, which embraces the Fort Worth Stockyards National Historic District and the northern part of downtown. The Stockyards continue to maintain old traditions with wooden sidewalks, brick streets, and a daily, real-live cattle drive that attracts tourists and locals alike.

Downtown Fort Worth

It's almost hard to swallow, but downtown Fort Worth just might be giving the Stockyards district a run for its money when it comes to attracting revelers, at least on weekends, when the streets come alive with partiers, shoppers, diners, and music lovers. The epicenter of all the activity is about 20 square blocks of renovated, refurbished, and renewed city center called Sundance Square.

TCU and Vicinity

The acres upon hilly acres upon which stately Texas Christian University now sits were once the hinterland outskirts of town. Now, they're prime real estate, just down the road from the Cultural District and minutes from downtown. Yet, thanks to the university, the area has its own distinct personality: The crisp, green lawns of the school, the lights of the football stadium, and a good concentration of clubs, bars, and hangouts lend the neighborhood a perpetually collegiate air.

Don't miss the daily cattle drive at the Fort Worth Stockyards National Historic District.

West Side Fort Worth

In many ways, Western Fort Worth is the heart of the city. This is the part of town where culture reigns supreme, be it in the form of world-renowned museums or a wide variety of food and shopping. Head over to Colonial Country Club and catch a few holes of the PGA's annual stop there in the summer. Many year-round activities and festivals take place in this section of town.

Greater Fort Worth

Glen Rose and Grapevine are beautiful, full of nature, country air, and fun activities. Arlington? Not so much. Made, it seems, almost entirely of concrete, asphalt, and gargantuan-scale tourist attractions, Arlington is the ultimate mid-city. It's just that those attractions happen to be some of the best in the world (the new Dallas Cowboys stadium, anyone?).

▶ WHEN TO GO

North Texas is at its best during autumn. This time of year, the prairie's ample, mature oak, maple, and pecan trees blaze with color, and the smell of burning mesquite logs fills the air as the weather gets colder. Fall also marks the beginning of football season. It may sound silly to the uninitiated, but the sport lends the air an extra crackle as high school, college, and pro teams kick off their seasons. The air is generally crisp but comfortable. Spring is also a lovely time here. Moderate temperatures and the smell of summer in the air encourage outdoor activities and several open-air festivals. Many visitors love the mild winters, but the leafless trees and dead grass come off as somewhat stark. Most of all, however, make all attempts to avoid the scorching heat of summer if you can.

Explore Dallas & Fort Worth

▶ THE TWO-DAY BEST OF DALLAS & FORT WORTH

Day 1: Dallas

▶ Start your day off with a genuine down-home breakfast at the All Good Café in the heart of historic Deep Ellum (you're going to need some energy for your big day ahead, so consider the chicken-fried steak and egg breakfast).

▶ Head down to the official Dallas Visitors Center at the Old Red Courthouse Museum and grab some maps and tourist information, then pop upstairs to orient yourself with a tour of the museum's History of Dallas County exhibit. The folks at the museum are extremely knowledgeable and friendly—this is the place to stock up on Dallas knowledge before heading out. This is also a good spot to ask directions to get to your next stop, the Arts District (it's also downtown, but a bit of a walk, so consider taking a Dallas Area Rapid Transit train).

▶ The Arts District will present you with several stellar choices. You probably won't be able to hit them all, so a good two-for-one option would be to see the Dallas Museum of Art and the Nasher Sculpture Center, which are adjacent to each other. While you can pay separately to enter either, combination tickets are available at discount prices at both the DMA and Nasher box offices. Another good choice is the Trammell and Margaret Crow Collection of Asian Art, which is free.

▶ You'll be tempted to stay in the Arts District for the remainder of the afternoon, and if that's your choice, try out the DMA's upscale Seventeen Seventeen restaurant for lunch, or for a big midday splurge, try Stephan Pyle's— a popular new spot just down the street.

▶ Should you choose to move on, a true Dallas experience awaits: Lunch at the Zodiac restaurant in the Neiman Marcus flagship store at the corner of Main and Ervay Streets. Make sure you work up an appetite by perusing the legendary racks of couture beforehand.

▶ If your legs are up for more exploring, Dealey Plaza and the Sixth Floor Museum—the site of the John F.

Dallas Museum of Art

TEN WAYS TO ESCAPE THE TEXAS SUN

- Head to one of the best malls in America, the **Galleria Dallas**, and hit up the indoor ice skating rink.

- Take a dip in the pool at **QuikTrip Park**, home of Independent Baseball's pro team the **Grand Prairie AirHogs.** Just behind the outfield, the pool allows you to see the action and stay cool.

- Hit up **Six Flags Hurricane Harbor** – one of the biggest water parks in the country. Or check out the indoor water park at **Great Wolf Lodge.**

- North Texas is full of lakes, and recreation at them ranges from skinny dipping to jet skiing. One of the biggest is **Lake Texoma**, about an hour-and-half drive north of the Metroplex.

- Catching a flick at Fort Worth's **Movie Tavern** is a great way to soak up a few hours of air conditioning – and a pitcher or two of beer.

- The rooftop pool at the **Joule Hotel** is cool in all senses of the word. Its eye-catching design makes it the hippest soak in town.

- While the outdoor exhibits may not escape the sun, the indoor penguin exhibit at the **Fort Worth Zoo** provide a fun educational respite that kids and adults both enjoy.

- Three words: **Joe T.'s margarita.**

- Both Dallas and Fort Worth boast dark, state-of-the-art **IMAX theaters.** Dallas' can be found at the **Museum of Science and Nature** in Fair Park; Fort Worth's is in the **Natural History Museum.**

the Grand Prairie AirHogs' new home

Kennedy assassination—are just a few blocks away.

▶ A 15-minute car ride from downtown, the Bishop Arts District is a low-key way to top off your day. Stroll along the picturesque, historic block until you reach Tillman's Roadhouse, where a blood orange margarita awaits. If you like a gussied-up roadhouse atmosphere, stick around for dinner. If not, Bishop Arts presents tons of dining options.

Day 2: Fort Worth

▶ First, you must indulge in Paris Coffeehouse's Texas-size breakfast. Then, get thee straight to the Museum of Modern Art, and give thyself plenty of time to peruse this amazing building and its world-class collection of post–World War II paintings, sculpture, video, and mixed media works.

▶ The next stop is that other world-famous museum, the Kimbell, whose Louis Kahn–designed walls just happen also to house one of the best museum restaurants in the country. Take a break and eat here, or send someone in your party up the street to pick up some Kincaid's burgers to go for a picnic on the lovely grassy park next to the Kimbell's reflecting pool.

▶ Then it's off for an afternoon of Old West history in the Stockyards. Make sure you get there in time for the Fort Worth Herd cattle drive, after which you can stroll the wooden sidewalks and see the sights.

▶ Shop for souvenirs, boots, hats, and belt buckles at places like M. L. Leddy's. Next, shake the dust off your boots and hunker down over a cold one at the White Elephant Saloon or Booger Red's Saloon before moving on to check out the Exchange building, where cattlemen once haggled over the price of steer.

▶ Hit up Cattleman's Steakhouse for a big slab of Texas steak—don't worry, you'll dance it off at Billy Bob's, the world's biggest honky-tonk, just down the road.

▶ If boot scooting isn't your thing, head downtown and grab a drink or dinner on the rooftop at one of Fort Worth's most popular restaurants, the always-buzzing Reata, which overlooks Sundance Square.

▶ From there, choose from any number of entertainment options, from the casual and understated (a brew or two at the Flying Saucer) to the swank (jazz and cocktails at Scat) to the fancy (a performance at Bass Hall).

DFW ON THE CHEAP

Try these budget-friendly options and you'll tour, eat, shop, and party like an oil tycoon during a boom – without having to worry about the bust.

MUSEUMS

The Amon Carter Museum features classic Western art as well as a more liberal interpretation of the genre. Free daily.

The Sid Richardson Museum's collection of traditional Western watercolors will get you in a Cowtown kind of mood. Free daily.

The Dallas Museum of Art features a consistently improving collection and some stunning traveling shows. Free Thursdays (5-9 P.M.).

The African-American Museum and **The Hall of State** are two of the best sights in Dallas' Fair Park.

SIGHTS AND RECREATION

Dallas' **McKinney Avenue trolley** is a cute throwback method of transporting yourself from downtown to McKinney Avenue – and it's free.

The **Dallas Mavericks** often release last-minute, nosebleed seats to home games, for a mere $8.

The **Fort Worth Water Garden**'s cool, frothy water sculptures are awe-inducing – and free.

The **Fort Worth Cats** baseball team has a long history – and as with seats as cheap as four bucks, you can be a part of it too.

FOOD

The AllGood Cafe's Two-Fer Tuesdays provide hearty, home style meals, one at full price, the cheaper one for free.

Kathleen's Sky Diner, known for its inventive take on upscale diner cuisine, is a Lovers Lane favorite, especially on Sunday nights, when entrees are half off.

Asian Mint will appeal to sushi lovers on $1 sushi nights (Monday and Tuesday).

Mama's Pizza offers a $7.50 lunch buffet with the best pizza in Fort Worth, and students fare even better – it's only $6.50 with student ID.

The Mansion on Turtle Creek is known for its stellar food and intensely expensive prices. But you can get in and out of there for $29 during the weekday lunch special. Worth every penny.

Tim Love's Love Shack provides the very Fort Worthian experience of eating a greasy, yet gourmet, burger smack in the middle of the stockyards. With its secret Love Sauce, the burger here is unique, and at around four bucks, it's cheap.

DRINKS

Check **pegasusnews.com**'s comprehensive drink specials site, which will match you up with drink specials in every neighborhood in the metroplex.

SIGHTS

Even though together they form an anchor for the cultural world of the South and Southwest—and, in some ways, for much of the country—Dallas and Fort Worth maintain very separate identities. Dallas, for instance, has catapulted itself into the world-class tier with dazzling speed, after years of being construed as "not quite there," and now the downtown Arts District, home to the Dallas Museum of Art, the Morton H. Meyerson Symphony Center, the Trammell and Margaret Crow Collection of Asian Art, and the brand new Performing Arts Center, has evolved into a cultural powerhouse, a must-see for every visitor. Fort Worth, meantime, has built up a world-class reputation in a quieter way. On one end of Fort Worth's cultural spectrum is the international cachet of the Kimbell Art Museum; the other end is manned by cowboys and rodeo queens.

There's history here, too, in both towns. The area's rich and sometimes strange past is reflected in its refurbished art deco buildings, Fort Worth's storied Stockyards, humble gravestones, and soaring towers. Sadly, much of that history centers on the somber Dallas block where President John F. Kennedy was shot and killed. But happier sights abound, too, such as Reunion Tower. One of downtown Dallas's most famous landmarks, the tower rises 560 feet above downtown, affording

HIGHLIGHTS

LOOK FOR TO FIND RECOMMENDED SIGHTS.

◖ Best Free Excursion: The **Dallas Museum of Art** is worth the price of admission, but if you're on a budget, check it out Thursdays from 5-9 P.M. or the first Tuesday of every month, when it's free to enter (page 35).

◖ Best Way to Wear Your Kids Out: It's a touch pricey, but the **Dallas World Aquarium** will thrill the young 'uns with its amazing indoor jungle habitat. It's huge — by the end of the tour even moms and pops will be tuckered out (page 37).

◖ Best Contemplation Spot: Meant as a study of color, space, and perception, Turrell's skyscape, "Tending (Blue)," at the **Nasher Sculpture Center,** fosters a quiet, contemplative feel in much the same way as Rothko's chapel in Houston. Turrell's space is also chapel-like, blissfully quiet as multicolored pastel lights slowly brighten and fade like the sun (page 37).

◖ Best Use of Livestock: Get a taste of the Old West by checking out the Fort Worth Herd, the world's only twice-daily cattle drive, in the **Fort Worth Stockyards National Historic District** (page 50).

◖ Best Place to Catch Your Breath: The Kimbell Art Museum is known as much for its architecture as for the art inside. Even the outside of the building reflects detailed forethought: The northern exterior features a portico and reflecting pool that open out onto a grassy, park-like area flanked by holly trees. On a sunny day, the effect is wondrous (page 57).

◖ Best Museum: For the new **Modern Art Museum of Fort Worth,** Japanese architect Tadeo Ando designed a contemporary cathedral to house one the best collections of post-World War II art in the world. Don't even think about skipping it (page 58).

◖ Best Gift Shop: The National Cowgirl Museum and Hall of Fame's first-floor shop is filled with kitschy items like "Bronco Babes" lunchboxes, boot-leather purses, and retro belt buckles. Just don't spend all your time there — you'll want to peruse the museum's many interactive exhibit that celebrate the lives of feisty Western women (page 58).

The Exchange Building is a stop on the daily cattle drive in the Fort Worth Stockyards.

© JONANNA WIDNER

visitors amazing 360-degree views from the observation tower.

Whether you want lofty views or a piece of down-home history, DFW boasts many locations to seek out and enjoy. The sights you see during your visit will demonstrate a unique type of Texas spirit: entrepreneurial, generous, sometimes failing, sometimes peculiar, but always striving for the best, and always proud.

Downtown Dallas

Map 1

DALLAS MUSEUM OF ART

1717 N. Harwood, 214/922-1200,
www.dallasmuseumofart.org

HOURS: Tues.-Weds. and Fri.-Sun. 11 A.M.-5 P.M.,
Thurs. 11 A.M.-11 P.M.

COST: $10 adult, $7 senior, $5 student, free under 12,
free after 5 P.M. Thurs. and first Tues. of each month;
joint ticket with Nasher Sculpture Center $16 adult,
$12 senior, $8 student

The Dallas Museum of Art was founded in 1903, and it has taken about 100 years for it to pull itself out of its status as a second-tier art institution and into world-class territory. The museum's first giant leap occurred when it finally found a permanent home in 1984 on Harwood Street, where it has anchored the Arts District ever since. The 2005 acquisition of major contemporary works from three prominent collectors cemented the transition to world-class, as have fantastic choices when it comes to traveling exhibits—recent examples include a blockbuster J. M. W. Turner

© DALLAS MUSEUM OF ART

Dallas Museum of Art

IF YOU RENOVATE IT, THEY WILL COME

The architecture of downtown Dallas has never exactly wowed. In the modern era, the general philosophy among those who have erected new buildings has been, "Get some glass and some steel. Now go up." And sadly, this town exhibits few qualms about tearing down the more interesting edifices (the amazing, mid-century **Dallas Grand Hotel**, which introduced elevator music to the world, currently teeters on the edge of extinction, for instance).

But there are still some gems to be seen. A few years ago, developers gobbled up several notable buildings in various states of disrepair, gussied them up, and converted them into fashionable mixed use retail/residential lofts. The buildings now hum with activity and life, and their unique architectural features make a for a fun subject of study on a quick lunch break or a leisurely walk. Here are four within a few blocks of each other to get you started:

Built in 1916 as a terminal for several local railways, the nine-story **Interurban Building**'s architectural details evoke the Chicago School. On the first floor, what was once a bundle of platforms and train tracks is now home to a busy café, bar, and grocery store.

In the early 2000's, renovators began restoring the lobby of the 100-year-old **Dallas Power and Light** building. Removal of seven layers of sheet rock revealed long-forgotten walls of onyx-colored marble, now the gleaming signature of the cavernous lobby. Further work inside and outside restored this prime example of gorgeous, gleaming Art Deco to its original glory.

Built in 1913 at the behest of beer baron Adolphus Busch as a companion to his hotel across the street, the **Kirby Building** is a stately nod to old-school Gothicism, right down (or up) to the rooftop gargoyles that guard the "Old Girl," as the building is known.

The mid-century **Republic Building,** now known as Gables Republic Tower, is actually two buildings: a 50-story former office and a 32-story building capped by a 150-foot spire. Both buildings are covered in a unique façade made of interlocking aluminum plates. It definitely stands out.

retrospective, an Olafur Eliasson show, and cutting-edge video art from Phil Collins (the artist, not the pop star).

The aforementioned 2005 procurement of 800 works (along with rights to future acquisitions) bolstered a decent permanent collection, which is divided along both temporal and geographic lines. The Art of Europe includes all the notable names—Picasso, Monet, Matisse, Degas, etc.—while the American collection features Wyeth, Sargent, Hopper, and O'Keeffe, among others. The countries overlap in the contemporary collection's works from Jasper Johns, Donald Judd, Matthew Barney, and an increasingly significant collection of German artist Sigmar Polke.

Two collections stand out as unique. First, the varied pieces of ancient indigenous and traditional art that comprise the Art of the Americas are stunningly comprehensive. The second, the Wendy & Emery Reves Collection, is notable more for its peculiarity. The collection is presented in a separate upstairs gallery that re-creates the living room of the Reves' good friend Coco Chanel, complete with priceless paintings from Toulouse-Lautrec, Cezanne, and Monet, among many other masterworks.

The museum houses two restaurants: the upscale Seventeen-Seventeen and the more casual Atrium Café. Different types of tours are available, including recorded or docent-led, for groups of any size. The GTE Collections Information Center, where visitors can download and print out information on the museum's works, is also a handy way to get to know the collection.

DALLAS WORLD AQUARIUM

1801 N. Griffin St., 214/720-2224,

www.dwazoo.com

HOURS: Daily 10 A.M.–5 P.M.

COST: $18.95 adult, $10.95 youth, $14.95 senior, free under 2

"Aquarium" might not be quite accurate: A multistory venue densely packed with flora and fauna, the main space at the Dallas World Aquarium is more like a mini-ecosystem, and it provides one of the most vivid and intimate zoological experiences available. At almost $20 per adult, this sucker had better deliver, and it does: Visitors wend their way through a verdant multilevel exhibit, gazing up as exotic birds whiz by the 30-foot waterfall, then gasping at eye-level amazements like crocodiles, stingrays, and tree sloths. The habitat provides up-close encounters with creatures large (panthers) and small (spiders, snakes, and lizards) and splinters off into side rooms, with individual aquariums devoted to different reef ecosystems from throughout the world. The reefs are a treat, full of colorful, exotic fish and strange sea creatures, but it's only a warm-up for the pièce de résistance: a 22,000-gallon overhead tank filled with sharks, manatees, and other creatures of the deep.

NASHER SCULPTURE CENTER

2001 Flora St., 214/242-5100,

www.nashersculpturecenter.org

HOURS: Tues.-Weds. and Fri.-Sun. 11 A.M.–5 P.M., Thurs. 11 A.M.–11 P.M.

COST: $10 adult, $7 senior, $5 student, free under 12, free after 5 P.M. Thurs. and first Tues. of each month;

© TEXAS TOURISM/KENNY BRAUN

Dallas World Aquarium

joint ticket with Dallas Museum of Art $16 adult, $12 senior, $8 student

Intended not just as a museum but as an artistic oasis amid the hustle and bustle of downtown, the Nasher Sculpture Center was designed by Renzo Piano as an open, airy, inviting space. With its five parallel stone walls and unique "roofless" design that allows indirect light to filter in from above, the building itself could be considered a sculpture. For the outdoor sculpture garden, Piano collaborated with landscape architect Peter Walker to create a seamless transition from the airy inner space to the verdant outdoor area, the museum's centerpiece. Unfortunately, while the building and grounds themselves are striking, both the temporary exhibits and permanent collection often lean toward the stale, despite being peppered with DeKoonings, Picassos, and Rodins. Some of the enormous outdoor sculpture collection feels dated, too, but it's definitely worth the price of admission to take a soothing stroll among the giant works, topped off by a bit of contemplation at the James Turrell skyspace.

A good way to check out the Nasher is to buy the Dallas Museum of Art/Nasher combination ticket, which offers a discounted price, or to attend the lovely Saturday Night in the City events, during which the museum stays open past dark and holds a party favored by the well-heeled and artsy alike.

TAKE A TOUR

The non-profit **Dallas Historical Society's** (3939 Grand Ave., 214/421-7500, www.dallashistory.org, call for schedule and a availability) tours are an excellent resource for discovering the city's overt charm as well as its hidden secrets. The knowledgeable and friendly Dallas-philes who lead the tours prove better ambassadors than the Chamber of Commerce, especially when it comes to the more eclectic aspects of Dallas' past.

The DHS' wide variety of tour offerings reflects that eclecticism. While the group offers a number of comprehensive tours that provide an historical overview, the best ones are more focused on specific aspects or themes of Dallas history, small windows of time, or singular events that helped define the larger picture of Dallas' past. Some suggestions:

The Extreme Dallas Tour gets to the nitty-gritty, underground details of Dallas' past. The tour visits things like the Pennsylvania Railroad engine that led the Robert F. Kennedy funeral procession in 1968, which is housed here, plus numerous other little secrets like the United States' Art Deco monument.

Music fans should check out the **Deep Ellum Walking Tour,** during which visitors walk the very red brick roads that scores of jazz and blues legends like Blind Lemon Jefferson and Robert Johnson traveled. Tour guide Marc Traynor knows his stuff, and he points out old speakeasies amidst new clubs, and hidden points of origin of today's bohemian Deep Ellum.

Alternative history buffs will be especially interested in the **Historic Oak Cliff Tour.** Separated from much of Dallas by the Trinity River and, for many years, along racial lines, Oak Cliff has always enjoyed its own flavor, much of it thanks to its distinct racial and cultural mix. Its contributions to Dallas' past are just as varied: Bonnie and Clyde once ran here, near where Lee Harvey Oswald lived and hid after allegedly shooting the president, down the road from the site of where the 7-11 empire was born.

Speaking of Oswald, perhaps the most popular tour, **Retracing the Steps of Lee Harvey Oswald,** is a chilling excursion that follows Oswald's route the day of the Kennedy Assassination, including the Texas Theater, as well as stops at his boarding house and other points of interest.

I.M. PEI'S GIANT "OOPS": DALLAS CITY HALL

World-renowned architect I.M. Pei has designed several lauded buildings in Dallas: His **Fountain Place skyscraper** (1445 Ross Ave.), for instance, is a modern, eye-bending, downtown beauty that soars to the sky amidst an oasis of frothy fountains. His **Meyerson Symphony Center** (2301 Flora St.) wonderfully fuses geometric shapes, curves and right angles somehow nestling together in beautiful symmetry. The three triangles that form his **Energy Plaza skyscraper** (1601 Bryan St.) pose a striking figure in the middle of downtown.

But his **Dallas City Hall** design at 1500 Marilla Street? Ugh. Clearly, it is ambitious design: The base of the wedge-shaped building – designed and built in the '70s – is much thinner than its top. The downtown-facing facade juts out sharply at 34 degrees, top-down, in an intimidating way over the "buffer zone" that separates the building from the closest street. The design was meant to be democratic and accessible, but, frankly, it's weird and also a pain in the butt (if you park on the street, it takes forever to walk across the buffer zone to actually reach the front doors). It's an intimidating effect, futuristic and secretive – no wonder it was used in the movie *RoboCop* and in the TV show *Lois and Clark* (both times as headquarters for monolith super-corporations). The *Dallas Morning News* City Hall blog called the building "a big doorstop balanced precariously on its tip," and commenters agreed with the disparagement, saying it looked more like "a manure spreader," and even "a punishment to all the senses."

The sad thing is, in theory, Pei's idea was a good one. The angled design helps keep the blazing Texas sun out of the windows, and the dramatic top-heavy sightline instills a sense of awe – how are the higher floors supported?

But even the $70,000,000 it took to build the thing couldn't save it. Which, of course, is all the more reason to go see it: How often do you get to see a mistake on such a scale? It may be a failure, but true to Texas form, at least it's on a gargantuan level.

OLD RED MUSEUM

100 S. Houston St., 214/745-1100,
www.oldred.org

HOURS: Daily 9 A.M.–5 P.M.

COST: $8 adult, $5 child, $6 senior

Long lying comatose and forgotten at the western base of downtown, Old Red finally started getting some attention a few years back and has been refurbished to its Romanesque Revival glory. Outside, the blazing red-colored limestone and signature turrets make this former Dallas County Courthouse immediately recognizable. Inside, a dramatic staircase leads to the second floor, which houses a museum recounting the history of Dallas County. Old Red also serves as home base for the Dallas Visitors Information Center, where you'll find maps, brochures, pamphlets, and a friendly staff ready to help you make the best of your trip.

REUNION TOWER

300 W. Reunion Blvd., 214/651-1234,
www.reuniontower.com

HOURS: Sun.–Thurs. 10 A.M.–10 P.M., Fri.–Sat. 9 A.M.–6 P.M.

COST: $2 adult, $1 child

Sometimes not-so-endearingly called "the Dallas phallus," this recognizable piece of the Dallas skyline has been taking locals and visitors alike to new heights since 1978. Standing around 560 feet high, the tower doesn't consist of much: Three concrete shafts hold elevators that take visitors to the top of the tower (a fourth is for mechanical storage), which is a ball-shaped giant geodesic dome ensconced in a network of flashing lights.

The ball holds three levels. The revolving restaurant Antares once comprised the entire second floor, but since then, a two-year renovation has combined it with the third-floor lounge; now, the new restaurant, called Fifty-Six, is helmed by none other than Wolfgang Puck. The first floor consists of an observation deck that provides the city's best views of Dallas, Fort Worth, and the surrounding environs.

SIXTH FLOOR MUSEUM/JFK SITE/ DEALEY PLAZA

411 Elm St., 214/747-6660,
www.jfk.org
HOURS: Tues.-Sun. 10 A.M.-6 P.M., Mon. noon-6 P.M.

JFK

Dallas is famous for a lot of things; sadly, one of them involves a terrible chapter in our country's history. The assassination of President John F. Kennedy occurred at 12:30 P.M., Friday, November 22, 1963 on the north side of Elm Street in downtown Dallas. The city has never forgotten it.

The city also has had a tough time reconciling its relationship with the historic tragedy. For many years, Dallas collectively tried to forget, even coming close to tearing down the Texas School Book Depository building, from which Kennedy's alleged assassin Lee Harvey Oswald fired his shots.

Fortunately, the Depository still stands. The building is a scar on the city − Elm Street is still highly trafficked, and it's an eerie feeling to drive past it on the way to work or for an evening on the town. But imagine if it weren't there, if it had been destroyed and replaced by a skyscraper or a strip mall. Would that have changed something in our collective memory? Would it have caused our national memory to fade in a different way? Would it have altered how we see the assassination?

Fortunately, we don't have to answer that question, as not only does the Depository remain, its infamous Sixth Floor has been transformed into an excellent museum. In fact, while much of the Dallas landscape has changed, plenty of sites relating to the Kennedy assassination remain. Here are some of the main ones.

THE SIXTH FLOOR MUSEUM

The Sixth Floor Museum is pricey, but well worth it. The self-guided tour begins with an extensive exhibit that puts Kennedy's presidency into social, historical, and political context − especially helpful for the younger folks who were not alive to experience it themselves. The comprehensive set of artifacts and displays set the stage for understanding the significance of what happened on November 22nd. The tour then moves on to a timeline of Kennedy's Dallas-Fort Worth visit, complete with detailed notes, photos, videos, and imagery. Finally, the assassination is covered, in chilling detail. There's no original evidence shown here, which is probably for the best, but a centerpiece is the actual, to-scale FBI model of Dealey Plaza designed for the Warren Commission. The most chilling display of all comes at the end of the tour; there, you'll find the "sniper's nest," recreated with book boxes to look just as it did the day Oswald supposedly fired out of it.

DEALEY PLAZA

Completed as a WPA project in 1940, Dealey Plaza is named for George Dealey, an early civic leader in Dallas and former publisher of the *Dallas Morning News*. Visitors with even the most casual knowledge of the Kennedy assassination recognize the Plaza, and today it teems with tourists and history buffs exploring its many notable sites, including:

Conspiracy Theorists: If you prefer not to pay the fee to get upstairs, or would like to supplement your museum experience, exploring Dealey Plaza is a fascinating way to spend anywhere from 30 minutes to a couple

COST: $13.50 adult, $12.50 youth, $7 senior, free under 5

It's often a startling moment for visitors when they first encounter the nexus of Houston and Elm Streets, the location where President John F. Kennedy, Jr. was shot to death on November 22, 1963. Suddenly, the black-and-white images familiar to so many of us change to color, and the Abraham Zapruder film comes to life. The sadly well-known panorama is all there: the grassy knoll, the triple underpass, and, of course, the Texas School Book Depository, from which the shots that killed Kennedy were fired by depository employee Lee Harvey Oswald (at least, according to some witnesses and the Warren Commission).

of hours. The truly adventurous should start with a chat with any number of conspiracy theorists who mill about at the base of the Depository building. These people may be considered to be crazy by some, and to be truth-seekers by others, but no matter what your personal theories about the JFK assassination are, they provide a never-ending flow of fodder. Some prove indeed to truly be wackos, while others actually are bona fide amateur historians. Take note: They also usually want money, so if you end up talking for a while, you might want end up throwing a buck or two in a donations jar or buying a pamphlet-it's all part of the experience.

The North Pergola/Grassy Knoll: Dealey Plaza is flanked by two pergolas-dramatic colonnades-that many people mistakenly think are Kennedy memorials. They are actually monuments to figures of Dallas history and pre-date the assassination. The pergola on the north side of Elm Street (the side by the Depository) is a memorial to Dallas founder John Neely Bryan. This is where Abraham Zapruder famously stood with his 8mm camera filming the motorcade and capturing the assassination on film. The North Pergola sits on the grassy knoll, from which many witnesses claim to have heard gunshots.

Wooden Fence/North Tower: At the top of the slope of the grassy knoll you'll find a wooden fence, the area where some witnesses claim they saw a puff of smoke shortly after the shots. The fence that currently stands is not the original-it long ago fell into disrepair and was replaced-but visitors can access both sides of it. If you walk around the back side of the fence, you will be near the railroad tower commonly called the "North Tower." A few witnesses also claimed to see mysterious men – including the famous "hobos" – milling around the fence and the North Tower that day.

X's: Two large white X's are taped to the pavement in the middle of Elm Street. Both mark the approximate spots where the two bullets that struck Kennedy hit. While many people think the X's are official markers, they are actually placed there by amateur historians. While it's extremely morbid to contemplate, the X's actually help bring the assassination into full perspective. When viewed from both the Sixth Floor and then the Grassy Knoll, for instance, it's easy to see how much more difficult Oswald's shot was than one would be from behind the fence.

Also rather morbidly, many visitors dodge cars and stand on the X's to have their pictures taken. If you attempt this, word of warning: Elm Street is still in use and heavily trafficked – such activity is not recommended.

John F. Kennedy Memorial: The smooth white walls of Philip Johnson's 30-foot concrete cenotaph melds seamlessly with Dealey Plaza's concrete pergolas, but stands out as a more streamlined, somber piece. The cenotaph consists of four walls, with airy entryways and no roof. The inside, meant by Johnson to be a place of contemplation amidst the bustle of downtown, centers on a single slab of marble bearing only three words: John Fitzgerald Kennedy. The monument can be found about two blocks east of where Kennedy was shot.

OSWALD AND RUBY SITES

Many of the sites associated with Lee Harvey Oswald can be found in Oak Cliff. A primarily residential area on the south side of Dallas, Oak Cliff is where Lee Harvey Oswald lived around the time of the assassination. Oak Cliff is also the area where Oswald allegedly killed Dallas Police Officer J.D. Tippit and where Oswald was arrested at the Texas Theater. Today, much of Oak Cliff struggles with poverty and crime, although that has improved somewhat in the past few years. The Bishop Arts District (near most of the Oak Cliff Oswald sites) neighborhood, for instance, has undergone a notable revitalization, although these changes have been criticized by some as gentrification.

Oswald Family Residence: From the street, it's tough to see the backyard of the Oswald Residence (212 W. Neely St.), where the well-known photos of Oswald holding his Carcano rifle were taken (of course, according to many, the photos were faked). Oswald's address was actually the top floor, 214 W. Neely. Nowadays the house is definitely worse for the wear, but it's still clearly recognizable.

Oswald's Residence, 1963: In November 1963, Oswald was living at a rooming house at 1026 N. Beckley Avenue, just south of Zang Boulevard. The house still stands in good condition today, and it's easy to drive by and see it (just don't knock on the door).

Site of Tippit Murder: Less than a mile southeast of the Beckley house you'll find this nondescript residential intersection (Corner of E.10th St, and Patton Ave.), where Oswald (or, again according to some theorists, someone else) shot and killed Dallas Police Officer J.D. Tippit somewhere between 1 and 1:15 P.M. the afternoon of the assassination. Tippit had been driving east down East 10th when he pulled over to talk to Oswald, according to witnesses, about 100 feet past the intersection with Patton Avenue. When he got out of the car to speak further, Oswald shot him.

Hardy Shoe Store/Texas Theater: After Tippit's shooting, Oswald slipped into the Hardy Shoe Store (213 W. Jefferson Ave.), where a clerk named Johnny Brewer noticed him acting peculiar. Oswald then popped back out and made the short walk down the street to the Texas Theater (231 W. Jefferson Ave.). He entered without paying for his ticket, and shortly afterward Brewer alerted the ticket taker to call the police. Oswald was arrested after a scuffle. The seat he was sit-

The School Book Depository actually sits in the middle of what was, pre-1963, already a historic site. Named after *Dallas Morning News* founder George Dealey, the park-like area commemorated both its namesake and the city's founder, John Neely Bryan, who had established his pioneer outpost on the spot in 1841. The area's open-air Bryan Colonnade (upon which Zapruder stood to film the motorcade) was built, along with other additions, as part of a Works Progress Administration (WPA) project during Franklin Roosevelt's presidency.

For decades after the assassination, Dealey Plaza and the School Book Depository saw very little in the way of official commemoration of such a world-changing event. The primary source of information about the assassination, in fact, was the handful of conspiracy theorists who gathered there daily and who still mill about near the grassy knoll today. Some of these are charlatans, hoping to hawk a few brochures, books, or videotapes. Others are genuinely passionate and knowledgeable about the subject. Others, like Robert Groden—who is responsible for painting the white "X's" that mark the exact spot on Elm

ting in at the Texas Theater now bears his name in gold leaf.

Oswald Murder Site: The basement where Jack Ruby shot Lee Harvey Oswald still exists underneath the building that once served as Dallas City Hall (2001 Commerce St., now the City Municipal Building). By all accounts, the site looks pretty much the same, with the addition of a second pair of glass doors, but it's tough to get down there without getting kicked out or possibly arrested, so don't try it. Similarly, the public is not allowed access to the fifth floor, where Oswald was being held before the attempt, thwarted by Ruby, to transfer him to the city jail. Still, the beautiful Beaux Arts structure is worth seeing, and a quick walk-by is worth it.

Former Site of the Carousel Club: Owned and operated by Jack Ruby, this semi-seedy burlesque bar, the Carousel Club (1312 Commerce St.), was long ago replaced by a modern office building across the street from both the Adolphus and Magnolia hotels. Still, if you walk by the site, it's eerie to notice just how close it is to other important sites like the old City Hall, where Ruby shot Oswald, and Dealey Plaza itself.

Campisi's Egyptian Lounge: While Campisi's (5610 E. Mockingbird Lane) by now has grown into a city-wide chain, its flagship still oozes history and dark ambiance. The Campisi's chain was begun by Carlo Campisi and his sons Joseph and Sam, who back in the day were well-known mob figures in Dallas. According to the House Committee on Assassinations, this is where Jack Ruby ate a steak dinner the night before Kennedy's death. It is still open, still family owned, and still easily identified by its mod "Egyptian Lounge" neon sign-although the place is 100 percent Italian, Joe Campisi kept the sign after he bought the place. You might recognize the current proprietor Carlo "Corky" Campisi and his daughters from the E! network's reality show *Wildest Party Parents*.

Oswald's Grave: Oswald is buried at Rose Hill Cemetery (7301 E. Lancaster Ave., Fort Worth) in Fort Worth underneath a simple marker that reads simply "Oswald." Don't ask cemetery employees where the grave is – their policy is to not reveal its location. In a weird twist, a comedian named Nick Beef purchased the plot next to Oswald so that he would be remembered as. . .the person buried next to Lee Harvey Oswald. The ploy worked, so now cemetery employees refuse to give directions to the grave of Nick Beef as well.

Street where the assassin's bullets found their mark—are a little of both.

When the School Book Depository company moved out of the building in 1970, Dallas didn't quite know what to do with the place. Many Dallasites called for the building's destruction, citing it as a painful reminder. That same year, the city took a huge step toward officially recognizing the assassination by unveiling the Philip Johnson–designed Kennedy Memorial. Consisting of 50-foot-high marble slabs that semi-enclose a contemplation area, the memorial is meant, according to the architect, "not as a memorial to the pain and sorrow of death," but as "a permanent tribute to the joy and excitement of one man's life."

The depository changed hands for several years, almost succumbing to an arsonist's fire in 1972, until Dallas County acquired the building in 1977. The Dallas County Commission used the bottom five floors as office space; the sixth and seventh floors remained empty.

Finally, in 1989, the Sixth Floor Museum opened, and Dallas began to come to terms with its place in a dark day in history.

© TEXAS TOURISM/KENNY BRAUN

John F. Kennedy Memorial in downtown Dallas

The museum does an excellent job of easing visitors toward a rather macabre ending—the sniper's nest, re-created with boxes positioned as they were on the day of the assassination. Much of the exhibit places Kennedy's presidency in social, cultural, and historical context before moving on to interactive stations featuring video of his speeches and footage of his entire visit to Texas. There are plenty of displays dedicated to the assassination as well, including the built-to-scale diorama of Dealey Plaza used by the FBI, journal pages from witnesses and doctors at Parkland Hospital, and a timeline of the actions of Lee Harvey Oswald, among hundreds of fascinating pieces. As a whole, the museum is good for those who remember as well as those who are too young to have experienced that time in history.

Uptown Dallas
Map 2

FREEDMAN'S MEMORIAL
Lemmon Ave. and Central Expy., 214/670-3284

It's kind of a mixed bag at the Freedman's Memorial. On one hand, the memorial's grand granite arches with poems etched into the entryway provide a touching tribute to the slaves and former slaves who were buried in the cemetery nearby. On the other hand, knowing that many of those graves were disinterred and moved during a rash of development during the 1960s doesn't exactly stir the soul. Still, the $2 million work is a beautiful, if belated, acknowledgement.

Park Cities
Map 3

SOUTHERN METHODIST UNIVERSITY
6425 Boaz Ln., 214/628-2000,
www.smu.edu

Officially chartered in 1911 (classes began in 1915), Southern Methodist University has grown into a focal point of higher education in the Southwest. The university's popularity and prowess is demonstrated by its billion-dollar-plus endowment, beautiful campus of green lawns, Ivy League–style buildings, and old-growth trees, as well as its consistent matriculation of professionally degreed students. It's also the home to the George W. Bush Presidential Library (which has met with some opposition from Dallas's less conservative population).

SMU has much to offer visitors. The university calendar is overflowing with lecture series, symposia, concerts, and exhibits. Many of the events are free or low-cost and/or open to the public. Athletic events are some of the most popular pastimes. Ever since enduring the severe "Death Penalty" punishment due to serious recruiting violations in 1985, the Mustangs football team has been known as subpar, though in late years it has bounced back, and hopes have risen for the future with the 2007 hiring of respected coach June Jones. Pre-game, many fans choose to tailgate or picnic along Bishop Boulevard before moving to Gerald J. Ford Stadium. The soccer team is also popular, having dominated its competition in recent years. SMU is a member of the NCAA's Division I Conference USA.

Another popular campus destination is the Meadows Museum, home of one of the world's largest collections of Spanish art. The neo-Palladian space provides a spectacular area in which to view Spanish art from the 10th to 20th centuries, including Picassos, Goyas, Riberas, and El Grecos, among many others.

Greenville Map 4

SWISS AVENUE
Runs southwest to northeast between Munger Blvd. and La Vista Dr.

There's no greater testament to the history of Dallas's grand opulence than historic Swiss Avenue. Gigantic historic mansions flank this wide boulevard, which runs for two-and-a-half miles smack through the middle of East Dallas. The street, with its more than 200 homes of varying architectural types, including Mediterranean, Prairie, Craftsman, Neoclassical, and others, is a must-see for lovers of 19th- and early 20th-century architecture. In the mornings and evenings, and on tolerable summer days, the sidewalks bear neighborhood denizens and gawkers alike as they stroll, jog, and walk dogs, enjoying the breeze rustling the leaves of the fully mature trees.

East Dallas Map 5

FAIR PARK
www.fairpark.org

Fair Park contains a city's worth of sports and entertainment facilities, historical sights, museums, and architectural delights, all rolled into one 277-acre complex. Built in 1936 for the Texas State Centennial (celebrating 100 years of liberty from Mexico), the Fair Park grounds and buildings are bedecked in amazing art deco style, with WPA-era murals, grand esplanades, and dramatic detailing. Aside from the delights they house, the buildings themselves are considered important historic works.

A favorite edifice is the Hall of State, a grand beaux arts structure with an entrance guarded by *The Tejas Warrior*, an 11-foot-tall gilded statue of a Native American brandishing a bow at the sky. The exterior of the building is inscribed with the names of 59 Texas luminaries of the past. Inside you'll find the "Hall of Heroes," with its six statues of Texas's most revered historical figures. The building now provides a home to the Dallas Historical Society as well as the G. B. Dealey Library and its three million historic documents.

Other highlights include the African-

the Hall of State in Dallas's Fair Park

COURTESY OF TEXAS HISTORICAL COMMISSION

© TEXAS TOURISM/KENNY BRAUN

the Texas Star Ferris wheel in Fair Park

American Museum, the Women's Museum, and the Science Place (a great choice for kids). A Fair Park Pass, available on the Fair Park website, gets you entry to these three and the Hall of State, plus four other museums on the grounds: the Age of Steam Railroad Museum, Texas Discovery Gardens, Dallas Aquarium, and Museum of Natural History.

Every year the grounds are home to the Texas State Fair, the largest of its kind in the country, attended by millions of visitors. It can seem odd to witness flip-flop–clad families scarfing down corn dogs and fried Nutter Butters in the shadow of the grand facades and statues that adorn the Hall of State, but then, Dallas has always prided itself on contradiction—that's part of the fun. Dramatically welcoming all State Fair visitors are two giant structures: a 52-foot-tall cowboy named Big Tex, and North America's largest Ferris wheel, called the Texas

Star, both of which lord over the fair's activities. Popular fair activities include auto shows, concerts, midway games, amusement park rides, animal shows, pig races, and pigging out on every type of food imaginable—fried.

Let's not forget the famous Cotton Bowl, recently renovated and expanded to 80,000 seats, that looms at the northern half of the park complex. Until 2008, the State Fair festivities involved the Red River Shootout, the annual football game between the University of Oklahoma and the University of Texas. That game moved to the new Dallas Cowboys' stadium in Arlington, but the Cotton Bowl still hosts the annual State Fair Classic between traditionally African-American schools Grambling State and Prairie View A&M. Frankly, the football teams usually aren't very good—but fans still pack the stadium for the spectacular battle of the bands at halftime.

LATINO CULTURAL CENTER

2600 Live Oak St., 214/670-3320,

www.dallasculture.org/latinoCulturalCenter.cfm

HOURS: Tues.–Sat. 10 A.M.–5 P.M.

COST: Free

Mexican architect Ricardo Legorreta crafted this stunning faux-adobe building that opened in 2003. The exterior performs a miracle: The shadow play created by Legorreta's angled walls intermingles with the building's sharp edges and even sharper colors, transforming the industrial blight of Live Oak Street into a bit of visual magical realism. The center itself is a focal point of Latino art, music, literary events, dance, and education.

South Dallas   Map 6

DALLAS ZOO

650 S. R. L. Thornton Fwy., 214/670-5656,

www.dallaszoo.com

HOURS: Daily 9 A.M.–4 P.M.

COST: $10 adult, $7 youth and senior, free under 2

Even though it covers a potentially daunting 95 acres of land, the Dallas Zoo's organized layout makes for a fun, easy, educational foray. The zoo is basically divided into two parts: the Wilds of Africa and ZooNorth. A stroll along the nature path at the Wilds of Africa takes visitors through river, desert, forest, mountain, brush, and woodland habitats filled with chimps, gorillas, crocs, and other African species. One mildly annoying feature, though, is that many of the other Wilds of Africa animals are only visible from the Monorail Safari.

ZooNorth is a great place to take kids, especially considering the highly interactive Lacerte Family Children's Zoo, where the little ones can clamber through a giant bird's nest or through an oversized "spider web."

It should be noted that despite its acreage, the zoo can come off as very small and disappointing as far as the number and variety of animals. The past several years have seen a revived effort to improve the grounds and facilities, including an initiative to recycle animal waste into power for the site. Still, even attempts to improve the zoo have sparked controversy, most recently when Jenny the Elephant was forced into smaller quarters while waiting for the expansion of the elephant habitat.

TEXAS THEATER

231 W. Jefferson Blvd., no phone

www.oakclifffoundation.org

Dallas has a conflicted relationship with the residuals from the Kennedy assassination. On one hand is the impulse to preserve the important historical structures associated with that fateful day. On the other, who wants to maintain and preserve painful reminders?

Such was the quandary faced when it came to one of the most iconic and recognizable buildings associated with the Kennedy murder: the Texas Theater, where Oswald sat in the fifth seat from the aisle, in the third-to-last row, watching *War Is Hell* as the Dallas Police Department closed in.

When it opened in 1931 as part of Howard Hughes' national chain, the theater was one of the fanciest and most technologically advanced in the country, and it opened with great fanfare as the anchor of the Jefferson Boulevard district. The place flourished, and even after the infamous November day in 1963, the theater continued to beckon patrons with its air-conditioning and signature sign that spelled out T-E-X-A-S in huge vertical neon letters.

Slowly, however, upkeep lessened along with attendance, and the interior grew shabby as fewer and fewer patrons showed up. The beautiful interior details and paintings were lathed over, and the Jefferson area suffered from a rough reputation, keeping moviegoers away. In 1989, the theater closed.

In the ensuing years, the historic spot narrowly escaped several dates with a wrecking ball, until finally rescued by a collaboration between the Dallas Summer Musicals group and the city in 2001. Since then, the venue has undergone well more than a million dollars in renovation and restoration, and the work continues. The theater now hosts special movie screenings, traveling theatrical shows, and local performing arts companies (there are no tours, so keep an eye out for events). And, while Dallas will never fully embrace its Kennedy history, at least the Texas Theater has begun to acknowledge it—even Oswald's chair has his name etched in it as a reminder.

THE VERY FIRST 7-ELEVEN
Corner of Edgefield Ave. and 12th St.

Dallas has long been populated with entrepreneurs, and when Joe Thompson took his shot in 1927, it paid off. Thompson started as a worker in an Oak Cliff ice house called Southland Ice Company when he realized that, given the restricted hours and far-flung locations of local grocery stores, there was a killing to be made selling "convenience items" like eggs, milk, and bread along with ice. Soon, Thompson was moving more sundries than ice, and he eventually bought Southland and set up shop. The original site remained a 7–Eleven until 1995; today, the old icehouse holds different occupants, but it's still the birthplace of an American institution.

Greater Dallas   Map 11

DALLAS ARBORETUM
8525 Garland Rd., 214/515-6500,
www.dallasarboretum.org
HOURS: Daily 9 A.M.–5 P.M.
COST: $9.50 adult, $6 youth, $8 senior
($6 every Tues.), free under 3

A peaceful oasis on the edge of White Rock Lake, the Arboretum covers 66 acres of real estate with endless swaths of flowers, trees, and other lush botanical delights. Each of the 12 different gardens has its own personality, sometimes wowing visitors with blazing colors, other times soothing with pastoral charm. The pecan grove provides a relaxing, tree-shaded picnic area, and kids will enjoy Toad Corners, with its oversize toad statues that squirt water. An afternoon stroll through the grounds proves a relaxing antidote to the glare and grime of the city, and makes downtown feel miles away, when really it's just down the road. On-site parking is $5 ($10 for valet), though there is off-site parking with a shuttle available during peak times.

LOUIS TUSSAUD'S PALACE OF WAX AND RIPLEY'S BELIEVE IT OR NOT!
601 Palace Pkwy., 817/263-2391 or 972/263-2391
HOURS: Mon.-Fri. 10 A.M.-5 P.M., Sat.-Sun. 10 A.M.-6 P.M.

COST: For all three sites: $30 adult, $18 youth, $26 senior and military; for two sites: $22 adult, $13 youth, $20 senior and military; for one site: $17 adult, $9 youth, $15 senior and military

A seven-foot Leaning Tower of Pisa and the life of Jesus depicted in wax are just a couple of the sometimes goofy, sometimes amazing sights at these two attractions under one roof. While it's a touch pricey, both of these spots keep the kids happy and the parents amused. If you only have time for one, choose the Palace of Wax; the Ripley's "odditorium" section relies a bit heavily on photos and two-dimensional displays. The recent addition of the **Ripley's Mirror Maze** supplies additional zing, but it's considered a third attraction and costs extra—believe it or not.

NATIONAL SCOUTING MUSEUM

1329 W. Walnut Hill Ln., Irving, 800/303-3047, www.bsamuseum.org

HOURS: Tues.-Sat. 10 A.M.-5 P.M., Mon. 10 A.M.-7 P.M., Sun. 1 P.M.-5 P.M.

COST: $8 adult, $6 youth, $6 senior, free under 4, $5 scouts

Scouting may be an old tradition, but this museum focusing on the history of the Boy Scouts of America is state of the art. Next door to the Boy Scouts of America's national headquarters in Irving, the site uses every inch of its 50,000 square feet, much of it dedicated to interactive displays and historic campsite dioramas. A shooting range, kayaking zone, derby car racetrack, and many other blockbuster activities keep the place well out of the dry, boring museum category. In addition, the museum tells the story of Boy Scouting by way of a robotic Lord Robert S. S. Baden-Powell, the founder of the Scouts, and 500,000 artifacts, including the very first Eagle Scout badge (it's too fragile to be shown consistently—call ahead to see if it's on display). If you and the kids aren't too exhausted, check out the art collection, which boasts the largest number of Norman Rockwell paintings under one roof, on your way out.

North Side Fort Worth   Map 7

◖ FORT WORTH STOCKYARDS NATIONAL HISTORIC DISTRICT

131 E. Exchange Blvd., 817/336-4373, www.fortworthstockyards.org

HOURS: Mon.-Fri. 11:30 A.M. and 4 P.M.

COST: Free

Fort Worth has not forgotten its history—rather, it's alive and well and can be enjoyed by all at the Stockyards. The Fort Worth Stockyards National Historic District is the actual hub of livestock commerce that gave Fort Worth its fame on the Chisholm Trail.

The original buildings, live music, and cowboys, all of which are still there, makes this a part of town that you don't want to miss. In fact, every day, history appears in the cobblestone streets of the Stockyards in the form of 15 braying longhorns and their drovers—the Fort Worth Herd. Cowboys decked out in authentic period gear guide the cattle along Exchange Boulevard, just like they did in the old days, as the great beasts groan and mew, kicking up dust—an impressive sight.

Downtown Fort Worth   Map 8

BASS HALL

525 Commerce St., 817/212-4200, www.basshall.com

This 10-story, 2,200 seat performance center, designed by David Schwarz and funded entirely by private funds, stands as the ostentatious crown jewel of downtown's revitalization. Built in 1998, the hall is guarded by two 50-foot limestone angels, trumpets lifted, as if heralding a new age of Fort Worth culture. In the entranceway, Jimmy Choos click alongside cowboy boots on the cut marble floors that lie underneath the lofty domed ceiling's trompe l'oeil clouds. The performance hall itself follows a horseshoe shape that provides excellent sightlines and even better acoustics, especially important, as it is now the permanent home of the Fort Worth Symphony Orchestra, the Van Cliburn International Piano Competition, the Texas Ballet Theater, and the Fort Worth Opera. The latter may have garnered Bass Hall's first major accolade—in 1998, *Travel + Leisure* magazine deemed it one of the top ten opera houses in the world.

FORT WORTH WATER GARDENS

1502 Commerce St., 817/871-5755

Architect Philip Johnson designed this downtown site, consisting of three unique water sculptures, as an oasis in the middle of downtown's concrete and skyscrapers. The three pieces are vastly different. The first is a still meditation pool, a plane of water as flat as glass that drops off over a 90-degree edge onto a sunken walkway. A more dynamic second pool is made of several small, spraying fountains, while the most popular is the "active pool," in which water falls down four terraced walls into a central square pool (you may recognize

THE TALE OF THE TIN CAN TOWER

There are many different advantages to the location of North Texas, but avoiding tornados isn't one of them. DFW sits in the thick of a wide swath of the Midwest known as **"Tornado Alley,"** and twisters here are more common in the spring than ticks on a hound dog.

Tornados often hit rural areas and, somewhat less commonly, suburban areas, but rarely do they hit downtowns. Yet that's just what happened on March 28, 2000, when an F3 tornado ripped through the skyscrapers of downtown Fort Worth.

Two people were killed by the storm, scores more injured, and a four-mile track of damage included 15 destroyed buildings, 17 damaged skyscrapers, and between $450-500 million dollars in damage. One of the worst hit buildings was the iconic 37-story Bank One Tower that overlooks Sundance Square. The building, one of the trademark silhouettes of the downtown skyline, sustained extraordinary damage – most of the windows were shattered, and that, combined with the interior damage, led most to conclude that rebuilding would be too dangerous and expensive. The fifth-tallest building in downtown Fort Worth, the tower was slated to be torn down.

But, miraculously, after sitting for about a year covered in plywood and metal – hence its adopted nickname the The Tin Can Tower – the building got a reprieve. Local developer TLC Realty purchased the building and completely restructured it, adding an octagonal facade and an even an extra 34 feet on the top floor. TLC then converted the interior into condos, with a few retail spots on the ground floor, and renamed the property simply, "The Tower." Today, with downtown hopping, the Tower stands at full capacity. The Tower also now measures as the fourth tallest tower in downtown (thanks to that extra 34 feet).

it from the 1976 film *Logan's Run*). The effect is both hypnotic and dramatic.

SUNDANCE SQUARE

Between 1st and 5th Sts., from Throckmorton St. to Jones St.

www.sundancesquare.com

Named after legendary gangster the Sundance Kid, Sundance Square is 20 square blocks of the newly redone downtown Fort Worth, replete with shopping, festivals, bars, restaurants, and sight-seeing. The square is a tourist haven, though locals also flock to it for its family-friendly activities and its fun, safe nightlife.

But it wasn't always that way. As a major stop on the Chisholm Trail, Fort Worth in the late 1800s endured its fair share of scallywags and debauched behavior, the most decrepit of which occurred in the downtown red-light district known as Hell's Half Acre, right around where Sundance Square sits today. This is where the Sundance Kid, Butch Cassidy and others of their ilk came to gamble, fight and, er, indulge in other carnal delights.

After years of gunfights, gambling and political stalling (after all, there's profit in sin), the town powers finally got fed up and began to crack down on the rowdy neighborhood. The area eventually cleaned up, and as time went on, the old bordellos and saloons were replaced by skyscrapers and hotels. By modern times,

BUTCH AND SUNDANCE

While neighboring Dallas boasts its own outlaw history with Bonnie and Clyde, Fort Worth brags of its own infamous pair. At the turn of the century, Robert LeRoy Parker, aka **Butch Cassidy,** and Harry Longabaugh, aka the **Sundance Kid,** tore through the West with the Wild Bunch on a killing and robbing spree made famous by the semi-ficitonal film *Butch Cassidy and the Sundance Kid*. While the pair moved about constantly, they spent a good amount of time in Fort Worth, especially in the gangsters' paradise known as Hell's Half Acre.

Filled with gambling, violence, drinking and prostitution, Hell's Half Acre might well have boasted the most debeauched behavior per square foot of any place west of the Mississippi. Butch and Sundance fit right in. While there, they and few others from the Wild Bunch gussied themselves up and popped into John Swartz's photography studio to get their portrait taken. The photo of the "Fort Worth Five," as they became known, ended up as one of the most recognizable relics of the Wild West.

It also got them into trouble. Some folks claim that the gang, feeling their oats, mailed the portrait to one of the banks they had robbed, which then turned it over to the Pinkerton Detective Agency. Others claim a passing lawman recognized the crooks' picture in Swartz's window. Either way, the photo made its way into Pinkerton hands, and it was used to track down the Wild Bunch, one by one. Pinkerton agents even distributed hundreds of copies in South America, where Butch and Sundance had fled. Sure enough, the two men were found in Bolivia, and killed by law enforcement.

Hell's Half Acre eventually succumbed to the progress of law and order, too, and many skyscrapers that house downtown Fort Worth's respected, international businesses sit atop the site of the boisterous old district. The gangsters have even grown respectable – when city fathers revitalized and refurbished downtown, they decided to name its central area, full of family-friendly shops and restaurants, Sundance Square.

Hell's Half Acre had grown into a downright respectable downtown.

And it was boring. At least until the Bass family got their hands on it. About a hundred years after the Half-Acre's heyday, one of Fort Worth's richest oil dynasties, the Basses, spearheaded a huge effort to revamp downtown into a viable entertainment district, a tourist draw, and a moneymaker. The Basses and the city worked together to refurbish the old Art Deco and turn-of-the-century style buildings and lured businesses, retail, and entertainment venues back downtown. They designated wide swaths of free parking, and created a security bike patrol with a visible presence.

Today, what was once known as Hell's Half-Acre is now a civic centerpiece. Simply walking around staring at refurbished buildings like the Worthington National Bank makes for a lovely, and cheap, pastime there. The WNB was built in 1914 and, even though it's a working bank, the building feels more like a meticulously crafted museum re-creation, with iron bars guarding the teller windows, authentic fixtures and décor, and custom-cut marble floors glossed to a high sheen. Other architectural highlights include the Knights of Pythias Hall, a red sandstone edifice replete with turrets and a giant knight, and the Jett Building, on the side of which you'll find Richard Haas' three-story-high mural depicting cowpokes driving cattle on the Chisholm Trail. The open expanse abutting Haas' piece often serves as the epicenter of year-round cultural and civic festivals and events, including everything from huge music fests to open-air movie screenings.

In addition to city-wide celebrations, shopping, nightlife and architecture, there's also culture. There's probably no better place for the Sid Richardson Museum, for instance, than such a historic locale. This Western art museum commissioned by a the legendary local oilman often falls under the radar in comparison to the Cultural Districts behemoths, but 50,000 visitors a year still visit the modest Sundance Square building that houses works by Remington, Russell, and others.

TARRANT COUNTY COURTHOUSE
100 W. Weatherford St., 817/884-1111

Surrounded by gleaming hi-rises, the dramatic Tarrant County Courthouse still commands attention. You might recognize the pink granite structure, built in an opulent American Beaux Arts style and topped with its signature clock tower, from the TV show *Walker, Texas Ranger*. Construction began on the courthouse in 1893 and didn't end until 1895, at a cost of over $400,000, thanks in part to the fees of the Kansas City firm who designed it, Gunn and Curtis Architects, and the cost of importing the granite from Austin. The townsfolk, disgusted at what they deemed an unnecessary extravagance, responded by ousting the entire Tarrant County Commissioners' Court, but nowadays, the building stands as a testament to the vision of Fort Worth's early citizens. Tours aren't given on a regular basis, but can be requested.

TCU and Vicinity   Map 9

ELIZABETH BOULEVARD

Elizabeth Blvd. between 8th and College Aves.

Much like Swiss Avenue in Dallas, Elizabeth Boulevard is rich in history and architectural eye-candy. The street, intentionally developed by John C. Ryan as a residential area for the town's oil gentry and professionals, saw its first house built in 1911. Ryan envisioned the neighborhood as an exclusive enclave to rival "Quality Hill," and even had ornate stone entry gates built to mark the area's special-ness. From there, house after house followed, each employing its own variation on any number of revival themes: Mission, Mediterranean, Georgian, classical and others, and some of them bordering on palatial. Smaller touches, such as tiled curb signs and streetlights, add to the rarified atmosphere here, and make a drive or walk down the street a pleasant diversion.

FORT WORTH ZOO

1989 Colonial Pkwy., 817/759-7555,
www.fortworthzoo.org

HOURS: Late Oct.-late Feb. daily 10 A.M.-4 P.M., late Feb.-late Mar. daily 10 A.M.-5 P.M., late Mar.-late Oct. Mon.-Fri. 10 A.M.-5 P.M., Sat.-Sun. 10 A.M.-6 P.M.

COST: $12 adult, $8 youth, $7 senior, free under 2

Well-funded and well-visited, the Fort Worth Zoo practically bursts with animals and activities. Founded in 1909, the zoo fell on hard times in the early 1990s as upkeep faltered and attendance dropped. Soon after, the non-profit Fort Worth Zoological Society took over fund-raising and management, and the zoo rapidly improved. Since then, almost every section of the zoo has seen expansion and restructuring, resulting in what amounts to an entirely new zoo—one of the best in the country.

The only downside: There are several days worth of premium exhibits—15 in all—so choices have to be made. If you only have a day or two, here are some suggestions:

Asian Falls: Carved out of an existing hillside, this is one of the zoo's most popular sites. Visitors make their way through a windy path that includes above-ground boardwalks from which to ogle elephants, rhinos, sunbears and various hoofstock animals, many of whom cool themselves in the waterfall-fed pools. Dramatic enough, but the real highlight is a pair of rare Malayan tigers, not to mention their feline counterparts across the ravine—a pair of gorgeous white tigers.

Cheetos Cheetahs: The good thing about the Zoological Society is its ability to raise funds from large companies; the flip side is that some of the zoo's most refined and exciting exhibits are plastered with reminders of the corporate side of things, like Frito-Lay's Cheetos. But even the biggest corporate intrusions are quickly forgotten at this exhibit. The area is divided into three separate sections accommodating three different species. The first is grassy forest clearing, home to African bongos, which are large antelope with dramatic spiraled antlers. The second is also a grassy plain dotted with hills and stands of trees, under which the zoo's group of cheetahs often lounge. The third is the warthog yard, where the hogs are often found cooling off in their mud pool.

Australian Outback/Great Barrier Reef: Sadly, the koala that's been on loan from the San Diego Zoo has been returned, but this exhibit still has plenty of wow factor, most

© FORT WORTH CVB

lions at the Fort Worth Zoo

notably the 10,000-gallon aquarium full of colorful fish, coral and sharks. The reef conjoins with the larger Australian Outback area, home to a number of kangaroos and wallabies.

African Savannah: Giraffes, rhinos, and ostriches compete for attention as visitors navigate the overhead boardwalks and ground-level sidewalks.

Komodo Dragons: They don't do much but loll in the sun, but these 7-foot Japanese reptiles are still somehow fascinating, as exemplified by the crowds they draw.

Texas Wild!: While it may not have the international appeal of some of the more exotic exhibits, the Texas Wild! habitat is a must-see for anyone interested in the land, flora and fauna of the Lone Star State. With its size and scope, Texas Wild! could well be a theme park unto itself, as visitors tour around the "habitats" of the state: the Texas Hill Country, High Plains and Prairies, Pineywoods and Swamps, Gulf Coast, Brush Country, and Mountains and Desert sections are filled with animals native to their respective areas. Expect to see armadillos, rattlesnakes, alligators and big cats, among many others species.

LOG CABIN VILLAGE

2100 Log Cabin Village La., 817/392-5881, www.logcabinvillage.org

HOURS: Tues.- Fri. 9 A.M.-4 P.M., Sat.-Sun. 1 P.M.-5 P.M.

COST: $3.50 adult, $3 youth and senior, free under 3

Tucked away among the trees in verdant Forest Park, Log Cabin Village is a highly interactive living history museum. Visitors can tour the 11 historic log structures, which were relocated from other parts of the state (many of them saved from destruction) and restored to their original look. Each structure embodies a different aspect of 19th-century life. You'll find a one-room schoolhouse, water-powered gristmill, smokehouse, blacksmith shop, herb garden and humble abodes. Along the way, authentically clad historical interpreters reenact prairie life with demonstrations of candle-making, weaving and spinning.

Local parents love the Village because children's prices are inexpensive and a visit will definitely kill an afternoon. For large groups, a number of different group tours and family programs are available, as well as summer camps and adult classes—check the web site for details.

OSCAR MONNIG METEORITE GALLERY
2950 W. Bowie St., 817/257-6277,
www.monnigmuseum.org
HOURS: Tues.- Fri. 1 P.M.-4 P.M., Sat. 9 A.M.-4 P.M.
COST: Free

This world-class facility on the campus of Texas Christian University appeals to the science nerd in everyone. Those in the astronomy know laud Oscar Monnig as one of the greatest meteorite collectors and scientists to ever live. His collection, donated to TCU between 1978 and 1986, is considered one of the best ever cataloged.

West Side Fort Worth   Map 10

AMON CARTER MUSEUM
3501 Camp Bowie Blvd., 817/738-1933,
www.cartermuseum.org
HOURS: Tues.- Weds. 10 A.M.-5 P.M., Thurs.
10 A.M.-8 P.M., Fri.-Sat. 10 A.M.-5 P.M., Sun. noon-5 P.M.
COST: Free

Fort Worth's celebrated oilman and philanthropist Amon G. Carter intended the museum that bears his name to house his 400-piece collection of Western art. He never counted on the vision and foresight of those who took care of his art after he was gone. Carter's collection contained some very important 400 pieces, to be sure, many of them bearing the name Remington or Russell, but, the museum's first director, Mitchell A. Wilder, drummed up a vision to surpass even that of his former boss. Carter had envisioned a vibrant museum devoted to Western art, but Wilder interpreted "Western" quite liberally, expanding the collection in unexpected directions. After he took the reins, one of the world's most important and comprehensive collections of American art was born.

The museum itself, designed by Philip Johnson, sits quietly atop a museum district hill and admission is free (both the location and cost as per Carter's wishes). Paintings, sculpture and works on paper from nineteenth- and twentieth-century artists as varied as Alexander Calder, Thomas Eakins, and Alfred Stieglitz are housed here next to twenty-first century video and photographic works from some of today's most well-known artists. The museum also owns more than 30,000 photographic prints, and is considered one of the most important photography repositories in the country—over 4,000 square feet of the museum is dedicated to photographic exhibits alone.

FORT WORTH BOTANIC GARDENS
3220 Botanic Garden Blvd., 817/871-7686,
www.fwbg.com
HOURS: Garden Center Mon.-Fri. 8 A.M.-10 P.M., Sat.
8 A.M.-7 P.M., Sun. 1 P.M.-7 P.M. (Daylight Savings Time),
Mon.- Fri. 8 A.M.-10 P.M., Sat. 8 A.M.-5 P.M.,
Sun. 1 P.M.-5 P.M. (Standard Time); Conservatory
Mon.-Sat. 10 A.M.-6 P.M., Sun. 1 P.M.-6 P.M. (Daylight
Savings Time), Mon.-Sat. 10 A.M.-4 P.M., Sun. 1 P.M.-4 P.M.
(Standard Time); Japanese Garden daily 9 A.M.-7 P.M.
(Daylight Savings Time), daily 10 A.M.-2:30 P.M.
(Standard Time)
COST: Conservatory $1 adult, $1 youth, $0.50 senior

Fort Worth Botanic Gardens

and children, free under 4;
Japanese Garden Mon.-Fri. $3 adult, $2 youth, $2.50
senior, free under 4, Sat.-Sun. and holidays $3.50
adult, $1 youth, $3 senior, free under 4

"Lush" doesn't even begin to describe it. With three different areas-the Garden Center, Japanese Garden, and Conservatory-and more than 2,500 species of flowers and plants, the Botanic Gardens overflow with color and life. Even though families flock to the verdant surroundings and special musical programs here, almost every path, nook, and corner provides a serenity to go along with the scenery. Favorites among the many gardens include the classic Rose Garden and the 7-acre Japanese Garden, with several picturesque wooden bridges crisscrossing koi ponds and creeks. Docent-guided tours are available.

FORT WORTH MUSEUM OF SCIENCE AND HISTORY

1501 Montgomery St., 817/255-9300,
www.fwmuseum.org
HOURS: Mon.- Fri. 8:30 A.M.-6 P.M.
COST: $8 general adult, $7 youth and senior, free under 3

This kid-friendly institution recently underwent a massive renovation, to mixed effect: Gone are the kitschy exhibits featuring antique dentist tools and cavemen performing surgery. In their place has sprung a more contemporary approach, with dozens of interactive stations where young 'uns can get their hands dirty and learn at the same time. The centerpiece of the museum is the IMAX theater (the first of its kind in Texas) and the newly refurbished, state-of-the-art Noble Planetarium. Call for times and prices for both, as they are subject to change.

◖ THE KIMBELL ART MUSEUM

3333 Camp Bowie Blvd., 817/332-8451,
www.kimbellart.org
HOURS: Tues.-Thurs. 10 A.M.-5 P.M., Fri. noon-8 P.M., Sat. 10 A.M.-5 P.M., Sun. noon-5 P.M.
COST: Free

The Kimbell may not be the largest museum in the world, but the quality of its collection wows art newbies and experts alike. A small but impressive collection of classic European works by the masters like Picasso, Caravaggio, El Greco, Rembrandt, Monet and other greats take precedence here. The quality over quantity philosophy applies to the rest of the collection, too, including a significant batch of antiquities as well as Asian, Pre-Columbian, African and Oceanic art.

The building in which these pieces are displayed, however, might be the Kimbell's most famously lauded work of all. Designed by Louis Kahn, the Kimbell building is immediately recognizable for its series of repeated barrel vaults that give the edifice a classical yet completely contemporary feel. The genius of the building, its coherence, symmetry and timelessness, simply cannot be overstated. Inside, the elegant design provides a seamless viewing experience. Four piers support the vaults at either end, eliminating obtrusive vaults in the exhibition area, and as the sun diffuses through the endless skylights, the aura is one of reverence.

Admission is always free, but the museum often charges for special exhibitions, which are half price all day on Tuesdays and after 5 P.M. on Fridays.

◖ MODERN ART MUSEUM
OF FORT WORTH

3200 Darnell St., 817/738-9215, www.themodern.org

HOURS: Tues.- Weds. 10 A.M.–5 P.M.

COST: $10 adult, $10 youth, $4 students and seniors; free under 12, free first Sunday of every month

Thanks mainly to the world-class Kimbell Art Museum, Fort Worth has always enjoyed a well-respected international reputation when it comes to art. With the Modern Art Museum of Fort Worth, that rep has skyrocketed. The Modern's permanent collection of top-tier sculpture, paintings, photography, drawings and mixed media work from the world's greatest artists will wow arties and novices alike. There are thousands of works by post-World War II artists like Andy Warhol, Willem deKooning, Martin, Yves Klein, Cy Twombly and Cindy Sherman—to name but a very few—in the permanent collection, but the museum fears neither risk nor wide range, especially when it comes to touring shows.

Then there's the building itself, such a perfect balance between aesthetic comfort and artistic setting that it transforms The Modern from a top museum to a house of visual worship. Designed by Japanese architect Tadeo Ando, the museum is guarded at the door by a massive Richard Serra sculpture that hints at the scale of the delights within. Inside, the cool, dark concrete walls, the smooth-surfaced reflecting pool, and the breeze circulating throughout the high-ceilinged pavilions are soothing and beautiful, but their main purpose is to give the art ample room, without drowning it out. That they do.

The Modern offers tons of educational opportunities and civic events in the form of classes, lectures, tours, a film series called Magnolia at the Modern, and other functions. Especially popular are the First Fridays series, which attracts visitors with evening happy hours and docent-led tours, and the excellent alternative music lineups provided by Spune productions. Call or check the website for details.

◖ THE NATIONAL COWGIRL MUSEUM
AND HALL OF FAME

1720 Gendy St., 817/336-4475, www.cowgirl.net

HOURS: Mon.-Sat. 9:30 A.M.–5 P.M., Sun. 11:45 A.M.–5 P.M.

COST: $8 general adult, $7 youth and senior, free under 3

This fun museum, one of the newest additions to the cultural district, is as refreshing and spunky as the women it celebrates. Housed in a nouveau Art Deco building that complements its big brother, the Will Rogers complex, the Cowgirl Museum is much more modern on the inside than you'd think. The three-tiered exhibit space kicks off with cool, glass-based murals that move as you do, a harbinger of the interactive concentration of the whole place. The museum's thousands of artifacts, photos, videos, and films paint a vivid picture of the strength, character and general giddyup of lady ropers, cowhands, barrel racers and their chaps-wearing ilk. Mind you, the celebration here doesn't center solely on ladies who were handy with a lariat: The focus expands, rightly, to feisty Western notables as disparate as Patsy Cline, Lady Bird Johnson and Georgia O'Keeffe.

WILL ROGERS MEMORIAL CENTER

3401 W. Lancaster Ave., 214/392-7469

Smack-dab in the middle of the cultural district, the 85-acre grounds of this center include a 2,900-seat auditorium, an impressive network of stock and equestrian grounds, and an

© FORT WORTH CVB

The National Cowgirl Museum and Hall of Fame

8,000-seat coliseum, the first of its kind in the world. Though the complex's trademark piece, the Landmark Pioneer Tower, is highly visible from the outside, its ornate Art Deco design only hints at the treats indoors: cowboy murals, terrazzo tile, and ornamental adornments embellish much of the interior. The center is used year-round for cultural and sporting events, but is perhaps best known for hosting the Southwestern Exposition and Livestock Show, attended by 800,000 people every year. Overall, the park Will Rogers sees around two million visitors a year—and most folks assume Rogers would've liked every single one.

Greater Fort Worth   Map 11

BUREAU OF PRINTING AND ENGRAVING

9000 Blue Mound Road, 817/231-4000, www.moneyfactory.gov/locations/section.cfm/25

HOURS: Aug.-May Mon.- Fri. 8:30 A.M.- 3 P.M. June and July Mon.- Fri. 8:30 A.M.- 5:30 P.M.

COST: Free

One of only two facilities that print US currency (the other is in Washington, D.C.), the Bureau tour is a fun, educational excursion that, ironically, won't cost you any money.

The tour winds through displays and exhibits that cover the history of US currency and its production process, but the best part is the elevated walkway above the production floor, from which visitors eyeball how money is made, literally. A few things to keep in mind: First, it's advisable to arrive at least 30 minutes before your tour is scheduled to begin, as there's a bit of security rigmarole to navigate beforehand. Second, the 45-minute tours fill up on a first-come, first served basis for walkup visitors and begin every half-hour. Those who have to wait can check out the Visitor Center's informational film, displays, and gift shop, so the wait isn't too boring. The final tour begins at 2 P.M., except in June and July, when the final tour begins at 4 P.M.

SIX FLAGS' HURRICANE HARBOR

1800 E. Lamar Blvd., Arlington, 817/640-8900, www.sixflags.com/hurricaneHarborTexas

HOURS: Vary

Texas summers can be, well, brutal, and a good way to beat the heat is to hit up Hurricane Harbor water park. The park opened two decades ago, and ever since then has been added rides and attractions of increasingly thrilling proportions, culminating in 2009's **Mega Wedgie,** in which thrillseekers drop four stories down a giant slide, only to be propelled back up another slide, then back down. A long time favorite is **Der Stuka,** with its 72-foot free-fall drop.

If that's not quite your speed, more mellow rides are available, including ones for very young children. Overpriced theme park food abounds here, of course, and no coolers are allowed, so expect to shell out some cash. Similarly, entry fees are expensive—check the web site for special deals, discounts, and passes. Prices and times vary seasonally and even day-to-day, so call or check the website for details.

SIX FLAGS OVER TEXAS

2201 Road to Six Flags, Arlington, 817/640-8900, www.sixflags.com/overTexas

HOURS: Vary

As the original birthplace of the theme park

Looney Tunes characters posing at Six Flags Over Texas

chain that bears its name, the Six Flags in Arlington holds a special place in the hearts of roller coaster lovers. Of course, nowadays, much of the park is taken up with corporate-themed screamers like Warner Bros.' Mr. Freeze and Superman coasters—which will do their job to set your heart pounding—but nostalgists will still find plenty of thrills in the Shock Wave (one of the first roller coasters to have two upside-down loops, and to go backwards), and the Judge Roy Scream, one of the last all-wood coasters in the country, which loops and lopes over eight acres of lakes. Prices and times vary seasonally and even day-to-day, so call or check the website for details.

RESTAURANTS

For years Dallas-Fort Worth dining has been all about the dichotomy of big and small. Some folks call the former "power dining"—we want the most illustrious chefs and the largest scoop of caviar. Venerable restaurants have long swept us off our feet with classic fare.

But slowly, DFW has begun to rediscover its neighborhoods, and in doing so, it has begun to embrace inventive menus filled with local, organic ingredients. The result has been scores of new hyper-local hangouts, each buzzing with friends and neighbors sharing small plates and big steaks.

As you might imagine, steakhouses here are about as ubiquitous as Starbucks—with the surplus of fine options for filets, sirloins, and T-bones in such abundance that meat eaters will practically be slobbering on the sidewalk. Meanwhile, if you prefer your meat hickory-smoked and slathered in sauce, there's always that other famous Texas cuisine: barbecue. No trip to DFW is complete without sampling what local restaurant critic Dotty Griffith calls "the most American food." For all the lovely upscale food to be had, a $6 barbecue brisket sandwich really can't be beat.

The other low-budget, high-cal cuisine for which DFW is known is Tex-Mex. For folks who grew up on this hybrid of American and south-of-the-border tastes, the gooey cheeses,

HIGHLIGHTS

LOOK FOR  TO FIND RECOMMENDED RESTAURANTS.

Best Celebrity Chef: Depending on how you look at it, Top Chef's Tom Colicchio is either the food world's brightest star or a cheesy fame-chaser. Either way, the Dallas satellite of his famed New York restaurant **Craft** is conceptually tight and surprisingly understated (page 63).

Best Retro Experience: Even though the zodiac-themed wallpaper and *Mad Men* aesthetic has long been replaced by bright colors and sleek tables, **The Zodiac** still evokes an era when there were ladies who lunched, and when they lunched, they wore hats (page 65).

Best Steak: Most high-end steakhouses don't provide TVs tuned to ESPN, but this is Dallas, remember? Settle into a cozy leather booth, order one of the best steaks in a town full of steaks, and bask in the boys' club atmosphere of **Bob's Steak and Chophouse** (page 71).

Best Downhome Cookin': Expect long lines at **Bubba's**, a neighborhood institution, especially after church on Sunday, when you can only pray they don't run out of fried chicken (page 75).

Best Neighborhood Place: The delightful, intimate, and highly praised **York Street** is so tucked out of the way, it's almost impossible to find, unless you indeed hail from the surrounding streets. One bite of chef Sharon Hage's New American cuisine, and its location will be seared into your memory (page 76).

Best Chicken-Fried Steak: Flavorful, fried in a light, crisp batter, and never greasy, the chicken-fried steak at the **AllGood Cafe**, a funky Deep Ellum cornerstone, comes in Frisbee-sized servings; it makes a great leftover breakfast the next day (page 81).

Best Barbecue: There's barbecue and then there's BBQ. Since 1910, **Sonny Bryan's** has been the latter, and nowadays about 36 bucks will get you meat, sauce, fixins, and sides for six people. It's worth it, too (page 84).

Best Use of An Exotic Animal: **Lonesome Dove** proprietor Tim Love's effusive creativity is no more apparent than in his varied use of kangaroo meat (page 85).

Best People-Watching: Before the tornado that blasted it from the top floor of the Bank One tower, Fort Worth institution **Reata** really had a view. No matter: Its new location on the admittedly lower rooftop of the former Caravan of Dreams provides a bird's-eye view of the goings-on at Sundance Square (page 86).

Best Burger: Nobody really knows the secret behind **Kincaid's** hamburger's, but considering the constant stream of patrons who frequent the venerable Camp Bowie spot, it doesn't matter (page 92).

Best Grocery Store: West Siders have loved the epicurean, locally owned **Roy Pope Grocery** since 1943 (page 93).

Live bands provide the soundtrack for a downhome meal at AllGood Cafe.

fried tortillas, and chili con carne sauces are second nature. Most Tex-Mex is affordable, even when coupled with a traditional margarita, but it has slowly made its way into middle and upper levels of cuisine.

With its fearless melding of flavors and aesthetics, Tex-Mex might just be the most democratic of foods, and that's the beauty of it: There are no boundaries here. From power dining to organic salads, from top chefs to taco carts, DFW leaves no palate disappointed.

PRICE KEY

$ Most entrées less than $10

$$ Most entrées between $10-20

$$$ Most entrées more than $20

Downtown Dallas   Map 1

RESTAURANTS

AMERICAN
CAPITAL GRILLE $$$

500 Crescent Ct., #135, 214/303-0500,
www.thecapitalgrille.com
HOURS: Lunch: Mon.-Fri. 11 A.M.-2:30 P.M.
Dinner: Sun.-Thurs. 5-10 P.M., Fri.-Sat. 5-11 P.M.

Nouveau-foodies and vegetarians need not bother entering the Capital Grille, the expertly run, classic high-end grill housed in one of Dallas's fanciest hotels. Steak lovers and those who long for the days of three-martini lunches, however, will feel right at home amid the glossy mahogany, the booths of stitched buttery leather, and the gleaming brass railings. An exercise in refined simplicity, the menu here represents a similar perfection of timeless aesthetic. The culinary centerpiece is definitely steak—dry-aged cuts, many of them accented only by au jus—along with seafood offerings and rich side dishes like béchamel creamed spinach. And you can expect four-star service, from the valet to the sommelier.

◪ CRAFT $$$

2440 Victory Park La., Ste. 100, 214/397-4111,
www.craftrestaurant.com/craft_dallas_style.html
HOURS: Lunch: Daily 11 A.M.-2 P.M. Dinner: Sun.-Thurs. 5:30-10:30 P.M., Fri.-Sat. 5:30-11 P.M.

Craft founder and culinary star Tom Colicchio may be best known for his intimidating presence on TV's *Top Chef,* but don't let his celebrity status fool you into thinking he's a lightweight. This is a man who's serious about creating great food, and the food at Colicchio's Craft is substantial, satisfying, and simple. As it is at Craft's New York flagship location, that simplicity doesn't mean simplistic; it translates into a focus on the food, rather than frou-frou trappings. This means letting dry-aged Japanese beef, sliced and served with a Bordelaise sauce, speak for itself. This also means unburdening fish and game from excess adornment, and creating garnishes that are detailed and thoughtful, but understated.

Because of Craft's emphasis on family-style dining, Dallas denizens may be more comfortable there than at any other fine-dining establishment in the city. The beauty of Colicchio's communal dining philosophy is the camaraderie and comfort it creates: How stuffy can you be when you're reaching across the table to spear a shared braised rib or nudging your neighbor to pass the risotto?

The irony is, all of this streamlined philosophy is not so simple on the pocketbook. There is a $100 steak on offer, for instance, and the wine list prices feel a bit unfriendly. Still, if you love food, a visit to Craft is essential.

A word about the menu: It's delightfully free of the cluster of adjectives that often weigh down menus at high-end eateries. The upside is you're spared the affected nonsense; the downside is it can be tough to know what you're getting. Ask your server for descriptions—at Craft they are friendly and knowledgeable, and are trained to fill in the blanks.

SCREEN DOOR $$$

1722 Routh St., 214/720-9111,
www.screendoordallas.com

HOURS: Lunch: Mon.-Fri. 11:30 A.M.-2 P.M. Dinner: Mon.-Thurs. 5-10 P.M., Fri.-Sat. 5 P.M.-midnight. Brunch: Sun. 10:30 A.M.-2:30 P.M. Tea: by reservation.

Located in the bustling, cosmopolitan One Arts Plaza, Screen Door is an oasis of Southern charm. It's hard to say whether Screen Door is an upscale take on down-home cooking or vice-versa, but either way, the cuisine here effortlessly combines chicken-fried goodness and modern flair. Hard to picture that kind of juxtaposition? Screen Door's afternoon tea sums up the combination nicely: Sure, there's meatloaf on the menu, but it's speckled with bits

FUEL CITY: THE BEST TACO YOU'LL EVER EAT AT A TRUCK STOP

Fuel City is the type of place street food obsessives dream about. Only, technically, **Fuel City** (801 S Industrial Blvd., Dallas 75207, 214/426-0011) is not on the street – it's a gigantic truck stop/gas station, lording over an unholy chunk of real estate at the nexus of Industrial Boulevard (the name says it all) and I-35.

It's not the most picturesque locale, but the atmosphere actually provides part of the fun. The parking lot is a scene in itself, as a constant stream of low riders and big rigs navigate around the pavement. Behind the building is a small grassy plot, home to a few longhorn cattle, and a swimming pool, home to several bikini-clad young women hired to hang out there. Seriously.

Once you're inside, however, you've reached taco nirvana. The taqueria is open 24 hours a day. Expect a line no matter what the clock says (word of great tacos travels fast in these parts). Two things are essential when you order: First, choose the moist, thick corn tortillas over flour, and second, try the picadillo, named the best

taco in Texas by venerable Texas Monthly magazine. You'll never encounter a more perfect mixture of flavors; spicy, chile-laced ground beef, soft potato chunks, and onions. The pastor taco comes in a very close second, with ada-style marinated beef, onion, cilantro, and a hell of a kick to it on the back end. The tacos all come with two types of salsa – tomatillo and red – about which there is much debate: Some say there's already such a perfect blend of flavors, the sauces are unnecessary. Others claim they'll send your palate into spasms of joy.

A stop at the *elotes* (a cup filled with roasted corn, sour cream, butter, lemon pepper and cayenne pepper) cart on your way out might seem indulgent, but this is Fuel City, so go for it!

The food at Fuel City is cash-only, but you won't need that much (the tacos top out at about $1.25 each), and don't forget to grab yourself a beer from the swimming-pool sized ice cooler or one of the many Mexican sodas available – either is a perfect chaser for the spicy meat and salsas.

of foie gras. There's also potpie—albeit with lobster meat and truffle corn puree.

Of course, there's no parsing the Southern-style atmosphere here. Even amid the hustle and bustle of downtown, the tastes and aura here evoke a breezy porch flanked by magnolia trees and lilting accents.

STEPHAN PYLES $$$

1807 Ross Ave., 214/580-7000,
www.stephanpyles.com

HOURS: Lunch: Mon.-Fri. 11:30 A.M.-2 P.M. Dinner: Mon.-Weds. 6-10:30 P.M., Thurs.-Sat. 6-11 P.M.

As one of the godfathers of upscale Southwestern cuisine, Stephan Pyles already enjoyed a fabled reputation as an innovator; with the 2006 opening of his eponymous restaurant smack in the middle of the arts district, he cemented his legacy. Pyles has created a menu that builds on his history of infusing American fine dining with Latin traditions and flavors, and the results have enticed the crème fraîche of Dallas's social crop. The menu (executed by executive chef Tim Byres) includes Pyles's famous giant Cowboy Ribeye, but it's the ample variations on ceviche that have pulled in scores of usually meat-hungry Texans every night. Other seafood is also copiously—and inventively—represented on the menu, along with creative spins on everything from gazpacho to poached pear. The decor is just as singular, its interwoven copper bands, updated Southwestern landscape photography, and antler sculptures reflective of what Pyles calls "New Millennium Southwestern cuisine."

⬛ THE ZODIAC $$$

Neiman Marcus, 1618 Main St., Sixth Floor,
214/573-5800, www.neimanmarcus.com

HOURS: Mon.-Sat. 11 A.M.-3:30 P.M.

Zodiac is a celebrated bastion of almost-lost elegance. While groovy zodiac-sign wallpaper once adorned the walls, the room now indulges in a more understated (and slightly more generic) modern sleekness, but the menu is much the same as it was back when socialite shoppers and oil barons made this *the* place to lunch. When you eat here, tradition suggests ordering the renowned Mandarin Orange Soufflé, preceded by popovers slathered with strawberry butter, but much of the menu (which still bears the touch of legendary chef Helen Corbitt) makes for a classic and luscious meal. Be aware that The Zodiac doesn't accept Visa or MasterCard.

FRENCH

THE FRENCH ROOM $$$

1321 Commerce St., 214/742-8200,
www.hoteladolphus.com/adolphus_dining.aspx

HOURS: Tues.-Sat. 6-9:30 P.M.

The French room is the gastronomic equivalent of *The Queen Mary* in its heyday—opulent, palatial, and ornate, but with the goods to back it up. Just entering the room is akin to traveling back to the high court of Versailles: The floor is a fine, green marble, the ceilings painted with chunky cherubs, the walls literally gilded. The food might as well be gilded, too, as rich and finely wrought as it is. Executive chef Jason Weaver grabbed the helm of this stately ship in 2005 and never deviates from his course of classic flavor and presentation—he merely, subtly, enfolds motifs from the most disparate locales into a cohesive richness. In less deft hands, his creations would amount to disastrous overindulgence, even hubris, but Weaver and his staff pull it off with élan. If you splurge on just one restaurant in Dallas, it should be this one. Jackets required.

The French Room

© DALLAS CVB

PUB FOOD
CAFÉ REMBRANDT 💲💲

703 McKinney Ave., 214/468-0073,
www.caferembrandtsdallas.com

HOURS: Lunch: Mon.-Fri. 11 A.M.-3 P.M. Dinner:
Mon.-Thurs. 5 P.M.-midnight, Fri.-Sat. 5 P.M.-2 A.M.

This Dutch pub (owned by an actual
Dutchman) is notable enough for its unique
selection of imported beers, but the menu is
intriguing, too, such that almost as many patrons drop by for *borrelhapjes* (beer snacks) as
they do Euro-brews. A visit is worth it either
way, as the space, housed in a giant old warehouse (and the former site of the infamous
Stark Club), is gorgeous, simultaneously airy
and intimate, and so is suitable for everything
from a cozy pub excursion to a boisterous burlesque show.

SEAFOOD
NEWPORT'S 💲💲💲

703 McKinney Ave., 214/954-0220,
www.newportsrestaurant.com

HOURS: Lunch: Mon.-Fri. 11:30 A.M.-2 P.M.
Dinner: Sun.-Thurs. 5-9 P.M., Fri.-Sat. 5-10 P.M.

Nowadays, the concept of freshly flown-in
fish in landlocked Dallas isn't such a big deal,
but when Newport's opened 20 years ago as
one of the first West End inhabitants, it provided the freshest seafood around. Even today,
when same-day catches from both coasts are
by no means scarce, Newport's still tops its
competition when it comes to *fruits de mer*.
Housed in a multitiered historic former brew-
ery, Newport's has long eschewed trendy decor
for timeless refinement in both aesthetic and
cuisine. Although there is plenty of meat on

the menu, the classic order sticks with the surf rather than the turf, a selection from the impressive wine menu, and a slice of the famous key lime pie.

TRULUCK'S ⓢⓢⓢ

2401 McKinney Ave., 214/220-2401,
www.trulucks.com

HOURS: Lunch: Mon.-Fri. 11 A.M.-2 P.M.
Dinner: Sun.-Thurs. 5-10 P.M., Fri.-Sat. 5-11 P.M.
Brunch: Sun. 11 A.M.-2 P.M.

Even amid the glitz and glam of McKinney Avenue, the bright green and blue light trimming Truluck's building is hard to miss, not so much for the sizzle of the neon light, but for the constant stream of Uptowners entering and exiting. There's a reason they're there: If you're craving crab legs in landlocked Dallas, Truluck's should be your number one choice. Inside, the well-lit, art deco interior is swank but welcoming, as is the service. It's a bit overpriced, but, since Truluck's almost always delivers a fine specimen from the ocean deep (thanks to their own fisheries in Florida and on the Isle of Capri), consider it a consistency tax.

STEAKHOUSE
DAKOTA'S ⓢⓢⓢ

600 N. Akard St., 214/740-4001,
www.dakotasrestaurant.com

HOURS: Lunch: Mon.-Fri. 11 A.M.-2:30 P.M. Dinner:
Mon.-Thurs. 5:30-10 P.M., Fri.-Sat. 5:30-10:30 P.M.

There's more than just aesthetics behind Dakota's sunken garden-patio dining area, found at the crowded nexus of skyscrapers known as One Arts Plaza. Seems the property now occupied by the classy eatery was once owned by the First Baptist Church, which contractually forbade future owners from selling alcohol "on the grounds." Dakota's proprietors circumvented the obligation through a little creative excavating, building *below* the grounds. A happy side result was Dakota's intimate, unique outdoor area, complete with ivy-laden walls and a lush fountain. And, of course, some of the best steaks around.

Y.O. RANCH STEAKHOUSE ⓢⓢⓢ

702 Ross Ave., 214/744-3287,
www.yoranchsteakhouse.com

HOURS: Mon.-Thurs. 11 A.M.-10 P.M., Fri. 11 A.M.-11 P.M.,
Sat. noon-11 P.M., Sun. noon-10 P.M.

One of the few non-chain restaurants in the tourist-y West End, the Y.O. Ranch Steakhouse leans heavily on cowboy cachet—as the stuffed animal heads and yee-haw decor proves. Expect the usual Texas attention to beef, along with wild game surprises like the signature buffalo filet mignon.

TEX-MEX
IRON CACTUS ⓢⓢ

1520 Main St., 214/749-4766,
www.ironcactus.com/dallas.asp

HOURS: Sun.-Weds. 11 A.M.-11 P.M.,
Thurs. 11 A.M.-midnight, Fri.-Sat. 11 A.M.-2 A.M.

The food at the Iron Cactus is fair-to-middling, but the view and the tequila can't be beat. Seriously, there's nothing more heavenly than grabbing a balcony table here at sunset—so much the better if the sun goes down around happy hour, when you should indulge in Dallas's most popular cocktail, the margarita. The concoctions here range from traditional to inventive, and all are made with fresh-squeezed lime juice and top-notch choices from the extensive tequila menu. If you prefer cutting straight to the source, try a flight of tequila, with three half-ounce samplers of your choice. Of course, with all of this booze, it's best to eat something. Choose carefully from this hit-or-miss menu:

Try the much-improved ceviche, or the ever-popular chile con queso—it's hard to mess up cheese.

Uptown Dallas
Map 2

AMERICAN

BREADWINNERS $$

3301 McKinney Ave., 214/754-4940,
www.breadwinnerscafe.com

HOURS: Breakfast and lunch: Mon.-Sat. 7 A.M.-4 P.M., Sun. 9 A.M.-3 P.M. Dinner: Tues.-Thurs. 5-10 P.M., Fri.-Sat. 5-11 P.M., Sun. 6-9 P.M.

First, a word of warning: If you're hitting up this charming brick-and-ivy spot for a weekend breakfast, you'll be hard-pressed to score a table in less than an hour. But if you're a fan of thick slabs of caramel-infused French toast or giant, savory crepes, it's worth the wait. For those in need of a bit of the hair of the dog, you can't beat the refreshing frozen peach Bellini, which serves to mitigate the pain of waiting. Breadwinners also serves up hearty lunch salads and an upscale dinner menu.

CAFÉ EXPRESS $

3230 McKinney Ave., 214/999-9444,
www.cafe-express.com

HOURS: Daily 11 A.M.-11 P.M.

Although it's a chain, Café Express is a handy spot for a quick, inexpensive lunch or dinner. The wide-ranging menu of soups, pastas, salads, and sandwiches is tailor-made for groups with disparate tastes or for those days when you just can't decide what you want. There's not really a bad choice here, but it's essential to pair your meal with the house-made limeade. There is a second location at 5307 Mockingbird Lane (214/841-9444).

EATZI'S $

3500 Oak Lawn Ave., 214/599-8602,
www.eatzis.com

HOURS: Daily 7 A.M.-10 P.M.

The epicurean groceries available are a delight, but they still play second fiddle to Eatzi's ample to-go offerings. The square footage of this place barely holds its huge deli (packed with things like Kobe meatloaf and crab cakes, as well as simpler fare), plus the grill, the salad bar, the sandwich bar, the pasta bar, and the pre-packed items, all of which supply restaurant-quality food to take back to your office, apartment, or hotel room. The convenience comes at a bit of a markup, but there are still deals to be had: The rotisserie chicken dinner, which comes with sides and cornbread, is a succulent steal, and every night around 9 P.M., patrons crowd like vultures around the pre-packed station, waiting for the evening "red dot" clear-out specials.

HUNKY'S $

4000 Cedar Springs Rd., 214/522-1212,
www.hunkys.com

HOURS: Mon.-Sat. 11 A.M.-9 P.M., Sun. 11:30 A.M.-9 P.M.

In Dallas, you don't crave just a burger—you crave a Hunky's. This 1950s diner-themed institution has held down its spot at the epicenter of gay Dallas long enough to be considered an institution. The made-to-order burgers, perfectly fried tater tots and onion rings, and handmade shakes are so beloved, you'll need good luck finding a table during lunch hour.

LOLA ⑤⑤⑤

2917 Fairmount St., 214/885-0700,
www.lola4dinner.com

HOURS: Tues.-Sat. 5:30–11 P.M.

Rather than succumb to urban trends, Lola has remained tucked away in a snug, remodeled old house, filled with warmth and traditional charm that is reflected in executive chef David Uygur's menu. The food here is stellar and consistent, less fanciful than many nouveau eateries but nonetheless fancy with thoughtful nods to French, Eastern, and Italian cuisines. A 40-page wine list bears shockingly reasonable prices, unlike the more expensive—and very popular—tasting room, where diners are treated to a prix fixe menu of 10 or 14 courses of mini servings of the main menu.

THE MANSION RESTAURANT ⑤⑤⑤

2821 Turtle Creek Blvd., 214/443-4747
HOURS: Breakfast: Mon.-Fri. 6:30–10:30 A.M., Sat.-Sun. 7–10:30 A.M. Lunch: Mon.-Sat. 11:30 A.M.–2 P.M. Dinner: Sun.-Thurs. 6–10 P.M., Fri.-Sat. 6–11 P.M. Brunch: Sun. 11:30 A.M.–2 P.M.

Ripples of fear surged through town in 2006 when The Mansion first began a belated retooling. After all, this may be the most storied, most respected restaurant in all of Dallas's history. It's here that so many heads of state have dined, where famed chef Dean Fearing perfected his tortilla soup, where power dining established its first Dallas foothold 28 years ago. The fear proved unfounded. The Mansion has not suffered a foolish attempt to keep up with trends; rather, it has been renovated, reenergized, and reinvigorated.

The feeling of exclusive luxury begins before you even step inside. While many four-star hotels feel the need to flash their opulence, The Mansion is tucked away in the lush Turtle Creek greenbelt. This place indeed served as the palatial estate of a cotton magnate, and the detailed touches still make it feel like home.

PARIGI ⑤⑤

3311 Oak Lawn Ave., #102, 214/521-0295,
www.parigirestaurant.com

HOURS: Lunch: Mon.-Fri. 11:30 A.M.–2:30 P.M.
Dinner: Mon.-Sat. 6 P.M.–10 P.M.
Brunch: Sat.-Sun. 10:30 A.M.–3 P.M.

For almost a quarter-century, Parigi has quietly carved a niche for itself in a town full of hyper-dining. Parigi's setting is snug, but nowhere near stuffy, with sky-high ceilings and a bright feel mirrored by its open kitchen. Many folks find Parigi's fresh, French take on dining an apt choice for a refined dinner, but don't overlook its lunch charm: It's the perfect place for anything from gourmet salad to a decadent chicken *cordon bleu*.

FRENCH
AURORA ⑤⑤⑤

4216 Oak Lawn Ave., 214/528-9400,
www.auroradallas.com

HOURS: Lunch: Mon.-Fri. 11:30 A.M.–2 P.M.
Dinner: Mon.-Sat. 5:30–10 P.M.

You can find Aurora in an unlikely, though upscale, strip mall that straddles the line between trendy Oak Lawn and ritzy Highland Park. The decor leans heavily toward the latter aesthetic, with Ultrasuede walls and the fanciest open kitchen you'll ever see. The menu lists toward French classics and is heavy on the indulgent, especially caviar.

ITALIAN

ARCODORO & POMODORO 💲💲

2708 Routh St., 214/871-1924, www.arcodoro.com

HOURS: Lunch: Tues.-Fri. 11 A.M.-2 P.M. Dinner: Tues.-Fri.
5-10 P.M., Fri.-Sat. 5:30-10 P.M.

Two Sardinian brothers own this spot—half
hip café, half refined for the stuffier set—and
they've done their island proud, serving up
toothsome versions of authentic Italian dishes,
much of it based on homemade pastas, but also
with a tasty nod to the seafood perfected in
their homeland.

BOLLA MODERN ITALIAN 💲💲💲

2927 Maple Ave., 800/921-8498,
www.stoneleighhotel.com

HOURS: Breakfast: Daily 7-10:30 A.M. Lunch: Daily
11 A.M.-2:30 P.M. Dinner: Tues.-Thurs. 6-10 P.M.,
Fri.-Sat. 6-11 P.M.

It's worth it to step into Bolla to check out the
newly revamped Stoneleigh Hotel. It's even
more worth it to snack on complimentary
small bites created by chef David Bull, who is
one fully pedigreed chef (after all, he's a James
Beard nominee, an *Iron Chef* contestant, and
the folks behind Bolla stole him away from
Austin's famous Driskill Hotel), during the
Wednesday and Thursday *L'Ora Dell'Apertivo*
(a fancy term for happy hour). As far as design
goes, no other restaurant in Dallas can com-
pare to the creative surroundings here, right
down to the giant "THE" salvaged from the
original Stoneleigh sign. Similarly, Bull pulls
classic Italian into the 21st century with a creative flair.

NONNA 💲💲💲

4115 Lomo Alto Dr., 214/521-1800, www.nonnadallas.com

HOURS: Mon.-Tues. 6-9 P.M., Weds.-Thurs. 6-10 P.M.,
Fri.-Sat. 6-10:30 P.M.

The buzz around chef/owner Julian Barsotti's
Nonna began well before the bistro's late-2007
opening, and with good reason. Although the
service is spotty, this is food with a good deal
of thought behind it, well-considered and
stunningly executed. The menu (comprised
of sustainable ingredients) changes nightly,
but expect handmade pastas, handmade sausages, delicate Nepalese pizza crusts and wonderful seafood, all in an elegant, minimalist
atmosphere.

MEDITERRANEAN

COSMIC CAFÉ 💲💲

2912 Oak Lawn Ave., 214/521-6157,
www.cosmiccafedallas.com

HOURS: Mon.-Thurs. 11 A.M.-10:30 P.M.,
Fri.-Sat. 11 A.M.-11 P.M., Sun. noon-10 P.M.

Cosmic Café's elaborate, colorful building
certainly stands out from the glitz, glam, and
commerce of Uptown, as does the delicious
vegetarian food and Zen-infused atmosphere.
The interior dining area of this casual café is
a bohemian oasis, though the tasty, thoughtful menu, influenced by Mediterranean and
Indian cuisine, appeals to all walks of life.
The samosas, dahl, and chutneys are to die
for. This is the perfect spot for a healthy lunch,
but be prepared to succumb to the slower pace
of the place.

SEAFOOD

HOOK, LINE, & SINKER 💲💲

3103 Lemmon Ave., 214/965-0707

HOURS: Sun.-Thurs. 11 A.M.-10 P.M., Fri.-Sat. 11 A.M.-11 P.M.

How this bustling faux fish shack—replete
with rusty boat gear, paddles, and other briny
accouterments—pulls off the miracle of serving deep-fried catfish that's almost greaseless
is anybody's guess, but why question a good

thing? Not that the menu is particularly light, what with ample cornmeal-fried delights like shrimp, hush puppies, and taters, or other goodies like oysters and gumbo. Thankfully, though the food may stretch your waistband, it won't stretch your budget.

SOUTHERN
LUCKY'S $

3531 Oak Lawn Ave., 214/522-3500,
www.croinc.com/luckys
HOURS: Daily 7 A.M.-10 P.M.

The breakfast scene at Lucky's, the welcoming corner diner in the midst of the gay-friendly Oak Lawn area, is as buzzing and social as a night out at the clubs down the street. The food is straightforward diner here—giant, gooey omelets, steak and eggs, large strips of bacon—but the crowd is definitely not straight, and the menu is all-encompassing. Despite the happy clatter around them, the staff remains friendly and efficient, and the kitchen is quick and handy with a griddle.

STEAKHOUSE
【 BOB'S STEAK AND CHOPHOUSE $$$

4300 Lemmon Ave., 214/528-9446,
www.bobs-steakandchop.com
HOURS: Mon.-Thurs. 5-10 P.M., Fri.-Sat. 5-11 P.M.

The nondescript windowless, low-lying building that houses Bob's Lemmon Avenue location is plunked on the very corner where the street starts getting, shall we say, sketchy. But the constant line of cars and ever-hustling valets tells the story of just how different it must be inside. Pass through these famous doors and there's an entirely different world—a man's world, really, with large leather booths flanked by dark walls and horse racing memorabilia. The stiff drinks and TVs (hey, this is Dallas, where watching sports is essential, even when you're fine-dining) only bolster the boys' club effect. It's actually the perfect environment to cut into the most celebrated steak in town, and you might even spot a celeb or two while you're doing it (if you consider Tony Romo a celebrity).

Park Cities
Map 3

AMERICAN
AUSTINUTS $

6915 Hillcrest Ave., 214/739-6887,
www.austinuts.com
HOURS: Mon.-Sat. 10 A.M.-6 P.M.

This Dallas satellite of Austin's favorite nut house is a godsend when you're looking for gift baskets, gourmet snacks, or just a tasty treat. Austinuts specializes in perfectly roasted and flavored nuts and fancy-pants chocolates, often presented in Texas kitchen-chic packaging. While the products are a bit pricey, they are stunningly good (and fresh!).

DUPRE'S SHORT STOP $

6920 Snider Plaza, 214/360-0311
HOURS: Mon.-Fri. 8 A.M.-6 P.M., Sat. 9:30 A.M.-2:30 P.M.

If you need a quick meal on the go, Dupre's is a great alternative to fast food. Tucked away in the swank Highland Park Village shopping center, this mostly takeout spot offers sandwiches, salads, soups, oven-ready meals, and even breakfast. Parking can be a bit of a hassle, but it's well worth it to avoid the high cost of many of the local restaurants, or if you just want a quiet evening meal without having to cook or order in.

GOFF'S HAMBURGERS $

6401 Hillcrest Ave., 214/351-3336,
www.goffshamburger.com

HOURS: Daily 11 A.M.–9 P.M.

Goff's is a Dallas institution, though it has moved from its longtime location on Lovers Lane and changed owners (the legendary former proprietor had a habit of peppering his patrons with insults before serving them their food). The patties are your general, well-seasoned beef variety, but it's Goff's hickory sauce, secret-recipe relish, and shredded cheddar that make the burgers so transcendent. The menu also includes hot dogs and a few other grill items, but most folks stick with the burgers—and wisely so.

HIBISCUS $$$

2927 N. Henderson Ave., 214/827-2927,
www.hibiscusdallas.com

HOURS: Mon.-Sat. 5-11 P.M.

Hibiscus has managed to quietly coerce the chophouse into the 21st century (a tough thing to do in Dallas). The traditional low lighting, leather furniture, and manly touches remain—and a steak, of course, is still a steak—so Hibiscus finds its niche with its chic Uptown vibe. This could be annoying or appealing, depending on your mindset, but the stunningly good steaks and sides eventually win everybody over.

KATHLEEN'S SKY DINER $$

4424 Lovers La., 214/691-2355

HOURS: Mon.-Fri. 7 A.M.-10 P.M., Sat. 8 A.M.-11 P.M., Sun. 8 A.M.-10 P.M.

Formerly known as Kathleen's Art Café, Kathleen's Sky Diner switched from a folk-artsy aesthetic to more of a concept café revolving around a travel theme. No matter what the motif, the spot is an excellent choice for a long lunch filled with updated comfort food, like the scrumptious meatloaf sandwich, or slightly more refined fare, such as bite-size ravioli with fresh tomato and basil sauce. Beware: Kathleen's is known for great food but occasionally rude service.

SOUTH PAW'S ORGANIC CAFÉ, SUPPLEMENTS, AND SMOOTHIES $

6009 Berkshire La., 214/987-0351,
www.southpawscafe.com

HOURS: Mon.-Fri. 7 A.M.–9 P.M., Sat. 9 A.M.-4 P.M.

South Paw's (the name refers to owner Reza Anvarian, who is a lefty amateur boxer) is proof that healthy food can be yummy. The food here comes courtesy of Luigi Troncoso, who once helmed the kitchen at the fine-dining establishment Trece, and though the fare here is much simpler and way less expensive, Troncoso's influence guarantees health food that transcends the usual pile of wilted alfalfa spouts on a plate. There's even an element of heartiness, as in the rotisserie chicken and tabbouleh sandwich. Of course, you've gotta try a smoothie-lightly sweetened with agave or honey, coupled with your choice of six different types of milk.

ASIAN

LITTLE KATANA $$

4527 Travis St., 214/443-9600, www.littlekatana.com

HOURS: Lunch: Mon.-Sat. 11 A.M.-2:30 P.M.
Dinner: Mon.-Sat. 5-11 P.M., Sun. 4-10 P.M.

Hip, hot, and heavy on the Uptown vibe, Little Katana's exposed brick walls and dark intimacy provide a good-looking framework for an exquisite meal. The inventive Japanese and Asian fusion dishes jazz up the mind and the palate, while the rich sushi creations defy the minimalism usually associated with the cuisine—to fabulous results.

MANGO THAI $$

4448 Lovers La., 214/265-9996,
www.mangothaicuisine.com

HOURS: Daily 11 A.M.-10 P.M.

D Magazine calls it "pop Asian" and the *Dallas Morning News* calls it "new Asian," but really, Mango Thai is just straight-up good. Located in the older shopping strip on Lovers Lane (beware—parking is a beast here), Mango fills the need for all things curry, spicy, and noodle-y in Park Cities. The service is straightforward and friendly, and the decor is casual but well thought-out with orange and blue walls and a modern feel.

BARBECUE

PEGGY SUE BBQ $

6600 Snider Plaza, 214/987-9188,
www.peggysuebbq.com

HOURS: Sun.-Thurs. 11 A.M.-9 P.M., Fri.-Sat. 11 A.M.-10 P.M.

The charming little hole-in-the-wall that houses Peggy Sue BBQ has barbecue in its brick and mortar. Before Peggy Sue opened in 1989, the spot was Peggy's Beef Bar, and before that, it was Howard and Peggy's. Peggy Sue has done its predecessors proud, maintaining a 1950s-type atmosphere and succulent, smoked meats (the ribs are especially tasty, pre-rubbed before they're smoked), along with fresh, perfectly steamed veggies.

COFFEE AND TEA

THE CULTURED CUP $

8312 Preston Center Plaza Dr.,
972/960-1521 or 888/VIP-TEAS,
www.theculturedcup.com

HOURS: Mon.-Sat. 10 A.M.-6 P.M.

Once you enter The Cultured Cup, you'll never want to leave. The atmosphere is warm and comfortable, but updated, neither prim nor precious. Similarly, the customer service is friendly, helpful, and generous—upon entering, you are usually offered a tea sampling of your choice and a plate of tea chocolates. Besides a huge selection of loose teas, the Cup also sells tins, gorgeous china teacups and sets, coffee accoutrements, and many other fun gifts and home items for every budget.

DRIP $

4343 Lovers La., 214/599-7800,
www.dripcoffeeco.com

HOURS: Mon.-Fri. 6:30 A.M.-8 P.M., Sat. 7 A.M.-8 P.M., Sun. 8 A.M.-6 P.M.

For too long, Park Cities dwellers were held in the grip of bad coffee, with few options when it came to a true, casual coffee shop. Drip changed all that. This casual yet modern place roasts its beans right on the spot, and you can taste the freshness in every latte. A small selection of other beverages and snacks is available, too.

FRENCH

BIJOUX $$$

5450 W. Lovers La., #225, 214/350-6100,
www.bijouxrestaurant.com

HOURS: Mon.-Sat. 5:30-10 P.M.

A gorgeous gem of a restaurant, Bijoux is opulent and expensive—and totally worth it. The food is slightly updated classic French—think cheese courses, coddled egg with caviar, arugula, foie gras, scallops, truffles—and is available in three- and five-course prix fixe menus, or in a whopping nine-course tasting menu. The service is impeccable; the wine menu features perfect pairings ranging from $34 to more than $600 a bottle. Sure, you might have to check your bank balance before you go, but with food, drink, and atmosphere this good, it's a satisfying splurge.

RISE NO. 1 $$$
5360 W. Lovers La., 214/366-9900,
www.risesouffle.com
HOURS: Tues.-Thurs. 11 A.M.-10 P.M., Fri.-Sat.
11 A.M.-11 P.M., Sun. 11 A.M.-9 P.M.

Never heard of a soufflé house? Rise No. 1 is
an excellent introduction to the eggy French
specialty. The menu here, of course, is mainly
soufflés, from the traditional ham and cheese
to an indulgent Maine lobster filling to sweet
dessert offerings like chocolate, ginger, and
raspberry. The wine menu is extensive and
available in very affordable flights—ask your
server for help, as the service is friendly and
well-versed in French food and drink.

MEDITERRANEAN AND MIDDLE EASTERN

CAFÉ ISTANBUL $$
5450 W. Lovers La., 214/902-0919,
www.cafe-istanbul.net
HOURS: Tues.-Fri. 11:30 A.M.-2:30 P.M. and 5-10 P.M.,
Sat. 11 A.M.-11 P.M., Sun. 11:30 A.M.-10 P.M.

The only establishment in the DFW area
serving solely Turkish cuisine, Café Istanbul
could easily rest on its laurels, but it doesn't.
Chef Erol Girgin serves a creative, savory
menu of Turkish classics as well as updated—
and slightly upscale—versions of traditional
foods like hummus, kebabs, and lesser-known
exotic delights.

FADI'S $$
3001 Knox St., 214/528-1800,
www.fadiscuisine.com
HOURS: Mon.-Thurs. 11 A.M.-9 P.M., Fri.-Sat. 1-9 P.M.,
Sun. 11 A.M.-8 P.M.

The storefronts on this side of town have a certain duality: If they face Knox Street, they are
cute and boutique-y; if they face the highway,
they invariably are in a strip mall. Fadi's falls
into the latter category, which is just fine, because this awesome Mediterranean diner isn't
about artifice, it's about hummus. And baba
ghanoush. And just about every Mideastern
dish you could think of, amazingly prepared
and served cafeteria-style. Quick, convenient,
and better than many four-star joints around.

PASTRIES

SPRINKLES CUPCAKES $
4020 Villanova St., 214/369-0004,
www.sprinklescupcakes.com
HOURS: Mon.-Sat. 9 A.M.-7 P.M., Sun. 10 A.M.-6 P.M.

Okay, Sprinkles Cupcakes is a chain. But if
there were ever a non-local place to recom-
mend, this is it. Sprinkles crafts the Platonic
ideal of cupcakes, moist and lip-smackingly
good, in a variety of inventive flavors, along
with new twists on the classics. The place is
almost always crowded, so you might want to
pre-order so you can jump to the shorter to-go
line. Or just pop in and grab one to munch
on while you window-shop along the Plaza at
Preston Center.

YUMMY DONUTS $
4355 Lovers La., 214/520-7680
HOURS: Weds.-Mon. 6 A.M.-noon

Chic, sleek, and with a twist of humor, Yummy
Donuts is a great place to grab something to
go, but an even better place to sit down and
linger. Why not, since the place has Wi-Fi,
piping hot coffee, and, of course, donuts? The
menu offers the classics like glazed, but you
can also find seasonally themed donuts and
mega-indulgent varieties like Moon Pie. For
those with less of a sweet tooth, there's a good
mix of breakfast sandwiches to keep you full
all morning.

SEAFOOD
CAFÉ PACIFIC $$$
24 Highland Park Village, 214/526-1170
HOURS: Mon.-Weds. 11 A.M.-10:30 P.M.,
Thurs.-Sat. 11 A.M.-11 P.M.

Café Pacific is what you'd expect from a Highland Park seafood eatery: upscale dining with upscale prices. The fresh, cleanly prepared seafood is worth a dent to your credit card, though, as one bite of the lobster, shrimp, and scallop ceviche will prove. Decor-wise, it's all "brass, glass, and class," as one local paper puts it, but at its heart, Café Pacific is a neighborhood place, dressed up but friendly.

HECTOR'S ON HENDERSON $$$
2929 N. Henderson Ave., 214/821-0432,
www.hectorsonhenderson.com
HOURS: Tues.-Sat. from 5:30 P.M.

Owned by former actor and consummate showman Hector Garcia, Hector's exchanges the stuffiness of power dining for the aura of a ritzy dinner show, complete with a full band that plays upbeat standards (Hector himself is known to sing a few tunes). The jazzy upscale menu pleases the crowd as well. Bracket your meal with the lobster-stuffed avocado to start and the crème brûlée candied apple to finish.

SOUTHERN
C BUBBA'S $
6617 Hillcrest La., 214/373-6527,
www.bubbascatering.com
HOURS: Daily 6:30 A.M.-10 P.M.

If you're seeking full-on Southern-fried vittles, Bubba's is the perfect destination. This is a place that's not afraid of a deep fryer, and puts it to best use making legendary fried chicken (Bubba's and its sister restaurant, Babe's, were named by *Southern Living* magazine as among the best places in the South for fried chicken). Tasty rolls, biscuit-centered breakfasts, and cobblers are popular, too. If you go during peak times, especially Sundays, expect to wait for a table or in the serpentine drive-through line, but it's well worth it.

STEAKHOUSE
DUNSTON'S $$
5423 Lovers La., 214/352-8320
HOURS: Mon.-Thurs. 11 A.M.-10 P.M., Fri. 11 A.M.-11 P.M.,
Sat. 5-11 P.M., Sun. 5-10 P.M.

Wood-paneled walls, old-school steakhouse art, busy carpet—Dunston's has been around since 1969, and it shows. The place is a true throwback, with wonderfully un-ironic atmosphere and patrons who have been regulars for 30 years. Sadly, the quality of the food has suffered with the times, but Dunston's is a must-see for an example of a real Texas open-grill steakhouse atmosphere. We suggest you grab a drink there.

TEX-MEX
MI COCINA $$
77 Highland Park Village, 214/521-6426,
www.mcrowd.com/micocina.html
HOURS: Sun.-Thurs. 11 A.M.-10 P.M., Fri.-Sat. 11 A.M.-11 P.M.

There is great debate among Dallas denizens as to whether Highland Park's Mi Cocina—or "Mico," as it is often called—is the real deal or just a "scene." If you like Tex-Mex, you'll most likely love Mico's *queso,* crispy shrimp tacos, and strong tropical-themed cocktails. Some purists, however, don't dig the "upscaling" of Tex-Mex, and the Highland Park Mico's chichi digs and beautiful people are considered by some to be heretical treatment of the cuisine. Either way, you've gotta check out

RESTAURANTS

TEX-MEX IS BETTER THAN SEX

For the uninitiated – or for those who like to eat, you know, healthy – a rundown of the cornerstones of Tex-Mex is perplexing: Processed cheese? Lard-laden refried beans? Vats of sour cream? What exactly is it about the combination of these ingredients that beckons to Texans so strongly? What makes Tex-Mex so special?

It can't be explained. You'll just know it when you taste it. Here are some suggested spots to begin your Tex-Mex education:

A little less junky than many of its ilk, **Manny's Uptown Texmex Restaurant** (3521 Oak Grove Ave, 214/252-1616) is a good place to start. This place is well-pedigreed (it's owned by a member of the Mi Cocina family), and its found in a cute frame house, tucked away from the hustle and bustle of Uptown. Inside, there's plenty of hustle and bustle, however, as the menu's specialty offerings like a luscious, spicy sunset dip (chile con queso with hot peppers) and a unique take on old faves keep the crowds coming consistently.

For a more straightforward approach, check out **Hererra's Café** (4001 Maple Ave., 214/528-9644), a family-owned BYOB place whose long menu can prove intimidating to the uninitiated. Stick to the basics until you get used to it. Try one of the many combination plates available, and make sure to include at least one beef enchilada, and make sure you don't fill up too much on the hot, hot salsa, fresh chips, and corn tortillas with butter before your meal arrives.

Good tortillas are key to good Tex-Mex, and at **El Ranchito,** (610 W Jefferson Blvd., 75208, 214/946-4238) they're made fresh on the festive, faux-authentic premises. From this base are built the cornerstones of the cuisine: crisp bean chalupas, peppery fajitas, and dense, classic enchiladas.

the Highland Park location (there are many across town), as it's one of the most Dallas-y experiences you'll have—eating tacos across the street from Jimmy Choo.

Greenville
Map 4

AMERICAN
LAKEWOOD LANDING ⓢ
5818 Live Oak St., 214/823-2410,
www.lakewood-landing.com
HOURS: Daily 3 P.M.-2 A.M.

The sign outside the Lakewood Landing advertises it as "an upscale dive," and that sums up the place nicely. This is a spot that doesn't take itself too seriously—despite the smattering of hipsters, you get the feeling the wood paneling covering the walls is not meant ironically. The Landing does, however, take its juicy, high-piled, nicely priced hamburgers seriously, and you should, too. If you stray from the burger,

the remainder of the menu is simple bar food, but it's, well, *really good* bar food. Thankfully, Dallas recently passed a smoking ordinance, so the cloud of smoke that once obscured the heat of the tasty jalapeño poppers and the freshly fried chips and salsa is gone for good.

◀ YORK STREET ⓢⓢⓢ
6047 Lewis St., 214/826-0968,
www.yorkstreetdallas.com
HOURS: Lunch: Weds. 11:30 A.M.-2 P.M.
Dinner: Tues.-Sat. 6 P.M.-10 P.M.

York Street may be the most consistently well-reviewed fine-dining establishment in a town full of them. Top-rated in *Zagat, Gourmet* magazine, and the *Dallas Morning News,* and noted in the *New York Times,* chef/owner Sharon Hage is a perennial James Beard nominee. Hage crafts inventive New American dishes with an acute eye for seasonal ingredients—you won't find her famous pan-fried okra in winter—on a menu so lively it practically dances. The hard-to-find spot is tiny, but its sleek interior and friendly service give off a feeling of welcome rather than exclusivity, manifested in the unexpected complimentary olives, nuts, and sherry that arrive as you do at your table—a nice touch in a restaurant full of them.

ASIAN
NANDINA 💲💲

5631 Alta Ave., 214/826-6300
HOURS: Lunch: Mon.-Fri. 11 A.M.-3 P.M.
Dinner: Daily 5 P.M.-3 A.M.

Billing itself as an "Asian tapas" restaurant, Nandina sometimes tries to be too much at once, but the menu's wide variety ultimately pleases. Tucked away on side street off Greenville Avenue, the place offers a cool, dark respite from the revelry going on a block away. Whether you'd like a full, lingering dinner of cocktails and unusual sushi, genuine dishes like 1,000-year egg, or a solution to your 3 A.M. drunken noodle craving, Nandina will have you covered. And they deliver.

ITALIAN
CAMPISI'S 💲💲

5610 E. Mockingbird La., 214/827-0355,
www.campisis.us
HOURS: Sun.-Fri. 11 A.M.-10 P.M., Sat. 11 A.M.-11 P.M.

By now Campisi's has a few locations scattered about the Dallas area, but the original location on Mockingbird Lane is really the only choice. That's not only because this Campisi's

has provided toothsome ravioli, lasagna, and pizza for decades; it's also because of the joint's history. Back in the day, Joe Campisi was rumored to be a major mafia crime boss, supposedly involved in the assassination of President John F. Kennedy. In fact, Jack Ruby—the man who shot Kennedy's assassin, Lee Harvey Oswald—ate a steak dinner here the night before Kennedy was killed. From the weird, inexplicable "Egyptian Lounge" sign outside to the dark interior, remnants of Campisi's mystery still infuse a dining experience there. Of course, some of the panache was lessened by the recent reality show *Wildest Party Parent,* which featured Joe's son Corky and his daughter Amber Campisi, fresh off a *Playboy* shoot.

MEDITERRANEAN AND MIDDLE EASTERN
CAFÉ IZMIR 💲💲

3711 Greenville Ave., 214/826-7788, www.cafeizmir.com
HOURS: Sun.-Mon. 5:30-9:30 P.M., Tues. and Fri.-Sat.
5:30-11:30 P.M., Weds.-Thurs. 5:30-10:30 P.M.

It's a shame the intimacy of Café Izmir discourages large groups, because the Mideastern tapas at this popular Greenville Avenue spot are perfect for sharing among a big bunch of friends—even more so on half-price "Tapas Tuesday," which also features great wine specials. Make sure to order an extra plate of Izmir's creamy hummus because you won't want to share, no matter how many people are at your table. Of course, thanks to Izmir's next-door casual deli, you can always take some home with you.

PUB FOOD
THE COCK AND BULL 💲💲

6330 Gaston Ave., 214/841-9111,
www.cockandbulldallas.com
HOURS: Mon.-Fri. 3 P.M.-2 A.M., Sat.-Sun. noon-2 A.M.

It's probably not easy to provide a genuine

The Cock and Bull serves up English pub food in the middle of the Big D.

English pub atmosphere, but The Cock and Bull rises to the occasion handily, with cozy if somewhat shabby—and dark—environs and a fine bar menu, including reliable blue plate specials on Sundays. For $6, the latter is more than just meatloaf; think instead grilled fish, pork chops, and hanger steak. Well, sometimes there's meatloaf, too. Just check the specials board to find out.

THE LIBERTINE $$

2101 Greenville Ave., 214/824-7900,
www.libertinebar.com
HOURS: Dinner: Mon.-Fri. 4 P.M.-midnight.
Brunch: Sat.-Sun. 11 A.M.-3 P.M.

A fine selection of beers, a casual atmosphere, and elevated pub grub make the Libertine a favorite destination for Lower Greenville denizens. The quasi-English decor, replete with brass bar and big comfy booths, belies both the beer and food menus, in a good way. The requisite nods to shepherd's pie and fish and chips are replaced, for instance, by a varied and inspired menu that's not too complicated, but definitely not simplistic. The popular steak sandwiches and portabella fries taste even better on Sundays, when the menu is half-price.

SEAFOOD

AW, SHUCKS $

3601 Greenville Ave., 214/821-9449,
www.awshucksdallas.com
HOURS: Sun.-Thurs. 11 A.M.-10 P.M., Fri.-Sat.
11 A.M.-11:45 P.M.

If you want something fried and cheap, hit up this quirky joint that has held down the same spot on Greenville Avenue for well more than two decades. Despite its bivalve-oriented name, the oysters at Aw Shucks are best avoided, but the fried-to-order shrimp and catfish will leaved you stuffed. Extra points for location (just across the street from the Granada Theater), atmosphere (simple wooden tables adorned only with condiments and a roll of paper towels), and convenience (payment is on the honor system, so there's no messing with the check).

LA CALLE DOCE $$

1925 Skillman St., 214/824-9900,
www.lacalledoce-dallas.com
HOURS: Mon.-Thurs. 11 A.M.-10 P.M., Fri.-Sat.
11 A.M.-11 P.M., Sun. 11 A.M.-9 P.M.

Even though it occupies a nondescript storefront in a landlocked city, La Calle Doce's clean, white walls and seafood-heavy menu evoke a breezy Acapulco café. Fish is king here, be it in filet, cocktail, or ceviche form. La Calle Doce caters to locals and is friendly to families—though many a happy hour margarita has been swilled here, no doubt.

SOUTHERN
GOLD RUSH CAFÉ $

1913 Skillman St., 214/823-6923

HOURS: Mon.-Sat. 7:30 A.M.-4:30 P.M., Sun. 8 A.M.-3 P.M.

If you're on the go or looking for hearty, simple, and cheap, the Gold Rush is the perfect little greasy spoon diner for breakfast or lunch. The eggy breakfast items are generously portioned, especially the taco meat omelet, but the tastiest treat is the hand-battered chicken-fried steak. Try it in sandwich form. You'd never know it from the fake brick decor and simple wooden tables, but this place has a storied past as a haven for hungover Dallas musicians and their aficionados.

WINE BAR AND TAPAS
THE GRAPE $$$

2808 Greenville Ave., 214/828-1981,
www.thegraperestaurant.com

HOURS: Dinner: Sun.-Thurs. 5:30 P.M.-10 P.M., Fri.-Sat. 5:30 P.M.-10:30 P.M. Brunch: Sun. 10:30 A.M.-2 P.M.

This down-the-block bistro has been around for almost 40 years and has maintained many of its original traditions, like the chalkboard menu, the much-lauded mushroom soup, and the dimly lit, tiny dining area. The Grape was Dallas's first wine bar, a fact reflected by the ample wine list and Euro-feel, but the food never comes second best in chef/owner Brian Luscher's kitchen. Luscher's brunches are especially celebrated, having won several mentions in national and local publications and "Best Brunch" awards in the local papers.

RESTAURANTS

East Dallas
Map 5

AMERICAN
GARDEN CAFÉ $

5310 Junius St., 214/887-8330,
www.gardencafe.net

HOURS: Tues.-Sun. 8 A.M.-2 P.M.

With its hippie-dippy charm and funky feel, the Garden Café is like a little piece of Austin in the midst of the Big D. The key to this little neighborhood spot is its adjacent namesake greenery, from which veggies, herbs, and greens are plucked fresh to order for patrons' omelets, salads, and sandwiches. Seating is available in the garden, and it's fun to lounge over a sunny lunch or all-day breakfast and watch the goings-on of this eclectic neighborhood street.

COFFEE SHOP
MURRAY STREET COFFEE $

103 Murray St., 214/655-2808,
www.murraystreetcoffee.com

HOURS: Mon.-Fri. 7 A.M.-9 P.M., Sat. 8 A.M.-6 P.M., Sun. 9 A.M.-2 P.M.

Murray Street Coffee is hip and sleek, but still comfortable. Head upstairs in this airy bi-level space and sip a giant latte or nosh on a bagel topped with farmers market arugula and tomatoes as you listen to one of the Wednesday night DJs. Or pop in on a Saturday morning for a mimosa and chat with owners Liz and Doug Davis, who combine a sharp eye for design, a good ear for music, and a penchant for hiring some of the friendliest baristas around.

RESTAURANTS

ITALIAN
CIVELLO'S RAVIOLISMO $$

1318 N. Peak St., 214/827-2989,
www.civellosraviolismo.com

HOURS: Mon.-Fri. 9 A.M.-3 P.M.

This family-owned and -operated takeout spot is a delight on otherwise bleak Peak Street. Chena and Phil Civello have supplied local eateries (such as the famous Campisi's) with superlative ravioli for years, and theirs is a convenient spot to grab a quick, easy, and yummy dinner. An 18-pack of ravioli will only set you back $4–6. Selection varies daily, and is always freshly made with everything from traditional beef/ricotta to the more inventive, like locally raised buffalo. Civello's also provides other pasta dishes and salads to go.

MEXICAN
MONICA'S ACA Y ALLA $$

2914 Main St., 214/748-7140,
www.monicas.com

HOURS: Lunch: Tues.-Fri. 11 A.M.-2 P.M.
Dinner: Tues.-Fri. 5-10 P.M., Sat. 5-11 P.M.,
Sun. 6-10 P.M., Brunch: Sun. 11 A.M.-3 P.M.

Entering Aca y Alla is a bit like walking onto the set of a Pedro Almodovar film. Bright sangria-red walls lend a colorful backdrop to equally colorful cocktails like watermelon margaritas and tequila Jell-O shots. Live Latin music lifts patrons up out of their glossy, jet-black seats and into a conga line. The lively proprietor, Monica Greene, chats with customers, her vivacious personality and striking figure evoking the larger-than-life Latin characters from the Spanish director.

And, as in Almodovar's movies, there's always a twist at this Deep Ellum mainstay where, to paraphrase Greene, things are not always what they seem. For instance, this particular Monica—a Mexico City native who arrived in the States in 1974—used to be Eduardo. Perhaps even more of a twist, however, is Monica's ability to serve up healthy

Monica's Aca y Alla, where Almodovar meets Tex-Mex

© JONANNA WIDNER

takes on Mexican and Tex-Mex food. Oh sure, there's plenty of sour cream and cheese to be had here, but there's also a clear emphasis on veggie options and lighter fare.

THE TACO JOINT ❶

911 N. Peak St., 214/826-8226,
www.thetacojoint.com
HOURS: Mon.-Fri. 6:30 A.M.-2 P.M., Sat. 8 A.M.-2 P.M.
Seems Austin's obsession with breakfast tacos finally made its way north up I-35 and planted its first flag in East Dallas. The Taco Joint's breakfast fare—made sans lard and trans fats has rapidly become a citywide favorite. Although the lunch menu is nothing to sneeze at, it's the morning combos of tortillas, eggs, black beans, cheese, and chorizo that lure scores of families in the mornings and hungover hipsters just before noon (on weekdays, breakfast ends at 11:45 A.M.; on Saturday, it's served all day). In fact, you might try going at an off time; otherwise, be prepared for the ravenous crowds elbowing for position at the salsa bar.

SOUTHERN

◖ ALLGOOD CAFE ❶❶

2934 Main St., 214/742-5362,
www.allgoodcafe.com
HOURS: Tues.-Sat. 9 A.M.-9 P.M., Sun.-Mon. 9 A.M.-2 P.M.
It doesn't get much more homey than the AllGood, a Deep Ellum stalwart owned by Texas music lover Mike Snider, who has covered the walls in cool old posters and flyers. Snider has been serving up some of the best country-style veggies, eggs, and chicken-fried steak since Deep Ellum was just a sparkle in some developer's eye, and he has speckled his grits-'n'-griddle menu with fresh, local ingredients and a few surprises. On most nights the place transforms into a primarily alt-country venue, so it's not uncommon to catch a show

© JONANNA WIDNER

The AllGood Cafe's chicken-fried steak breakfast has cured many a hangover.

there at night, then shuffle over the next morning for a late and hearty breakfast.

COWBOY CHOW ❶❶

2801 Commerce St., 214/742-2469,
www.cowboychow.net
HOURS: Lunch: Mon.-Sat. 11 A.M.-2 P.M. Dinner: Thurs.-Sat. 5-9 P.M. Brunch: Sun. noon-4 P.M.
The home-on-the-range aesthetic of Cowboy Chow, the brainchild of the folks behind the ever-popular Twisted Root Burger Company, would be a little cloying were the brisket not so moist, the pot pie not so flaky, and the "mashed tater parfait" not so doggone tasty. The atmosphere here borders on theme-park cowboy, but the decent prices (try the "Recession Menu," where everything is $7) and true-to-Texas flavors (Dr. Pepper–laced barbecue sauce, anyone?) allow the proprietors to pull it off.

South Dallas Map 6

AMERICAN

BOLSA $$

614 W. Davis St., 214/367-9367,
www.bolsadallas.com
HOURS: Mon.-Thurs. 11 A.M.-10 P.M.,
Fri.-Sat. 11 A.M.-11 P.M., Sun. noon-10 P.M.

While much of Dallas's dining tradition tends toward see-and-be-seen and large-scale finery, Bolsa occupies a comfortable neighborhood niche, and the neighbors have taken quite kindly to it. The café, which doubles as an epicurean grocery, is located in a former auto repair garage and the chatty buzz of the nighttime crowd gives the impression of familiar comfort. Ditto the food: Chef Graham Dodds clearly recognizes the connections between the Mediterranean culinary aesthetic and Texas's ample supply of fresh organic ingredients, and walks the walk: "No freezer, no fryer" is Bolsa's motto.

So, for Dodds, fresh means *fresh,* a concept that turns simple into sumptuous. The popular bruschetta, for instance, intermingles inventive toppings like figs and honey, or salmon and crème fraîche, all of which stand out with the extra zing of the newly procured. Pizzas are popular here, too, for similar reasons, with the unique flatbread base deftly holding local cheeses, veggies, and meats.

CLIFF CAFÉ $$

901 Fort Worth Ave., 214/393-4141,
www.belmontdallas.com
HOURS: Sun.-Mon. 7 A.M.-9 P.M.,
Thurs.-Sat. 7 A.M.-10 P.M.

Breakfast is the time to be at Cliff Café. True, the lunch and dinner menus' unique comfort food like buffalo-bleu cheese cheddar mac are all savory delights, but really, how can you pass up a breakfast that offers sweet potato pecan pancakes? Even though the offerings have a down-home touch, Cliff Café is actually located in the swank, modern boutique Belmont hotel, which rose like renovated phoenix from the ashes of what was once a bit of a flophouse.

HATTIES $$

418 Bishop Ave., 214/942-7400, www.hatties.net
HOURS: Lunch: Mon.-Sat. 11:30 A.M.-2:30 P.M. Dinner: Tues.-Sun. from 5:30 P.M. Brunch: Sun. 11 A.M.-2:30 P.M.

Housed smack in middle of the charming storefronts that make up the core of the Bishop Arts district, Hatties pours on the upscale Southern charm. The bistro specializes in grown-up comfort food in a refined but comfy atmosphere (which tends to get a bit loud, especially on weekends). Make sure to order the four-cheddar mac 'n' cheese.

THE STUDIO BAR AND GRILL $

1135 S. Lamar St., 214/928-9844,
www.studiobaronlamar.com
HOURS: Mon.-Thurs. 11 A.M.-3 P.M., Fri. 11 A.M.-midnight, Sat. 2 P.M.-midnight

Although the South Lamar district is slowly gaining steam, the dining choices have lagged a bit. Fortunately, the Studio Bar and Grill fills much of the gap, providing lunch-y sandwiches and apps, plus pub food dinner, all at pretty reasonable prices.

TILLMAN'S ROADHOUSE $$

324 W. 7th St., 214/942-0988,

www.tillmansroadhouse.com

HOURS: Lunch: Tues.-Fri. 11:30 A.M.-2 P.M., Sat.
11 A.M.-3 P.M. Dinner: Tues.-Thurs. 5:30-10 P.M.,
Fri.-Sat. 5:30-11 P.M.

You won't find any stray tobacco juice on the knotted wood floor of this particular roadhouse; considering proprietor Sara Tillman's fancy take on classic Texas aesthetic (culinary and otherwise), you're more likely to encounter a spot of stray truffle oil. Surrounded by repurposed barn wood and distressed leather, the crowd at Tillman's is as happily raucous as any roadside tavern ruffians, but it's telling that the social lubricant here is blood orange margaritas, often found astride a bowl of venison Frito pie or a plate of chicken-fried hanger steak.

Ah, yes, that chicken-fried steak. Amazingly crisp, not lying flat across the plate like most, but piled gloriously high and enmeshed in a mountain of whipped garlic potatoes, this is the kind of meal you dream about on cold winter days. And that savory combo of comfort and cuisine forms the crux of Tillman's appeal.

COFFEE SHOP
OPENING BELL ●

1409 S. Lamar St., #12, 214/565-0503,
www.openingbellcoffee.com

HOURS: Mon.-Thurs. 7 A.M.-10 P.M., Fri. 7 A.M.-midnight,
Sat. 9 A.M.-midnight, Sun. 10 A.M.-3 P.M.

Despite its slightly cloying Wall Street theme, Opening Bell is a welcoming, hang-out-all-day kind of spot, tucked into an intimate corner of the gargantuan South Side on Lamar building (a former Sears & Roebuck distribution warehouse, now refurbished into a mixed-use development). Bypass the meager food offerings and grab a comfy couch and a latte as you catch

FRIED COKE?

Of all the colloquial culinary oddities you can find in Texas, the **deep-fried food competition** at the State Fair of Texas might just take the cake – as long as the cake has been dipped in batter, submerged in eight inches of cooking oil, and then covered with ice cream and chocolate.

Though the State Fair begins in late September and only lasts until the end of October, the competition actually begins a few weeks before that, when dozens of food vendors unveil the artery-clogging concoctions they've been cooking up for an entire year, pitting them against each other for the Big Tex Awards. For the public, the competition is a lighthearted affair, but for the most part, it's serious business: The winners enjoy a huge amount of publicity, which drives customers to their booths by the thousands.

Hence, the escalating creativity. Past winners have created fried banana pudding, fried Nutter Butters, and fried peanut butter and jelly sandwiches. By current standards, these actually seem pretty pedestrian, because in recent years, contestants have cranked it up a notch, producing things like fried Coca-Cola (a three-year winner), chicken-fried bacon, and something called the Donkey Tail, which involves a hot dog split down the middle, filled with cheese, wrapped in a tortilla, deep-fried, and then covered in chili.

If all of this sounds decadent, well...it is. And if it sounds disgusting, well...some of it is. But for the most part, the indulgent treats usually range from pretty good to downright mind-blowing, and the fun of eating them in the shadow of Big Tex makes them taste all the much better.

one of the many local musical acts that perform here amid the concrete walls and exposed ductwork. A second location opened in 2008 in the Mosaic building, downtown.

WINE BAR AND TAPAS
CAFÉ MADRID ⑤⑤

408 N. Bishop Ave., #108, 214/942-8272, www.cafemadrid-dallas.com

HOURS: Tues.-Sat. 5-11 P.M.

Anyone can throw together a table full of small plates, but the folks at Café Madrid know the ins and outs of true tapas. There is an Uptown location, but the one in Bishop Arts can't be beat for saffron-infused, authentic ambience (right down to the occasionally indifferent waitstaff, a la Europe, which is one of the few drawbacks here). On busy nights, friends gather at tables crowded with traditional Spanish fare (a shockingly good blood sausage, well-considered cheeses, perfect tortilla Española), along with a few curveballs (the goat cheese balls fried in honey, for instance). Skip the wine list and order a few pitchers of the balanced, boozy sangria, which pairs well with everything.

Greater Dallas   Map 11

BARBECUE
🄲 SONNY BRYAN'S ⑤

2202 Inwood Rd., 214/357-7120

HOURS: Mon.-Fri. 10 A.M.-4 P.M., Sat. 10 A.M.-3 P.M.

No trip to Dallas would be complete without a trip to the original Sonny Bryan's, which opened in 1910. And no trip to Sonny Bryan's would be complete without loosening a notch on your belt buckle to make room for chopped beef sandwiches and fat, juicy sausages, all dripping with Sonny's signature smoky sauce. Settling into one of the school desks they've utilized as seating here for decades might feel weird at first, but once the first piece of heavenly meat hits your taste buds, you'll forget where you are anyway.

TEX-MEX
AVILA'S ⑤⑤

4714 Maple Ave., 214/520-2700

HOURS: Lunch: Mon.-Sat. 11 A.M.-2:30 P.M. Dinner: Mon.-Thurs. 5-9 P.M., Fri.-Sat. 5-10 P.M.

The parking sucks, the location might be called "light industrial," and the decor won't win any awards, but none of the dozens of people who call this place their lunchtime home care. Avila's is Tex-Mex in all its gooey glory. It's impossible to go wrong ordering any of the enchilada platters, sided by smoky refried beans and Spanish rice, but the special board is really where it's at, especially when the brisket burrito makes an appearance.

North Side Fort Worth

Map 7

RESTAURANTS

AMERICAN

C LONESOME DOVE $$$

2406 N. Main St., 817/740-8810,
www.lonesomedovebistro.com

HOURS: Lunch: Tues.-Sat. 11:30 A.M.-2:30 P.M.
Dinner: Mon.-Sat. 5-11 P.M.

Generally, it's wise to steer clear of restaurants named after popular movies, but with Lonesome Dove, it's safe to make an exception. Chef Tim Love has created an adventurous bistro menu that both celebrates and updates Western flavors. It's located in the Stockyards historical district, but that doesn't mean the food is limited to steak. You're as likely to order quail, elk, or boar here—all exquisitely prepared—as you are beef. But while the menu is modern, the decor is pure Old West, with a tin ceiling, a long wooden bar, and chefs in cowboy hats visible in the open kitchen.

SARSAPARILLA SALOON $

140 E. Exchange Ave., 817/625-1822,
www.oldetymemercantile.com/sarsaparilla-saloon.htm

HOURS: Mon.-Fri. 10 A.M.-6 P.M., Sat. 10 A.M.-7 P.M.,
Sun. noon-6 P.M.

Located in the Stockyards, the Sarsaparilla Saloon fits right into its Old West surroundings. It's an offshoot of the Old Tyme Mercantile, purveyors of 19th-century reproduction cowboy duds, and the Sarsaparilla is itself a re-creation of an old-fashioned saloon. The simple menu features just a few fresh-made sandwiches. The real draw here is dessert: shakes, malts, and sundaes, of course, but also decadent choices like pecan pie and cheesecake.

STEAKHOUSE

CATTLEMEN'S STEAKHOUSE $$$

2458 N. Main St., 817/624-3945,
www.cattlemenssteakhouse.com

HOURS: Mon.-Thurs. 11 A.M.-10:30 P.M.,
Fri.-Sat. 11 A.M.-11 P.M., Sun. 1-9 P.M.

When viewing all those longhorns on the hoof at the Stockyards gives you a deep hankering for a thick steak (but no desire to bust your wallet paying for it), swing the family on in to Cattlemen's Steakhouse, a Fort Worth institution for more than half a century. There are more than a dozen different steaks on the menu (ranging from Porterhouse to chicken-fried) to slake your thirst for red meat. There's even a six-ounce hunk of steak on the children's menu (after all, you gotta teach 'em young). Kids and adults alike will dig the atmosphere of unpretentious Old West kitsch, too.

TEX-MEX

JOE T. GARCIA'S $$

2201 N. Commerce St., 817/626-4356,
www.joets.com

HOURS: Mon.-Thurs. 11 A.M.-2:30 P.M.,
Fri.-Sat. 11 A.M.-11 P.M., Sun. 11 A.M.-10 P.M.

Back in the day, the only way to access the dining area at Joe T. Garcia's was to walk though the kitchen. Now occupying a full city block, Joe T's is more like a Mexican restaurant theme park than an actual Mexican restaurant. Strolling mariachis, opulent decor, a poolside outdoor seating area, and seating for 1,000 make it a sure bet that a meal here will be memorable. The menu is not the draw—dinner offerings are limited to fajitas or enchiladas. Well, actually, maybe it's the *lack*

© JONANNA WIDNER

Joe T. Garcia's

of menu that's the draw: Joe T's has been famous for doing a few things but doing them amazingly well. Plus, you'll need to eat after indulging in the strong margaritas.

Downtown Fort Worth   Map 8

AMERICAN
AFTERNOON TEA AT THE
ASHTON ⑤⑤⑤

610 Main St. (in the Ashton Hotel), 817/332-0100,
www.theashtonhotel.com

HOURS: Thurs.-Sat. 2-4 P.M.

Dressing up is part of the fun at the Ashton Hotel's afternoon tea, served in the 610 Grille. The lush fabrics and burnished woods of the Grille make for an elegant setting for the tea service. Traditional tea accompaniments such as finger sandwiches, house-made scones, and petit fours will make you feel like you've stepped into another time and place,

as does the historic luxury of the Ashton overall. Reservations are required 24 hours in advance.

ⓒ REATA ⑤⑤⑤

310 Houston St., 817/336-1009,
www.reata.net

HOURS: Lunch: Daily 11 A.M.-2:30 P.M.
Dinner: Daily 5-10:30 P.M.

Reata was originally located atop a skyscraper—until a tornado blew through and swept it away in March 2000. But like a phoenix rising from the ashes—or at least from the debris—this Cowtown favorite has been reborn in Sundance Square. With a rooftop patio and tables that offer plenty of privacy, Reata is rightly celebrated as one of Fort Worth's most romantic fine-dining spots. The Southwestern menu matches the decor and offers a slate of updated regional favorites from the South and the West—grits and chicken-fried steak both appear on the menu—alongside with traditional Mexican dishes.

ASIAN
THAI TINA'S 💲💲

703 N. Henderson St., 817/332-0088

HOURS: Sun.-Thurs. 11 A.M.–9 P.M., Fri.-Sat. 11 A.M.–10 P.M.

Who knew the hot spot in Tex-Mex and steak-obsessed Cowtown would be a tiny hole-in-the-wall Thai joint? While outside Thai Tina's looks like a bunker, inside is a colorful world of zingy duck dishes, sweet-sour sauces, and pad thai up the yin-yang. The entrée offerings here are plentiful; in fact, you might find yourself overwhelmed. Thai Tina's classic choices—a pad thai, say, or crab Rangoon—are transcendent, but don't fear experimenting (especially with the duck!).

BARBECUE
ANGELO'S 💲

2533 White Settlement Rd., 817/332-0357, www.angelosbbq.com

HOURS: Mon.-Sat. 11 A.M.–10 P.M.

At Angelo's, the pit produces some of the best barbecue in Texas. The brisket is moist and tender while the meat falls from the rib bones—but give the sides a pass. Although the sawdust on the floor may be long gone, the atmosphere at Fort Worth's most historical place to worship at the altar of 'cue is still profoundly unpretentious—plasticware and Styrofoam plates and a space that looks less like a restaurant and more like a warehouse.

© JONANNA WIDNER

Angelo's barbecue is a staple of the Fort Worth diet.

But the legion of regulars wouldn't have it any other way.

ITALIAN
FERRÉ 💲💲💲

215 E. 4th St., 817/332-0033, www.ferrerestaurant.com

HOURS: Mon.-Thurs. 4-10 P.M., Fri.-Sat. 4-11 P.M.

With an interior that is sleek and stylish, Ferré feels more Big Apple than Cowtown. The flavors of Tuscany are what you'll find here: An open-fire grill gives the steaks and other meats a smoky edge. A stone-fired pizza oven guarantees the pizzas come out shatteringly crisp. House-made pastas show off the kitchen's commitment to freshness and intriguing mixes of ingredients (like the sweet potato gnocchi with applewood bacon). The location, near Sundance Square and across the street from Bass Hall, makes it a good spot for pre-performance dining.

WINE BAR AND TAPAS
ZAMBRANO WINE CELLAR ⑤⑤
910 Houston St., 817/850-9463,
www.zambranowines.com
HOURS: Mon.-Fri. 4:30-11 P.M. (kitchen closes at 9 P.M.),
Sat. 5:30 P.M.-1 A.M. (kitchen closes at 10:30 P.M.)

With more than 300 wines available (50 by the glass), you probably won't make it all the way through Zambrano Wine Cellar's extensive wine list—but you'll probably have fun trying. Zambrano's menu is tailored to enhance the wine drinking experience, and features house-made pizzas, sophisticated cured meats, and a couple of different entrées each night. The knowledgeable staff can help steer you toward a bottle that fits your taste and pocketbook, whether you're a seasoned wine drinker or a raw newbie. While the bar is open late, the kitchen closes most evenings around 9 P.M.

TCU and Vicinity
Map 9

AMERICAN
BISTRO LOUISE ⑤⑤⑤
2900 S. Hulen St., 817/922-9244,
www.bistrolouise.com
HOURS: Lunch: Mon.-Sat. 11 A.M.-2 P.M. ,
Dinner: Tues.-Thurs. 5:30-10 P.M.

Bistro Louise boasts "New American Cuisine with a Mediterranean attitude," which is an accurate take on the cuisine here: American ingredients romanced by the flavors and preparations of Spain, France, and Italy. Chef-owner Louise Lamensdorf is committed to high-quality ingredients and bold flavors. The restaurant's cheerful European inn–style decor provides a refreshing change from the Western theme of many of Cowtown's other upscale restaurants, as does its locale away from many of the town's hot spots. Bistro Louise gets raves for its wine list and its brunch.

CARSHON'S DELI ⑤
3133 Cleburne Rd., 817/923-1907,
www.carshonsdeli.com
HOURS: Mon.-Sat. 9 A.M.-3 P.M.
(dining room closes at 2:30 P.M.)

Yes, there are Jews in cowboy country. And 80 years ago, one of them went and started a deli. Although the bare-bones atmosphere at Carshon's is nothing to *kvell* about, the pastrami, corned beef, and other deli meats are as authentic a deli experience as you'll find in the area. For the most authentic New York–style deli experience, try the chopped liver, though the Reuben is the most popular item on the menu. Come hungry—portions are big. Open for breakfast and lunch only.

DUTCH'S ⑤
3009 S. University Dr., 817/927-5522,
www.dutchshamburgers.com
HOURS: Mon.-Sat. 11 A.M.-10 P.M., Sun. 10 A.M.-10 P.M.

Texas chef Grady Spears' burger joint draws 'em in with grilled all-natural beef burgers in a range of sizes and toppings. The mini sliders, with grilled onions and cheddar cheese, are great for soaking up some of the fruits of Dutch's better-than-average beer list. Non beef-eaters have choices here, too, including a flavorful grilled chicken sandwich festooned with green chiles. Lots of chrome and steel give this spot in a historic building near TCU a nice retro feeling.

PICNIC TIME

Fort Worth's many excellent restaurants, laid-back attitude and less congested urban space make it a perfect for picnicking. Here are some suggestions for melding some of the town's best food with some its most picturesque spots:

Grab a fabulous sandwich from the **Carshon's Deli** and head to the Cultural District, where the grassy park behind the Kimbell Art Museum makes for a lovely place to idle.

There may be no more romantic spot in town than the Botanic Gardens. Pack up some gourmet to go from **Bistro Louise** and indulge amidst the petals of the Rose Garden.

Spiral Diner creates some of the most imaginative and tasty vegan vittles around. Couple your bean burger and fresh coconut limeade with a sunny **Forest Park** excursion.

RAILHEAD SMOKEHOUSE $

2900 Montgomery St., 817/738-9808,
www.railheadonline.com

HOURS: Mon.-Sat. 11 A.M.-9 P.M.

You'd think that the Railhead Smokehouse, with its authentic Texas barbeque, would be found amid the cowpokes and boot-scooters of the Stockyards, but this joint sits quietly in a nondescript building smack in the middle of a parking lot, near the cosmopolitan Museum District. Inside, however, it's a genuine Texas smokehouse, with brisk but friendly service, simple wooden tables, neon beer signs, dark plank walls, and mesquite-tinged air. For less than $10, you can choose from a variety of traditional BBQ favorites: moist, smoky brisket, its edges crusted with caramelized bits of the Railhead's heavenly, balanced sauce; chopped beef sandwiches falling apart under the weight

of their own juices; red-hot ribs battling plump sausages for space next to a pile of mustard-y potato salad. All of it goes great with a cantaloupe-size beer goblet full of icy Lone Star beer.

SPIRAL DINER AND BAKERY $

1314 W. Magnolia Ave., 817/332-8834,
www.spiraldiner.com

HOURS: Tues.-Sat. 11 A.M.-10 P.M., Sun. 11 A.M.-5 P.M.

Cowtown can be hard on a vegetarian—let alone a vegan. But the Spiral Diner is a happy exception to that rule. Voted 2007's Best Restaurant of the Year by *Veg News* magazine, Spiral Diner features vegan-ized versions of Southwestern favorites like biscuits and gravy, *migas,* taco salads, and two different kinds of burgers, all made with as many organic ingredients as feasible. Although service can be spotty, an extensive beer list is the icing on the vegan cupcake—speaking of which, leave room for some of Spiral's luscious baked goods or house-made vegan ice cream.

BREAKFAST
OL' SOUTH PANCAKE HOUSE $

1509 South University Dr., 817/336-0311

HOURS: Daily 24 hrs.

Every great city has a great breakfast place, and in Fort Worth, it's the straightforward, diner-y Ol' South Pancake House. Since it's open 24 hours, sooner or later you'll see every demographic saunter in: late-night party people in the wee hours, working men and women during the week, families and couples on the weekends. The German pancakes, as big as your head and sweet-tart with lemon juice and powdered sugar, are what the cognoscenti are eating here. Forget about IHOP.

COFFEE SHOP

PARIS COFFEE SHOP $

700 W. Magnolia Ave., 817/335-2041,
http://pariscoffeeshop.net

HOURS Mon.-Fri. 6 A.M.-2:30 P.M., Sat. 6-11 A.M.

Don't come to the Paris Coffee Shop expecting croissants and café au lait. Instead, you'll find hearty Texas-style breakfasts like biscuits and gravy and country ham, along with fluffy pancakes and golden waffles. Weekends bring both out-the-door lines and red-eye gravy. At lunchtime, the menu switches to classic diner fare. With an atmosphere as welcoming and old-fashioned as the 80-year-old Paris Coffee Shop's, bet on the pies—which are to a Texan what a fine croissant is to a Parisian—to be spectacular.

HOMESTYLE

MASSEY'S RESTAURANT $

1805 8th Ave., 817/921-5582

HOURS: Mon.-Sat. 11 A.M.-9 P.M., Sun. 11 A.M.-3 P.M.

The chicken-fried steak at this local favorite is a big draw, battered, fried, and served with white gravy, but the fried catfish and fried chicken bring 'em in, too. It's not just the entrées that are given the FryDaddy treatment, though—you can also get fried okra, fried squash, and (although not fried) some of the best biscuits in the region.

ITALIAN

BRIX PIZZA AND WINE BAR $$

2747 S. Hulen St., 817/924-2749,
www.brixpizzeria.com

HOURS: Mon.-Sat. 11 A.M.-10 P.M., Sun. 4-10 P.M.

The new pizzeria on the block, Brix gets its pedigree from owner Daniele Puelo, who really knows his stuff. The pizzas here are Neapolitan style—light, crisp, and perfectly fired in the wood oven, with simple but tasty toppings. For those not craving a pie, the menu features a healthy slate of apps and main dishes, many of which take advantage of the wood-fire oven.

MEDITERRANEAN AND MIDDLE EASTERN

KING TUT $

1512 W. Magnolia Ave., 817/335-3051

HOURS: Mon.-Sat. 11 A.M.-2:30 P.M. and 5:30-9 P.M., Sun. noon-6 P.M.

If you're looking for good Middle Eastern food in Fort Worth, King Tut, a hole-in-the-wall Egyptian restaurant on funky Magnolia Avenue, fills the bill nicely. Regulars rave about the hummus, baba ganoush, and falafel (though less so about the service, which can be a bit slow when the restaurant is busy). To cap off your meal, enjoy an authentic Turkish coffee with one of King Tut's traditional Middle Eastern desserts, rich and sweet with honey.

PASTRIES

SWISS PASTRY SHOP $

3936 W. Vickery Blvd., 817/732-5661

HOURS: Tues.-Fri. 6:30 A.M.-5:30 P.M.,
Sat. 7 A.M.-4 P.M.

If the only thing the Swiss Pastry Shop sold was its renowned Black Forest cake—layers of meringue, whipped cream, and shaved chocolate—people would still flock to this simply decorated, old-fashioned bakery. But the Swiss Pastry Shop also has a full roster of superb pies, cookies, and cakes, all at reasonable prices. The shop also puts out a good lunch: sausages, soups, and sandwiches. If you're not getting it to go, head here when you have time to dawdle; service can be slow.

© JONANNA WIDNER

Get a tasty meal for cheap at King Tut.

TEX-MEX

CARO'S $

3505 Bluebonnet Cir., 817/924-9977,
www.caros.biz

HOURS: Mon.-Fri. and Sun. 11 A.M.-2 P.M. and 5-9 P.M.,
Sat. 11 A.M.-9:30 P.M.

The folks at Caro's, a Fort Worth stalwart on cute little Bluebonnet Circle since 1952, bill themselves as the only restaurant in town that doesn't use a steam table, microwave, or can opener, and they recently converted to using zero-trans-fat oil, but that doesn't mean the place is good for your waistline. The yummy, puffy tacos, however, are good for your soul. The menu here is fairly standard Tex-Mex, done fresh and right. The enchiladas rank up there with the best, but don't skip the tacos, either—try one of the nicely priced Manager's Specials, which has both.

HOT DAMN! TAMALES $

713 W. Magnolia Ave., 817/926-9909,
www.hotdamntamales.com

HOURS: Mon.-Fri. 11 A.M.-5 P.M.

Purists may scoff, but the lard-free tacos at Hot Damn! are fluffy and moist and come in intriguing varieties, including ancho pork and beef and jalapeño, as well as several vegan- and vegetarian-friendly varieties like fresh corn and poblano as well as wild mushroom and Texas goat cheese. (Don't forget to save room for chocolate, cherry, and roasted pecan tamales for dessert, by the way.) Hot Damn! is mostly a mail-order and takeout operation, but a tiny four-table restaurant serves up ta- male plates and other Mexican favorites. If you find the dining area occupied, do yourself a favor: Pick up a couple dozen tamales and take them home.

West Side Fort Worth   Map 10

RESTAURANTS

AMERICAN

CURLY'S CUSTARD $

4017 Camp Bowie Blvd., 817/763-8700

HOURS: Sun.-Thurs. 11 A.M.-9 P.M., Fri.-Sat. 11 A.M.-10 P.M.

Don't call it ice cream. Paradoxically richer and yet lighter than ice cream, frozen custard is softly served, and at Curly's you can have your vanilla or chocolate flavor custard "concrete" style, with your choice of a rainbow of candy and fruit toppings whipped in. On nice days, enjoy your custard outside in Curly's grassy, park-like yard. Curly's also serves a mean Frito pie.

FRED'S TEXAS CAFÉ $

915 Currie St., 817/332-0083,

www.fredstexascafe.com

HOURS: Daily 10 A.M.-midnight

Fred's Texas Café is a classic roadhouse—a great place to grab a beer and a stellar burger while relaxing in kitschy gold booths or listening to live music on the spacious patio. The food is better than you'd ever expect in the midst of such a dive-y atmosphere. "Outlaw Chef" Terry Chandler's most famous creation may be the fiery Diablo Burger, but the half-pound Fredburger is nothing to sneeze at. Not into burgers? Fred's also features steaks, Tex-Mex favorites, and some of the best quail dishes(!) in the region.

GALLIGASKIN'S SUBMARINE SANDWICH $

5817 Camp Bowie Blvd., 817/714-0383,

www.resercom.net/141

HOURS: Mon.-Sat. 7 A.M.-9 P.M.

Conditioned as we are to chain sub sandwich shops that boast of their healthiness, it's easy to forget the joys of a real overstuffed made-to-order sub sandwich. Galligaskin's features a slate of more than 20 hot and cold subs, from egg salad to—yes—chicken-fried steak. The Fort Worth cognoscenti like the cheesesteak and the meaty Italian cold-cut varieties. And forget a bag of chips as an accompaniment—Galligaskin's features hand-cut fries as well as other deep-fried treats (try the mushrooms, with a side of ranch dressing, for extra trashy goodness).

KINCAID'S $

4901 Camp Bowie Blvd., 817/732-2881,

www.kincaidshamburgers.com

HOURS: Mon.-Sat. 11 A.M.-8 P.M.

Sure, you can have a thick, juicy, char-grilled hamburger almost anywhere (okay, maybe not), but you can't beat the original location of Kincaid's for a truly unique experience. Rub shoulders with what feels like all of Fort Worth as you chow down on Kincaid's oozingly flavorful burgers at the long, stand-up counters that run the length of this former grocery store, "where friends meet to eat." The mid-century grocery store trappings remain intact, making for a charmingly retro atmosphere. Spend your extra calories on the onion rings instead of the fries, and you might as well throw in a house-made shake while you're at it—not that the best burger in town needs any accompaniment.

MONTGOMERY ST. CAFÉ $

2000 Montgomery St., 817/733-8033,

www.themontgomerystcafe.com

HOURS: Mon.-Sat. 6 A.M.-2 P.M.

Old-fashioned service, a bottomless cup of coffee, and nearly unbelievably inexpensive prices—what more can you ask from a 60-year-old breakfast/lunch place? Delicious food? Montgomery St. has that, too. Go for the regional specials, like biscuits and gravy and grits to accompany your eggs and juicy thick-sliced ham. Atmosphere is early oilcloth, but with the friendly service and low prices, nobody really cares.

◖ ROY POPE GROCERY

2300 Merrick St., 817/732-2863,
www.roypopegrocery.com

HOURS: Mon.-Sat. 8 A.M.-7 P.M.

Even in a town that takes its time shedding the past, Roy Pope Grocery is a throwback. This neat neighborhood epicurean grocery, which has been around since 1943, is known for its excellent meat selection, not to mention hard-to-find foodstuffs and gourmet cheeses and deli items. Premade to-go and daily hot meals round out the offerings. Things get really old-school, however, when it comes to service: The grocery still delivers groceries, in cardboard boxes, to your door.

ASIAN
JAPANESE PALACE ⬤⬤⬤

445 Highway 80 W., 817/244-0144

HOURS: Sun.-Thurs. 5-10 P.M.,
Fri.-Sat. 5 P.M.-midnight

The serene pond that greets you on your arrival to Japanese Palace is just one indicator that you're in for an exotic experience. Be prepared for a wait, but you'll enjoy spending that time in the bizarre lounge, where pictures of nude women and other kitschy decor abound. In the restaurant itself, you can choose from traditional Japanese floor seating or chairs around a big hibachi grill, where the chefs do performance cooking. The Japanese Palace also offers some of the better sushi in town—you

can often circumvent the wait by requesting a seat at the sushi bar.

SZECHUAN ⬤⬤

5712 Locke Ave., 817/738-7300

HOURS: Sun.-Thurs. 11 A.M.-9:30 P.M., Fri.-Sat.
11 A.M.-10:30 P.M.

With a huge menu encompassing more than 150 items, ordering at Szechuan can be a daunting experience. But relax—you almost can't go wrong with any of the Chinese dishes here, especially the "Chef's Suggestions" at the front of the menu. This is a good choice for vegetarians and health-conscious diners; Szechuan offers several meatless dishes and a large selection of entrées cooked without oil. Lunch specials are a bargain.

FRENCH
SAINT-EMILION ⬤⬤⬤

3617 W. 7th St., 817/737-2781,
www.saint-emilionrestaurant.com

HOURS: Tues.-Thurs. 6-9 P.M., Fri.-Sat. 6-10 P.M.

There's French, and then there's *French*—and Saint-Emilion definitely qualifies as the italicized version. This Fort Worth mainstay sticks closely to the überclassic French fare; think sweetbreads, fois gras, and things tartare, all worked with a Gallic magic. For years, Valentine's dates, prom couples, and anniversary celebrators have flocked to the intimate digs and prix fixe goodies here, and both the atmosphere and cuisine have been honed to perfection.

GERMAN
EDELWEISS ⬤⬤

3801 Southwest Blvd., 817/738-5934,
www.edelweissrestaurant.com

HOURS: Tues.-Thurs. 5-10:30 P.M., Fri.-Sat. 5-11 P.M.

Sometimes you want to go to a dark, quiet

place and have a nice conversation. That's not when you should go to Edelweiss. Instead, head there when you're in the mood for a raucous evening of chicken dancing; listening to traditional German music (sometimes on an authentic alpenhorn); drinking a wide variety of hard-to-find German beers; and consuming massive plates of schnitzel, wurst, spaetzle, and other hearty Bavarian dishes. While the food may be uneven sometimes, Edelweiss owner Bernd Schnerzinger makes sure everyone has fun.

ITALIAN
FORTUNA ITALIAN RESTAURANT ⑤
5837 Camp Bowie Blvd., 817/737-4469
HOURS: Mon.-Thurs. 11 A.M.-10 P.M., Fri.-Sat. 11 A.M.-11 P.M.
A solid menu of basic Italian entrées, along with pizza and pastas, is what you'll find at this family-owned restaurant. The prices are good for the quality, and the extensive menu means you will probably find exactly what you're craving.

ITALIAN INN RIDGLEA ⑤⑤
6323 Camp Bowie Blvd., 817/737-0123,
www.theitalianinn.com
HOURS: Sun.-Thurs. 5-10 P.M., Fri.-Sat. 5-11 P.M.
Romance is what you'll find at the Italian Inn. Sit in a closed-door private booth and canoodle with your honey, or choose a table where you can take in the sights and sounds of the singing waitstaff. Either way, the atmosphere at this below-street-level spot is dark and cavernous. The food is definitely as old-fashioned as the romance: Veal marsala, eggplant Parmesan, and big plates of pasta are what you'll find here. The graffiti on the walls of the booths from previous lovers' visits inspires some, but isn't everyone's cup of tea.

JOE'S ⑤⑤
6818 W. Camp Bowie Blvd., 817/738-6937
HOURS: Sun.-Thurs. 11 A.M.-10 P.M., Fri.-Sat. 11 A.M.-11 P.M.
Joe's doesn't deliver, which is a shame, since the atmosphere here borders on that of a condemned Dairy Queen. But, oh, is the pizza worth a drive to pick up your to-go order: perfect thin crust, topped generously with traditional ingredients and a balanced sauce. There's not an ounce of gourmet pretension with these pies—just plain ol' family-owned tradition.

MAMA'S PIZZA ⑤
5800 Camp Bowie Blvd., 817/731-6262,
www.mamaspizzas.net
HOURS: Mon.-Thurs. 11 A.M.-10 P.M., Fri.-Sat. 11 A.M.-11 P.M.
Mama's sat in a warehouse-type building on Camp Bowie for many years before finally moving to a much more inviting locale just up the road. The wooden booths and bustling atmosphere are a great improvement, but the pizza has never needed an upgrade, thanks to the just-the-right-thickness crust that's brushed with garlic butter and a slightly sweet sauce that gives the pies here their unique taste.

SARDINE'S RISTORANTE ITALIANO ⑤⑤
509 University Dr., 817/332-9937,
http://sardinesftworth.com
HOURS: Sun.-Thurs. 5-11 P.M., Fri.-Sat. 5 P.M.-midnight
Go here for the atmosphere: Antiques, candlelight, a dark and cozy lighting scheme, and nightly jazz make Sardine's one of the most romantic restaurants in Fort Worth. The menu is traditional Italian, along with specialties like chateaubriand. The pastas, especially the seafood choices, are dependably good. Sardine's also can accommodate large parties, but service can be spotty.

SEAFOOD
J&J OYSTER BAR $

612 University Dr., 817/335-2756

HOURS: Sun.-Thurs. 11 A.M.-10 P.M., Fri.-Sat. 11 A.M.-11 P.M.

Friendly and just slightly dive-y, J&J is the place to go when you want a plate of briny, sparkling oysters and a cold schooner of beer. To follow that up, order the grilled snapper or something from J&J's slate of Southern favorites, like a fried oyster po' boy (with addictive hand-cut fries), a mound of boiled crawfish, or a bowl of gumbo. Hit the popular patio to cool off with a pitcher of beer on a hot day, and you won't be sorry.

LAMBERT'S $$$

2731 White Settlement Rd., 817/882-1161, www.lambertsfortworth.com

HOURS: Dinner: Mon.-Thurs. 5-10 P.M., Fri.-Sat. 5-11 P.M. Brunch: Sun. 11 A.M.-3 P.M.

As straightforward as its motto—"Steaks. Seafood. Whiskey."—Lambert's menu features natural beef steaks along with decadent family-style side dishes like the justly celebrated cauliflower gratin. The live oak grill and smoker lead to succulent creations like smoked prime rib and brown sugar–crusted rib eye. The atmosphere is dark and comfortable but modern, with witty nods to Cowtown culture like a rack of saddles suspended from the ceiling and trophy heads mounted behind the bar.

OVATION $$$

6115 Camp Bowie Blvd., 817/732-8900, www.ovationrestaurant.com

HOURS: Weds.-Thurs. 6-11 P.M., Fri.-Sat. 6 P.M.-midnight, Sun. 6-10 P.M.

The upscale food's got soul at Ovation, where you can dine on Southern favorites like fried catfish, gumbo, and braised oxtails, all tricked out with updated flavors and top-notch ingredients. Don't miss the chicken and waffles—fried chicken and Belgian waffles served with collard greens and sweet potato French fries. The nightly live music, usually gospel, jazz, or blues, draws a boisterous crowd to this big space located in a strip mall. On weekends, be prepared for a wait.

SOUTHERN
DREW'S PLACE $

5701 Curzon Ave., 817/735-4408, www.drewsfortworth.com

HOURS: Mon. -Thurs. 10:30 A.M.-7 P.M., Fri. 10:30 A.M.-8 P.M., Sat. 10:30 A.M.-6 P.M., Sun. 11 A.M.-4 P.M.

The smothered pork chops at Drew's Place have been known to make grown men weep. This family-owned home-cooking lunch spot in the Como section of Fort Worth features great soul food at amazingly low prices. Entrées like catfish, Buffalo wings, and chicken-fried steak all come with two sides (make sure one of them is the collard greens). There's not much atmosphere here, but with a plate of soul food goodness and a big glass of sweet tea in front of you, you won't much care.

TEX-MEX
EL FENIX $$

6391 Camp Bowie Blvd., 817/732-5584

HOURS: Daily 11 A.M.-10 P.M.

Although it's no longer family-owned, the 90-year-old El Fenix chain of Mexican restaurants still serves up solid Mexican comfort food. There is universal acclaim for their chips and salsa, perfect accompaniments to El Fenix's slate of potent margaritas, including one blended with a swirl of sangria, for those who can't decide between the two. Enchiladas are a specialty here; order them by themselves or as an element on one of El Fenix's many combination plates while you bask in the cheesy matador atmosphere. Olé!

THE ORIGINAL MEXICAN EATS CAFÉ $

4713 Camp Bowie Blvd., 817/738-6226

HOURS: Daily 11 A.M.–9 P.M.

Tex-Mex, old-school style, is what you'll find at The Original Mexican Eats Café, Fort Worth's oldest Hispanic-owned restaurant. The prices are reasonable and the portions of enchiladas, nachos, fajitas, and other Mexican favorites are large. The refried beans here are particularly good, rich and creamy. "Bare bones" is the best way to describe the atmosphere, which looks as if it hasn't changed since Franklin D. Roosevelt dined here during his presidency.

Greater Fort Worth   Map 11

ITALIAN
PEROTTI'S PIZZA $

6136 Southwest Blvd., 871/377-2202, www.perrottispizza.com

HOURS: Sun.–Weds. 10 A.M.–10 P.M., Thurs. 10 A.M.–11 P.M., Fri.–Sat. 10 A.M.–midnight

When you can't decide between pizza and "grinders" (East Coast lingo for sub sandwiches), Perotti's has got you covered. The secret to this family-owned spot's delicious pizza? Freshly house-made crust—garlicky, thick, and deep-dished to perfection. Grinders come in hot and cold varieties, but the meatball sandwich is king here. There's a slate of pastas, too.

PICCOLO MONDO $$$

829 Lamar Blvd. E., Arlington, 817/265-9174, www.piccolomondo.com

HOURS: Lunch: Mon.–Fri. 11:30 A.M.–2:15 P.M. Dinner: Mon.–Thurs. 5:30–10 P.M., Fri.–Sat. 5:30–11 P.M., Sun. 5–10 P.M.

Piccolo Mondo has never let its strip mall locale hinder it. In fact, considering that much of Arlington is asphalt and concrete, the location is rather suitable in some sense. It doesn't match, however, the elegance of the surroundings and deliciousness of the Italian fare that lies within. Expect straightforward, classic Italian pastas with a touch of seafood here. No trendy molecular cooking or overwrought descriptions to throw you for a loop—just excellent service, friendly atmosphere, and well-executed food. A couple quick caveats: Piccolo Mondo is one of the most popular places in town, so be prepared for a lively buzz. And the restaurant features piano entertainment during peak times, seven days a week, so if that sort of thing annoys you, best to avoid it.

MEDITERRANEAN
GEORGE'S SPECIALTY FOODS $

4424 White Settlement Rd., 817/737-0414

HOURS: Tues.–Sat. 9:30 A.M.–5 P.M.

This Greek grocery and café has sat quietly on a nondescript stretch of White Settlement Road for decades, silently beckoning to lovers of dolma, baklava, and gyros (they're the best in town). While there are a few tables at this unassuming spot, it serves takeout clientele admirably, along with epicureans in search of olive oils, olives, and other imported goodies.

NIGHTLIFE

Considering Texas's brassy reputation, is it any wonder this is a population that likes to go out? When it comes to hanging out at clubs, bars, lounges, discos, sports bars, or any other gathering spot, you can count on DFW denizens of all stripes to be there en masse. Night owls here don't wait for the weekend—there are simply too many places to go.

A good place to start is with a band—the DFW area has a long, intimate relationship with live music. Many Dallasites, for instance, are lured out into the night by the long row of live music venues that make up Lower Greenville Avenue, while Fort Worthers indulge in the town's long legacy of small,

intimate stages and unexpected venues like the Modern and even grocery stores.

Twists on the usual bar games are popular, too: Trivia nights abound, as do karaoke nights (even some with live backing bands), Golden Tee tournaments, and retro video games. Even a version of Texas's extensive underground poker scene has wriggled its way above ground: The cards fly once or twice a week at poker night at many different places (not for cash, of course—winners get gift certificates or other prizes).

A few things to remember: In Dallas, parking will most likely be a hassle no matter where you go, so bring extra cash for valet

NIGHTLIFE

HIGHLIGHTS

LOOK FOR ◖ TO FIND RECOMMENDED NIGHTLIFE.

◖ **Best Jukebox:** After listening to the jukebox at **Adair's Saloon**, with its lonesome downhome country classics from the likes of Johnny, Waylon, and Patsy, you just might end up with more than a single tear in your beer (page 99).

◖ **Best Bar Games:** With 24 beers on tap, a bank of HD and old-school video games and Skee-ball, think of **Barcadia** as an adult Chuck E. Cheese's (page 106).

◖ **Best Grownup Bar:** More than just a hotel bar, **The Library Bar**'s cozy leather chairs, upscale bar menu, and nightly jazz piano give it a comfy, but mature, air (page 108).

◖ **Best Dive Bar: Ships** is tiny, cheap, and bedecked with an inexplicable nautical theme. In other words, it's the perfect dive (page 109).

◖ **Best Gay Cowboy Bar:** Beautifully melding two of Dallas' storied demographics – cowboys and gay men – **The Round-Up Saloon**'s dancefloor hosts a lotta same-sex line dancing (page 114).

© LIBRARY BAR

The Library Bar

or be prepared to walk. Fort Worth's parking situation is much easier to contend with, especially in the free lots and garages that surround Sundance Square. Second, though a few after-hours dance clubs speckle the scene, state law dictates that alcohol-serving establishments must close no later than 2 A.M., and most close a few minutes before that. Finally, smokers should be aware that Dallas adheres to a strict smoking ban.

Live Music

THE AARDVARK

2905 W. Berry St., 817/926-7814,
www.the-aardvark.com
HOURS: Mon.-Thurs. 11 A.M.-2 A.M., Fri.-Sat.
11:30 A.M.-2 A.M.
`Map 9`

The Aardvark sports a prime location just across the way from Texas Christian University, so it's no surprise that its spacious digs can fill up quickly, especially since it's a top booker of local bands.

ACROSS THE STREET BAR

5625 Yale Blvd., 214/363-0660,
www.acrossthestreetbar.com
HOURS: Tues.-Sat. 7 P.M.-2 A.M.
`Map 3`

This SMU hotspot consistently draws the college crowd with five nights a week of music that, although varied, falls on the conservative side of things (you'll more likely catch a reggae band, say, than a punk band). It's a good size for a borderline dive, but when weekends come around, be ready to stand shoulder-to-shoulder.

 ADAIR'S SALOON

2624 Commerce St., 214/939-9900,
www.adairssaloon.com
HOURS: Daily 11 A.M.–2 A.M.
`Map 5`

Adair's is what you might call a neighborhood honky-tonk. This family-owned hole-in-the-wall has Texas atmosphere to spare, with gimme caps stapled to the ceilings along with graffiti-scribbled walls, ceilings, and floors. The Adair family has a few rules posted, the most famous one being "You dance with the one who brung ya or you don't dance at all," and it's easy to follow such advice with such a stellar jukebox. Filled with classics and hidden tracks from Patsy Cline, Bob Wills, and

© JONANNA WIDNER

Head up to the Balcony Club to catch some live jazz.

Ernest Tubb, among many other legends, the jukebox might just be the best in Texas. The bands that play here on weekends are cut from similar cloth.

BALCONY CLUB

1825 Abrams Rd., 214/826-8104
HOURS: Daily 5 P.M.–2 A.M.
`Map 4`

Pop up the wrought-iron stairs to the second story just above the much larger Lakewood theater and you'll find the dark, quirky, and just slightly cramped Balcony. The club serves a popular brunch and strong cocktails, but is best known for its jazz, provided by the trios and quartets who crowd the tiny stage that abuts the front door. Music begins around 9:30.

BROOKLYN JAZZ CAFÉ

1701 S. Lamar St., 214/428-0025,
www.brooklynjazzcafe.com
HOURS: Sun.–Thurs. 11 A.M.–midnight, Fri. 11 A.M.–2 A.M.,
Sat. 5:30 P.M.–2 A.M.
`Map 6`

Like the eclectic borough it's named after, Brooklyn Jazz Café is a varied little scene. The handsome red brick space is simultaneously cozy and open, and one of the most racially mixed crowds in Dallas enjoys several entertainment options under Brooklyn's roof, such as a game area, a quieter beautiful back patio, and spoken-word performances. The club's core will always remain based in jazz, and the lineup here challenges music lovers with a constant, varied flow of different types of the genre.

THE CAVERN

1914 Greenville Ave., 214/828-1914,
http://thecaverndallas.com

NIGHTLIFE

NIGHTLIFE

© JONANNA WIDNER

Club Dada has been a cornerstone of Deep Ellum for two decades.

HOURS: Daily 6 P.M.–2 A.M.

Map 4

Patterned after the famous Liverpool club of the same name, this Greenville Avenue mainstay is indeed dark, insular, and often packed. While most venues on this street lean away from live music and more to the preppy side of things, the Cavern hosts an eclectic assortment of acts, from hip-hop nights to Southern rock quartets to lounge singers. Upstairs is a laid-back loft with comfy chairs, video games, and often a DJ.

CLUB DADA

2720 Elm St., 214/742-3400,
www.myspace.com/clubdada

HOURS: Tues.–Sun. 5 P.M.–2 A.M.

Map 5

One of the few surviving clubs left over from Deep Ellum's most recent resurgence in the late 1980s/early '90s, Club Dada is a funky reminder of the neighborhood's roots and serves as an epicenter for eclectic music and art. Most nights, Dada's entry is guarded by a doorman known only as "Beard," a Deep Ellum institution who has been checking IDs, gathering cover charges (when there is one), and running off ruffians at the club since it opened in 1986. Inside, the red brick walls, ramshackle booths, and framed music posters lend Dada its atmosphere of downtown coolness. At the bar you'll find a friendly, efficient bar staff—sporting everything from Mohawks to nouveau-greaser pompadours—slinging free-flowing Shiner Bock and hard "root beer" shots. The club has a hipster vibe, but it's friendly and devoid of attitude; really, it's the music that matters most. The small stage has been home to local-heroes-made-good like Edie Brickell and New Bohemians, Reverend Horton Heat, and the Dixie Chicks, as well as countless popular national acts. Whether you're looking to chill on the lush, roomy back courtyard with a cool acoustic act and a cold beer or sweat inside with a high-powered punk trio and a potent cocktail, Dada is still the place to be.

CURTAIN CLUB

2800 Main St., 214/826-2336,
www.curtainclub.com
HOURS: Thurs.-Sat. 9 P.M.-2 A.M.
`Map 5`

The spacious but nondescript interior isn't really much to look at, but it has always been about the music anyway at the Curtain Club. Back in the day, this space housed the cream of the Deep Ellum crop, the ample stage room hosting the biggest local acts and smaller national ones. Nowadays, the Curtain is the epicenter of the hard rock scene and battle of the bands competitions.

THE DOUBLE-WIDE

3510 Commerce St., 214/887-6510,
www.thedoublewidebar.com
HOURS: Mon.-Fri. 5 P.M.-2 A.M., Sat.-Sun. 7 P.M.-2 A.M.
`Map 5`

Replete with revolving tornado atop the roof, the Double-Wide's half-ironic nod to Texas's trashy cachet lulls hipsters and music lovers from across the city. Surrounded on all sides by wood paneling and old-school beer signs, the main room always hops with tattooed scenesters, while across the patio, a second, sparsely fitted room features the stage, graced by local and smaller touring groups. Entering for the first time, you might feel like you've just crashed an intimate gathering of friends, but don't worry—soon you'll feel right at home with the help of the alternative, alt-country, indie rock, and punk

© JONANNA WIDNER

Hit the Curtain Club for hard rock and heavy metal.

NIGHTLIFE

bands on the bill and an ice-cold PBR in your hand.

THE FAIRMOUNT

600 W. Magnolia Ave., 817/420-9455,
www.thefairmountlive.com
HOURS: Mon.-Fri. 4:30 P.M.-2 A.M., Fri.-Sat. 6 P.M.-2 A.M.
`Map 9`

If Americana's your thing, the Fairmount's where you need to be. Everything about this spot is Texas cool, right down to the tin roof and interior detailing built from reclaimed barn wood. The bands, who play every night of the week, follow suit, churning out a hearty mix of classic country, alternative country, and other forms of roots music. There's ample room for dancing, or pool tables and two bars for wallflowers.

GILLEY'S DALLAS

1135 S. Lamar St., 214/421-2021,
www.gilleysdallas.com

HOURS: Fri.-Sat. 6 P.M.-2 A.M.

Map 6

The original Gilley's (made famous in the John Travolta classic *Urban Cowboy*) outside of Houston was cutting-edge in its day, but compared to its namesake in Dallas, it was just a rundown old honky-tonk. The new, updated version is a huge venue, tailor-made for C&W boot-scooting and swilling whiskey. If you want a genuine sawdust-floor dive, this ain't it, but with its swank space and modern cowpoke atmosphere, you won't find any other country joint that reflects Dallas better than this. The folks who patronize the place are friendly, but the prices definitely aren't, so take advantage of the free cover before 8 P.M. and the early free dance lessons—besides, you'll need to learn a

DEEP ELLUM'S MUSICAL LEGACY

Dallas loves music. We're not just talking that of the C&W variety – Dallas loves rock and blues, hip-hop and avant-garde, jazz and alt-country. Dallas loves to hear about music, talk about music, think about music, make music, and, most importantly, to listen to live music. And no discussion of Dallas and music would be complete without including the history of the neighborhood just east of downtown, bordered to the north by Pacific Street, to the south by Canton Street, to the west by Exposition Avenue, and the east by I-75: Deep Ellum.

Deep Ellum's history goes back to the days when it was a stop on the "chitlin' circuit," back when African-American blues and jazz artists traveled the South, playing clubs in the black parts of segregated towns. In those days, the busy cobblestone streets full of con men and preachers, the two-story brick pawns shops and juke joints, the readily available opiates and the even more readily available audience lured many a bluesman: "Leadbelly" Ledbetter, Robert Johnson, Bessie Smith and Blind Lemon Jefferson all lived and/or performed there.

Sadly, over the years Deep Ellum lost its panache as a hopping locale full of music and mystique. In the mid-20th century it fell into disrepair and transformed into an industrial neighborhood, home to warehouses and empty buildings. But in the late 1980s and early 1990s, a new generation discovered the gritty streets anew, and dozens of bars, art galleries and music venues began popping up. Suddenly there was a scene.

New legends began: There was the rock club Trees, where Nirvana performed just before hitting the mainstream jackpot, and where Kurt Cobain got in a fistfight onstage (recorded for posterity – you can find it on YouTube). There was the Good-Latimer traffic tunnel, coated in graffiti and street art. And there were the bands, whose energy and intensity lured thousands of people to Deep Ellum every night. Some of those bands hit it big: The Reverend Horton Heat, Edie Brickell and New Bohemians, the Old 97s, the Polyphonic Spree.

And, as it did back during Deep Ellum's first musical renaissance, the scene began to die. No one knows quite why. Some say it was an uptick in crime, others attribute it to oversaturation. Most likely, the scene ended ultimately because that's what scenes do, but for whatever reason, the buzz dwindled. One by one, clubs shuttered their storied doors, and even the Good-Latimer tunnel was destroyed to make room for a DART (Dallas Area Rapid Transit) station.

These days, while its vibrancy may have tarnished, the ghosts of Deep Ellum's history still make themselves known. The neighborhood is quieter now, but you can still feel a backbeat vibrating in the streets, barely perceptible. Several establishments – Monica's Aca y Alla, Club Dada, the AllGood Café – are still viable, and with its planned retail base, the very DART station responsible for the end of the tunnel might just kick start a new chapter in Deep Ellum's history. If not, there's still plenty of history to fall back on.

few two-step and line-dancing moves before you hit the floor. Oh, and yes, there is a mechanical bull.

THE GRANADA THEATER

3525 Greenville Ave., 214/824-9933,
www.granadatheater.com

Map 4

For fans who eschew the homogeneity common to corporate-owned venues like the House of Blues and Palladium across town, the Granada is the best place in Dallas to see a show, hands down. The place oozes history, with dramatic murals, a spacious balcony, and detailed interior architecture, but still connects with current audiences, thanks to the lovingly painted psychedelic ceiling.

Unfortunately, despite its obvious character, the Granada struggles against its counterparts. With bigger resources and far-reaching contracts, two cross-town venues—the Palladium and the House of Blues— snag most of the traveling shows that come through town. Still, the Granada manages to put together a consistently sizzling lineup of indie acts, roots music, and local biggies. Check the Granada's website—if you're in town and if they've booked a band you like, don't miss it.

J&J BLUES BAR

937 Woodward St., 817/870-8337,
www.jjbluesbar.com
HOURS: Fri.-Sat. 8:30 P.M.-2 A.M.

Map 8

On the outside, J&J's is a dead ringer for the tin-shack juke joint in the film adaptation of *The Color Purple*. On the inside—well, it's about the same, actually, whenever one of the locally grown blues bands takes the stage and gets the crowd to put some boogie in its woogie amid the roadhouse decor. Add a usually

reasonable cover charge and cold, cheap beer, and it's no wonder the place has been around for 20 years.

LOLA'S

2736 W. 6th St., 817/877-0666,
www.lolasfortworth.com
HOURS: Daily noon-2 A.M.

Map 8

When Lola's took over the spot formerly known as 6th Street Live in January 2008, Fort Worth didn't just gain a revamped venue—it also gained the services of one of the metroplex's best concert promoters. Lance Yocom usually books top-name indie bands in Denton (north of Dallas-Fort Worth), with occasional forays into the big cities and Austin, but his Fort Worth presence increased dramatically as the spot's only booking agent. Yocom's indie taste is exquisite, and his contacts run deep—Lola's has already stolen several touring indie acts that usually go to Dallas, and continues its string of strong local bands.

THE MOON BAR

2911 W. Berry St., 817/926-9600,
www.themoonbar.com
HOURS: Tues.-Fri. 4 P.M.-2 A.M., Sat.-Mon. 7 P.M.-2 A.M.

Map 9

The Moon is dark, dive-y, and a touch more hipster-casual than its neighbor The Aardvark. The tiny stage here manages to fit the biggest in local bands.

THE PALLADIUM BALLROOM

1135 S. Lamar St., www.thepalladiumballrom.com
HOURS: Vary by showtime

Map 6

The bad news is that the Palladium is a cavernous, sterile, corporate-owned venue with complicated, expensive parking and cruddy

NIGHTLIFE

acoustics. The good news: The Palladium provides a much-needed venue for the middle- to upper-market touring shows, of which Dallas gets its fair share. The ballroom holds about 2,500 general admission patrons, who, despite the drawbacks, often sell the place out for newer acts such as Interpol, M.I.A., and My Morning Jacket, and older faves like Tom Waits, Morrissey, and the Lemonheads. Even though the sightlines are favorable and the three bars ensure you won't wait in line for drinks, the place still sometimes feels like a warehouse gussied up for a prom. Not so for its smaller, more intimate upstairs club called the Palladium Loft, which houses smaller-draw national tours and tons of local groups. The Loft actually enjoys what its big-brother venue downstairs doesn't—character—and while the varnished wood and exposed ductwork may be a bit out of sync with some of the grittier bands who play there, the super-cool downtown view from the balcony brings everyone together.

POOR DAVID'S PUB

1313 S. Lamar St., 214/565-1925,
www.poordavidspub.com
HOURS: Wed.-Sat. 7 P.M.-2 A.M.
Map 6

For more than 30 years, the stage at Poor David's has served as a launching pad—or sometimes, a home roost—for Texas's top roots music talent. The club began in 1977 on McKinney Avenue, relocated as a Greenville Avenue institution for 20 years, then nestled into the burgeoning entertainment district on South Lamar Street a few years ago. Owner David Card has an ear for the type of musicians so special that they transcend local scenes. The list of luminaries who have frequented Poor David's, then, is impressive but not surprising: Lyle Lovett, Jerry Jeff Walker,

Robert Earl Keen, Jr., The Dixie Chicks, Nanci Griffith, and so many others. Even today, no matter what night you pop in, the band performing will be special.

RIDGLEA THEATER

6025 Camp Bowie Blvd., 817/738-9500,
www.ridgleatheater.com
HOURS: Vary by showtime
Map 10

Metal, metal, metal: This landmark theater opened in the 1950s as a movie house, went under in the early '90s, and then was resurrected as the region's premier venue for bands featuring double bass drums and flying V's. The Ridglea's retro environs create a cool backdrop for all varieties of the hard rock ilk: Goth, grindcore, and dramatic Marilyn Manson types (with a smattering of other fairly large names from other genres) all have found a home here, in a landmark that might not have survived otherwise.

SCAT JAZZ LOUNGE

501 Houston St., 817/870-9100,
www.scatjazzlounge.com
HOURS: Tues.-Fri. 5 P.M.-2 A.M., Sat. 6 P.M.-2 A.M.,
Sun. 7 P.M.-1 A.M.
Map 8

Local jazz man Ricki Derek may be best known for his smooth, suave, old-school lounge shows, which he performs at scattered Dallas venues. Anyone who's caught a Derek show knows he's a finely polished throwback who can croon Sinatra songs with the best of them. It's no surprise, then, that Derek's Scat Jazz Lounge is a tip of the fedora to the Rat Pack days. As in his own stage demeanor, Derek got the details right: a speakeasy-esque alleyway entrance under a retro sign; comfy booths; small, candle-lit tables. The effect is classy and of a certain time, but not in a

© JONANNA WIDNER

Sons of Hermann Hall is the house of local and national country mavericks.

hackneyed kind of way. The same goes for the music—top-notch local jazz, with an increasing presence of national acts.

SONS OF HERMANN HALL

3414 Elm St., 214/747-4422,
www.sonsofhermann.com
HOURS: Weds.-Sat. 5 P.M.-2 A.M.
Map 5

Proudly housed in a renovated building that dates back to 1911, Sons of Hermann Hall stands as a stalwart symbol of the evolution of Texas music. Inside, the decor is all genuine torch and twang, with a nice long bar,

shuffleboard, and—most importantly—tons of room to scoot a boot. Folks like Marcia Ball, Jimmie Dale Gilmour, and Townes Van Zandt are but a few of the legends who have graced the stage here, but the hall is home to a large pack of young guns, too.

WHITE ELEPHANT SALOON

106 E. Exchange Ave., 817/624-8273,
www.whiteelephantsaloon.com
HOURS: Mon.-Thurs. 2 P.M.-midnight,
Fri.-Sat. noon-2 A.M., Sun. noon-midnight
Map 7

In its 100-year history, the White Elephant has seen its share of a-cussin' and a-fightin'. In fact, the Elephant was the backdrop for the most famous shootout in Fort Worth history, between former city marshal Jim "Longhair" Courtright and gambler Luke Short. The two had long shared a rivalry that culminated on February 8, 1887, when their guns went to blazin',' leaving Short dead.

Nowadays, the saloon sees its share of tourists and country music fans, both of whom flock to this Stockyard institution for its history, Texas music bands, and genuine Cowtown atmosphere—as the dozens of cowboy hats nailed to the walls attest. You probably won't see a bar fight (though it's not to be ruled out), but you'll definitely see guys in Wranglers and Stetsons boot-to-boot with those in suits and ties, which is about as Fort Worth as it gets. And, if you're lucky, you'll catch the reenactment of the Courtright-Short duel, staged every February 8.

NIGHTLIFE

Bars

BAR BELMONT

901 Fort Worth Ave., 214/393-2300,
www.belmontdallas.com
HOURS: Sun.-Weds. 4-11 P.M.,
Thurs.-Sat. 4 P.M.-midnight
Map 6

Featuring one of the city's best views of down-town, Bar Belmont fancies itself a modern lounge. The mod furniture and low, pastel lighting might support that theory, but in reality, Bar Belmont is a laid-back, comfortable place. It's updated but not stuffy, and boasts a particularly good bar menu. If you're looking to escape loud joints filled with Golden Tee machines, but also want to skip the Uptown snoot, Bar Belmont is an excellent place.

◖ BARCADIA

1917 N. Henderson Ave., 214/821-7300,
www.barcadiadallas.com
HOURS: Mon.-Sat. 4 P.M.-2 A.M., Sun. 11 A.M.-2 A.M.
Map 4

With its bank of vintage video games and Skee-Ball, huge choice of beers, and 1950s motif, Barcadia consistently draws a crowd looking for a laid-back good time. The vibe here is casual, but definitely not dingy, with a constant stream of energy thanks to the young, hip crowd. Beware: At peak times, the line for Skee-Ball can be long; wait it out while people-watching on the always-packed porch.

BILLIARD BAR

1920 Greenville Ave., 214/826-7665
HOURS: Mon.-Sat. 5:30 P.M.-2 A.M.,
Sun. 5:30 P.M.-midnight
Map 4

Other Dallas pool halls may have a bit more room or better felt, but none compares to the Billiard Bar for atmosphere and location. True, this Greenville Avenue mainstay once cornered the market for retro-swank stick-and-cue environs, but now comes off as a bit faded. Still, the regulation-size tables are just fine, the sticks are straight, and the hip bar staff always plays good music.

BILLY MINER'S SALOON

50 W. 3rd St., 817/877-3301,
www.cyberrodeo.com/billyminers
HOURS: Mon.-Thurs. 11 A.M.-11 P.M., Fri.-Sat. 11 A.M.-1 A.M.,
Sun. noon-11 P.M.
Map 8

Used to be you could settle onto a wooden bar stool at Billy Miner's for a cold beer and free peanuts, the shells of which could simply be tossed on the floor. Restaurant regulations forced the Miner folks to end the latter tradition, but the storied saloon still maintains its casual Western vibe. It's not such a loss anyway—the beer and burgers here beat the peanuts, hands down.

BOOGER RED'S

105 E. Exchange Ave., 817/624-1246
HOURS: Mon.-Thurs. 11 A.M.-10 P.M., Fri. 11 A.M.-1 A.M.,
Sat. 9 A.M.-1 A.M., Sun. 9 A.M.-10 P.M.
Map 7

Named after a legendary Texas bronc buster, Booger Red's takes Fort Worth's Wild West aesthetic to kitschy extremes, from the saddle barstools to the bordello-red walls to the large buffalo derriere that sticks out from the mirror behind the bar. Said derriere is the namesake of the Buffalo Butt Beer that is served here alongside a large variety of tequila and an excellent food menu.

© JONANNA WIDNER

Booger Red's, home of saddle barstools and Buffalo Butt beer

THE CHAT ROOM PUB

1263 W. Magnolia Ave., 817/922-8319,
www.thechatroompub.com
HOURS: Mon.-Fri. 4 P.M.-2 A.M.,
Sat.-Sun. 6 P.M.-2 A.M.

Map 9

It self-deprecatingly bills itself as "easily Fort Worth's eighth best bar," but as a laid-back neighborhood hangout, The Chat Room ranks far higher than that. It sits in a frankly ugly, square, squat building on cute little Magnolia Avenue, but inside you'll find a cozy, friendly pseudo-dive with wood paneling and Formica floors, friendly bartenders, and even Fort Worth microbrew Rahr Beer on tap. The atmosphere is thick with hipster cachet—gimme caps and pearl-snap button shirts abound—but not in a particularly snooty way. Perhaps that's because patrons find themselves having too much fun playing Skee-Ball, pinball, or pool to bother with irony. Definitely check to see if there's a band playing; while the Chat isn't primarily a music venue, the choosy proprietors put their excellent taste to good use booking the occasional indie/local band, so the tunes are always top-notch.

COSMO RESTAURANT AND BAR

1212 Skillman Ave., 214/826-4200
HOURS: Daily 5 P.M.-2 A.M.

Map 4

Maybe the denizens of Lakewood feel so comfortable at Cosmo because with the thrift-store couches, dark lighting, and lava lamps, it feels like an extended version of their hipster living rooms. That's what makes Cosmo such a popular destination—it's cozy and comfy, but still has an edge to it. Adding to the living room–writ-large sensation are the movie screens showing classics of all genres, the friendly familiarity of the patrons, and the free-flowing PBR. Cosmo serves pizza that will do in a pinch, but don't consider it a dinner destination.

NIGHTLIFE

FLYING SAUCER

111 E. 4th St., 817/336-7468, www.beerknurd.com

HOURS: Mon.-Sat. 11 A.M.-2 A.M., Sun. noon-2 A.M.

Map 8

The Flying Saucer is part of a small North Texas chain, but given the charm and popularity of the downtown Fort Worth location, you'd never know it. Found in a freestanding historic building, this three-story beer house stays constantly crowded, as brew enthusiasts ranging from hippies to defense contractors gather to sample the 100 beers on tap.

GEZELLIG

2010-C Greenville Ave., 214/826-1700,

www.gezelligbar.com

HOURS: Mon.-Fri. 4 P.M.-2 A.M., Sat.-Sun. noon-2 A.M.

Map 4

According to its owners, *gezellig* is a term that people in Amsterdam use to describe a cool place that makes you feel welcome. In Dallas, the definition should be expanded to "a cool place with fantastic bar sandwiches and fun jazz and funk bands." Of course, any place that freezes the lines from the keg to the tap—to keep the beer extra cold—should be considered the most welcoming spot there is.

LEE HARVEY'S

1807 Gould St., 214/428-1555

HOURS: Daly 3 P.M.-2 A.M.

Map 6

Yep, this semi-dive is named for Lee Harvey Oswald, whose taxi ride from the School Book Depository to his Oak Cliff home on November 22 passed near here. This name's irreverence extends to much of the attitude at this popular casual locale. While the jukebox swings wildly from obscure 1980s new wave to Prince to local alt-country, clientele of all types hang out at the picnic tables in the large outside yard or dance in the almost shack-like inner sanctum.

◖ THE LIBRARY BAR

3015 Oak Lawn Ave., 214/521-5151

HOURS: Mon.-Thurs. 2 P.M.-midnight,

Fri.-Sat. 2 P.M.-1 A.M., Sun. noon-11 P.M.

Map 2

Elegant and stately, but not stuffy, the Library Bar is an oasis of good taste in flashy Uptown, and in that sense it's a microcosm of the Melrose Hotel in which it's found. On any given night, a piano might tinkle in the background, or perhaps an unobtrusive jazz singer might scat in the corner as patrons sit in overstuffed leather chairs and sip their sidecars or imported beers. Bookshelved walls hold hundreds of volumes of the classics, though one suspects the only thing anyone reads in here is the menu, which offers

VALET PARKING

You might notice that, for a town so taken with its cars and freeways, and so big on space, Dallas has very few places to park. No matter where you go, no mater what your activity, you'll end up in a parking bind at some point. Matter of fact, at some locales, such as certain areas of McKinney Avenue, there are literally no parking spots, no parking garages and no parking lots to be found. Definitely try to find a spot, but know that often you can circle your destination for hours and never succeed. Sometimes, you'll end up giving in and plunking down your $8-10, plus tip, then watching someone else park your car in a valet lot two feet away.

It's frustrating as hell, but you should be prepared nonetheless. Factor parking costs into your travel budget, and arm yourself with parking cash.

upscale bar food like five-spice calamari and venison chili. A nice way to enjoy the Library is to take advantage of Tuesday night's "classic cocktails and jazz," with $4 old-school drinks and a relaxed atmosphere.

POUR HOUSE

2725 W. 7th St., 817/335-2575,
www.pour-house.com
HOURS: Mon.-Sat. 11 A.M.-2 A.M., Sun. noon-2 A.M.
`Map 10`

A friendly favorite downtown regulars bar, the Pour House was forced out of its 13-year home abutting Sundance Square in 2008. Fortunately, owner Chris Matatall found new digs in the burgeoning 7th Street area, so this local-favorite sports bar should maintain its casual and upbeat vibe, complete with some of the best pub grub you can find.

◖ SHIPS

1613 Greenville Ave., 214/823-0418
HOURS: Daily 10 A.M.-2 A.M.
`Map 4`

Like any good dive bar, Ships has a story. The original owner was a sailor (hence the requisite nets 'n' anchors theme on the walls). His girlfriend helped manage the place, which, for its location and clientele, bore little trouble, perhaps thanks in part to the no-cussing rule. Somewhere along the way in the mid-1970s, sadly, trouble caught up to the place, and the girlfriend shot and killed the owner.

Not much has changed at Ships since then, not even the jukebox, which is stuck in some year that probably predates much of the clientele's birthdates. The proportions haven't changed, either—the place is as cramped as a submarine—and it looks as if the felt on the pool table hasn't been replaced since the Cold War. This is still a beer-and-wine-only, cash bar. Oh, and that no-cussing rule? It's still in effect. And they mean it.

SLIP INN

1806 McMillan Ave., 214/370-5571
HOURS: Mon.-Sat. 7 P.M.-2 A.M., Sun. noon-2 A.M.
`Map 4`

Don't let the cracked vinyl booths and location next to a dingy convenience store fool you—the Slip Inn isn't a true dive bar, because no true dive bar has Morrissey on the jukebox and a hip-hop DJ on weekends. Therein lies the brilliance of the Slip Inn: its ability to meld a come-as-you-are aesthetic with a hip, underground Brooklyn feel. Dance nights on weekends pack the joint.

NIGHTLIFE

Clubs and Lounges

BILLY BOB'S TEXAS

2520 Rodeo Plaza, 817/624-7117,
www.billybobstexas.com

HOURS: Mon.-Thurs. 2 P.M.-midnight,
Fri.-Sat. noon-2 A.M., Sun. noon-midnight

Map 7

It's billed as the world's biggest honky-tonk, and they ain't foolin'. At around 100,000 square feet, Billy Bob's feels more like an indoor amusement park than a club. Consider the concert hall, 32 drink stations, barn-size gift shops, full restaurants, and indoor rodeo with live bull riding if you need any convincing of the Texas-size proportions of this place.

Still, Billy Bob's is always about the music. Country music, to be exact. While the concert hall sees some of Nashville's best acts, as well

BILLY BOB'S TEXAS: THE WORLD'S LARGEST HONKY-TONK

Billy Bob's doesn't have a mechanical bull. Let's just get that straight right off the bat.

If you're thinking mechanical bull, you're thinking Gilley's – the Pasadena, TX honky-tonk made famous by the John Travolta movie *Urban Cowboy*. But you're on the right path: Gilley's *used* to be the world's largest honky-tonk. Until Billy Bob's came along.

In April 1981, Billy Bob Barnett opened his namesake club in an old cattle barn. With 127,000 square feet of space (enough for 6,000 people), dozens of bar stations, and – forget some wannabe mechanical bull – an entire indoor rodeo arena, Billy Bob's soon made a name for itself as a Texas-sized destination.

It's almost impossible to describe the scale of Billy Bob's – it's more like an amusement park than a nightclub. It helps to know a bit about the place's history. As a cattle barn, the Billy Bob's building held about 1,200 pens. During World War II, the building served as an airplane factory, and after that it served as a department store so large the stock boys wore roller skates to get around faster.

With a place that big, and with so many entertainment options to offer, it's tough to navigate. So here's a handy guide to the World's Largest Honky-Tonk:

- **Cover Charge:** Sun.-Tues. $1 before 7 P.M., $3 after 7 P.M., Weds.-Thurs. $1 before 8 P.M., $4 after 8 P.M., Fri.-Sat. $1 before 5 P.M., $6.50 and up (depending on performer) after 6 P.M.

- **Parking:** Billy Bob's own parking lot spans 20 acres – it's advisable to use it, although there are other lots in the area, as the neighborhood can get a little rowdy after sundown. Parking is free Monday through Thursday. Weekend parking rates are as follows: Self-parking: Fri. $5 after 4 P.M., Sat. $4 after noon, Sun. $4 after 8 P.M.; Valet parking: Fri. $7 after 6 P.M., $6 after 6 P.M.

- **Got Kids?:** Although it's a honky-tonk, Billy Bob's is quite family friendly, and a popular destination for moms, pops, and their kids. Visitors 17 years old or younger must be present with a parent or guardian. Guardians must be at least 30 years old and have a signed consent form, available on the Billy Bob's web site. Visitors over 18 must present ID at the door (only 21 and up are allowed to drink alcohol, of course).

- **Dance Instruction:** Line dancing: Thurs. 7-8 P.M., free. Other beginner and intermediate lessons in different genres are available on a rotating schedule for around $5. Check the web site for details.

as a few classic rock shows, it's the lariat-laced dance floor—complete with mirrored saddle in place of a disco ball—that sees the most action here. Billy Bob's is a place where line-dancing never died, where the Cotton-Eyed Joe and two-stepping set the pace, and where strangers still ask each other to dance.

8.0

111 E. 3rd St., 817/336-0880,
www.eightobar.com
HOURS: Mon.-Weds. 10 A.M.-midnight, Thurs.-Sat.

10 A.M.-2 A.M.

`Map 8`

It's all about location at 8.0, which is lucky enough to boast a comfy, casual patio right in the heart of Sundance Square. It's not all about the outdoors here, however: 8.0 has long been a favorite spot for mingling singles and folks out for dance floor booty-shaking. The excellent martinis are a draw, too, though recent bookings by the edgy Spune Productions draw in the beer and bedhead crowd as well.

- **Bull Riding:** You can't go to Billy Bob's without checking out the rodeo; after all, there's nothing better than dancing the Cotton-eyed Joe and then popping over to watch a 2,000-pound bull tossing around the 150-pound man on his back. Fri.-Sat. 9 P.M. and 10 P.M., $2.50.

- **Food:** Barbeque, Tex-Mex, and fried finger foods are available at the restaurant, although it's a touch overpriced and nothing to write home about.

- **Concerts:** Billy Bob's has two stages: The smaller one, for house bands and the like, is in the middle of the complex, between two dance floors. The larger stage, where huge country stars, classic rock bands, and even some pop bands play, sits at the end of the larger dance floor.

- **When music, dancing, and the rodeo aren't enough:** The video game arcade, and Handprint Hall of Fame (with prints from everyone from George Strait to Ringo Starr), pool tables, and Dry Goods Store (a.k.a. the gift shop) round out the Billy Bob's experience.

BILLY BOB'S TRIVIA:

- Four movies have been filmed at Billy Bob's:

Baja Oklahoma, *Necessary Roughness*, *Over the Top*, and *Pure Country*.

- The rhinestone-encrusted saddle that serves as a dance floor disco ball is from the Dolly Parton movie *Rhinestone*.

- Billy Bob's is about three times the size of the original Gilley's.

- Some parts of the floor at Billy Bob's are sloped, dating back to the days when the building served as a cattle barn — sloped floors were easier to clean.

- Country singer Merle Haggard set a world record at Billy Bob's by buying the entire house a beer.

- The Gatlin Brothers, Willie Nelson, and Waylon Jennings all played the opening week at Billy Bob's.

- Country greats George Strait and Rick Trevino both got their starts at Billy Bob's. Strait was an opening act and Trevino won a talent show there.

- After the *Urban Cowboy* craze died down, Barnett and his co-owner struggled to keep the club open. Billy Bob's closed in 1988, but fortunately re-opened under new ownership and has been going strong ever since.

NIGHTLIFE

ESCAPADE 2001

10701 Finnell St., 214/654-9950

HOURS: Weds.-Sun. 8 P.M.-4 A.M.

Map 11

Escapade 2001 is one of those mega-clubs with several separate clubs within, each featuring a different type of music. What makes Escapade unique is its six different dance areas catering solely to varieties of Latin music, from rancheras to reggaeton. The humming energy here is infectious, as the vast dance expanses are filed with both revelers and a super light show. Despite its size, Escapade is consistently packed on weekends, with hundreds of patrons happily shelling out $12 (ages 21 and up) to $20 (for the under-21 crowd) for a chance to boogie on the ample dance floors. If you want to get your cumbia on sans such expense, try getting there before 9 P.M., when entry is free.

GHOSTBAR

2440 Victory Park, 214/790-9909,

www.n9negroup.com/#/ghostbardallas/main

HOURS: Mon.-Fri. 5 P.M.-2 A.M.,

Sat.-Sun. 8 P.M.-2 A.M.

Map 1

Before heading to ghostbar, the expansive, ultra-swank club that sits atop the 33rd floor of downtown Dallas's W hotel, you have to make some decisions. Do you want to spend $20–40 in cover charges? Do you want to spend that on your first round of drinks? Do you want to dance among the $30,000 millionaires? It all sounds so bad, but you have to remember, ghostbar is an *experience,* like Six Flags or the Eiffel Tower. On the right night, with the right mix of people, and the right DJ, ghostbar's uber-modern decor and scantily clad waitresses can make for a downright transcendent night.

LIVING ROOM BAR

2440 Victory Park, 214/397-1400

HOURS: Daily 6 P.M.-2 A.M.

Map 1

While its upstairs sibling, ghostbar, plays the flashy role, the W Hotel's downstairs lounge feels more grown-up. Oh sure, there's a slightly pretentious, cougar-y vibe in the air—after all it's the W—but the cool purple-hued furniture and expertly concocted cocktails, though pricey, provide a relaxing oasis in the middle of Victory Park.

LIZARD LOUNGE

2424 Swiss Ave., 214/826-4786,

www.thelizardlounge.com

HOURS: Thurs.-Sun. 9 P.M.-4 A.M.

Map 5

Okay, so it's the kind of place with a shot bar and bikini-clad go-go girls (not the retro kind, either), but if you want to dance to live DJs, slither down to the Lizard Lounge and stay after hours, because the pumping music makes up for the cheese factor. If house and hip-hop don't appeal, try the goth-themed "The Church" night on Thursdays and Sundays.

SUITE

4515 Travis St., 214/520-9135,

www.suitedallas.com

HOURS: Thurs.-Sat. 10 P.M.-2 A.M.

Map 3

Dark, exclusive, and intense, Suite is a 300-person-capacity club that caters to the rich and those aspiring to be. Strangely, there's no cover charge, but expect to shell out that extra dough for bottle service—around $350 a pop. And, since many of the tables are reserved for bottle service patrons, don't expect to find a seat any other way. You might not need one: Suite sets itself apart from other generic "ultralounges" with its surprising selection of out-of-town and underground DJs, so the dance floor is commonly packed.

ZUBAR
2012 Greenville Ave., 214/887-0071,
www.thezubar.com
HOURS: Sun.-Fri. 5 P.M.-2 A.M., Sat. 6 P.M.-2 A.M.
Map 4

With its banquette tables and sponge-painted walls, Zubar would almost give off a restaurant feel if it weren't for the excellent DJs and dance space. With above-average hip-hop and house, two different rooms, and a classy vibe, Zubar is an energetic spot that's a perfect compromise between a cavernous dance club and a tiny bar. Honestly, the clientele here tend toward the young and the wasted, but if you're in the mood to boogie without making too big a night out of it, check this place out.

Gay and Lesbian

BILL'S HIDEAWAY
4414 Buena Vista Ave., 214/559-2966,
www.billshideawaydallas.com
HOURS: Daily noon-2 A.M.
Map 3

Yes, indeed, this little-house-turned-piano-bar is hidden away, which is all the more reason its three decades of existence are a surprise. Bill's longevity is a testament to its popularity. Day in and day out, folks surround the bar's lovely grand piano to listen to some of the best local ivory ticklers in town, or to sing during open mic nights (check the website for schedules). The latter evenings are hardly amateur hour: Frequented by local performing arts gods and goddesses, the open mics often provide star-quality entertainment at bar prices—and there's never a cover charge. The verdant and relaxing back patio beckons to those less interested in Broadway, and while the main bar doesn't open until 4 P.M. on Sundays, the patio bar opens at noon to soothe those in need of a bit of hair of the dog.

BUDDIES II
4025 Maple Ave., 214/526-0887
HOURS: Daily 1 P.M.-2 A.M.
Map 2

God only knows what became of Buddies I, because Buddies II has been around as long as anyone can remember. While a few blocks away, Sue Ellen's corners the glitz and glam market, Buddies II is all about the low-lit, neighborhood bar feel. That's not to say there's not some showmanship: In the summertime, BII opens up its back deck and swimming pool for water volleyball and other exploits. Year-round, there's a weekly rotation of drag queen shows, dance events, and their infamous "barely legal" shows.

DALLAS EAGLE
2515 Inwood Rd., 214/357-4375, www.dallaseagle.com
HOURS: Sun.-Thurs. 4 P.M.-2 A.M., Fri.-Sat. 4 P.M.-4 A.M.
Map 11

As Dallas's favorite bear club, Dallas Eagle isn't for everyone (hint: If you don't know what a "bear" is, you probably don't want to go). It's

NIGHTLIFE

definitely a specific scene, catering to an older crowd and those who celebrate the old-school queer aesthetic. Perhaps the club's theme nights say it all: "Shirtless Tuesdays" lead to "Underwear Wednesdays" and beyond.

JR'S BAR AND GRILL

3923 Cedar Springs Rd., 214/528-1004,
www.caven.com/jrsbardallas.htm
HOURS: Tues.-Sat. 11 A.M.-2 A.M., Sun.-Mon. noon-2 A.M.
Map 2

Once one of the only gay bars on what's known as "The Strip," JR's is now the flagship in Caven Enterprise's fleet of queer-oriented night spots. Even as a number of gay hangouts have cropped up around it, this lively, boy-friendly spot is still the place to go in the Cedar Springs neighborhood—a night out usually involves it in one way or another. The crowd is flirty, friendly, and mixed—folks of all stripes are welcome. And, yes, it is named after the character from the TV show *Dallas*.

◖ THE ROUND-UP SALOON

3912 Cedar Springs Rd., 214/522-9611,
www.roundupsaloon.com
HOURS: Daily 3 P.M.-2 A.M.
Map 2

Before there was *Brokeback Mountain*, there was the Round-Up, where that singular Dallas inhabitant, the gay cowboy, can go to two-step, shuffle, and waltz. Since 1980, the Round-Up has corralled thousands of patrons sporting checked shirts, tight jeans, and giant belt buckles, patrons who've spent many an evening dancing to the 24–7 C&W played by live DJs. The musical mix sashays from classic country to nouveau-Nashville, making a fine backdrop for chatty patrons at any of the six different themed bars. Even if you're not much

of a country fan, don't worry—the crowd here is friendly and fun, and most folks will even teach you to dance if you ask.

STATION 4

3911 Cedar Springs Rd., 214/559-0650,
www.caven.com/station_4dallas.htm
HOURS: Daily 9 P.M.-4 A.M.
Map 2

It's a good thing Station 4 is the size of a Wal-Mart, because it's the only real dance club in the middle of Dallas's gay district. This spot is exactly what a classic gay dance club should be—enormous, with different stations to keep the attention-deficient crowd pleased, and an absolutely killer lighting system. The latter makes up for a lack of imagination in the music department—think bass-heavy oomph-oomph-oomph house—but the energy here flows as freely as the vodka and Red Bull.

SUE ELLEN'S

3014 Throckmorton St., 214/559-0650,
www.caven.com/sue_ellensdallas.htm
HOURS: Mon.-Fri. 5 P.M.-2 A.M., Sat.-Sun. 2 P.M.-2 A.M.
Map 2

For years the girl bar Sue Ellen's played little sister to its always-hopping brother bar, JR's, up the street, but in 2007 Sue Ellen's moved to different digs and finally found her own identity. The new Sue Ellen's is a bi-level club straight out of *The L-Word*. The massive first floor opens to a glassed-in dance floor flanked by two bars, pool tables, and a car-size video monitor. Upstairs, the DJ lords over her kingdom from the second-story DJ booth. Up here, the glass soundproofing keeps the cacophony to a minimum, allowing for lower-key acoustic and rock acts to keep the crowd that buzzes around the two bars occupied.

ARTS AND LEISURE

World-class museums, art galleries, the performing arts, and almost every kind of recreation under the sun (and indoors, too)—such is the arts and leisure landscape of Dallas-Fort Worth. People of all stripes will find their to-do lists full every day, no matter what the season (although the summer heat puts a slight damper on things): Art lovers will discover famous works by the masters in museums and edgy works from up-and-comers in local galleries; sports fans can join 30,000 others at a Mavs game or 3,000 people to watch the Fort Worth Cats scrap it out. In between, there's history, beauty, and fun.

Any discussion of DFW arts must begin with Fort Worth's Cultural District. While Dallas's Arts District boasts a stunning new home—consisting of four Pritzker Prize winners in a row—for the Dallas Opera, symphony, several theater and dance companies, and many others, Cowtown's art museums have always enjoyed a quiet superiority to accompany their world-class reputations.

Outdoorsy types will love the jogging, hiking, and biking to be had in the Katy Trail greenbelts, or the numerous recreation opportunities at places like Burger's Lake. And, of course, Dallas has always been sports crazy, from the inception of the Dallas Cowboys in 1960 to the newest local franchise, the Major

HIGHLIGHTS

LOOK FOR **(** TO FIND RECOMMENDED ARTS AND ACTIVITIES.

(**Best Learning Experience:** The **Frontiers of Flight Museum** will blow your mind with its collection of planes and aviation paraphanalia (page 117).

(**Best Underappreciated Performing Arts Group:** Helmed by Jaap van Zweden, the **Dallas Symphony Orchestra** is edgy, cool, and right on target (page 121).

(**Best Surprise:** Who knew Fort Worth enjoyed such a vibrant theater scene? The town boasts several excellent companies, but for a taste of the unusual, try the **Hip Pocket Theatre** (page 122).

(**Best Movie Theater:** Forget sticky floors and uncomfortable seats – try bean-bags, couches, and La-Z-Boys. The **Inwood Theater** shows arthouse films and special midnight classic screenings in the comfiest surroundings around (page 123).

(**Best Cultural Event:** Draped in a dramatic history, the **Van Cliburn International Piano Competition** is one of the most respected competitions of its kind, and a rare chance for experts and novices alike to enjoy the world's best classical pianists (page 125).

(**Best Annual Event:** Combining social tiers of all kinds, the resources of the Cultural District, and genuine Western traditions, the **Fort Worth Stock Show and Rodeo** just might be the Fort Worth-iest of all activities (page 127).

(**Best Bad Team:** Major League Baseball's **Texas Rangers** usually stink, but the team's ballpark is beautiful, tickets are cheap and plentiful, and with some of the best bats in the league, fireworks are guaranteed (page 137).

(**Best Place to Explore:** Hiking the **Fort Worth Nature Center and Refuge** will take you through shady woods and critter-laden wetlands – a quick, convenient way to escape the city for a few hours (page 138).

(**Best Driving Range:** It's not really just a driving range – **Top Golf** is more like an interactive video game, spread out over several acres (page 141).

© LANDMARK THEATRES

Inwood Theater

League Soccer team FC Dallas. On a smaller scale, the metroplex is the proud home of a trio of minor league baseball teams, whose intimate stadiums and family-friendly prices lure many a fan. And don't forget the rodeo: DFW provides ample choices for the "national sport of Texas," from the Mesquite Rodeo to the Black Rodeo. No matter which one you choose, no trip to the area is complete without catching a glimpse of the sport's masterful riders.

The Arts

MUSEUMS
DALLAS FIREFIGHTERS MUSEUM
3801 Parry Ave., 214/821-1500,
www.dallasfiremuseum.com
HOURS: Weds.-Sat. 9 A.M.-4 P.M.
COST: $4 adult, $2 youth
Map 5

It's hard to imagine a time when Dallas only needed one firehouse, but the Firefighters Museum takes you back to that day. Filled with memorabilia like vintage equipment, helmets, and a pump truck dating back to 1911, the museum is housed in Dallas's first firehouse, a handsome brick building directly across the street from Fair Park.

FIRE STATION #1
Corner of 2nd and Commerce Sts. 972/262-4479,
www.fwmuseum.org/exhibits/150.html
HOURS: Daily 9 A.M.-8 P.M.
COST: Admission varies by exhibit
Map 8

Any exploration of Fort Worth should start at this site, which served as a working fire station from 1907 to 1980. Today, it holds the "150 Years of Fort Worth History" exhibit, which features artifacts, letters, and memorabilia chronicling the city.

◖ FRONTIERS OF FLIGHT MUSEUM
6911 Lemmon Ave., 214/350-3600,
www.flightmuseum.com
HOURS: Mon.-Sat. 10 A.M.-5 P.M., Sun. 1-5 P.M.
COST: $8 adult, $5 youth, $6 senior, free under 3
Map 11

Second only to the National Air and Space Museum in archival research and artifacts, the Frontiers of Flight Museum is a must-see. Its bright new space in a colossal former hangar has rightfully raised the museum's profile, as well as given its fine collection an appropriate home. The museum's displays provide an excellent overview of the history of aviation. The wide-ranging collection, from a restored World War I Sopwith "Pup" to items on loan from NASA's Apollo 7 mission to a series of deployed ejection seats, is a jaw-dropper.

TRAMMELL AND MARGARET CROW COLLECTION OF ASIAN ART
2010 Flora St., 214/979-6430, 214/821-1500,
www.crowcollection.org
HOURS: Tues.-Weds., Fri.-Sun. 10 A.M.-5 P.M.
COST: Free
Map 1

This museum was always a family affair. For years, Dallas's most well-known real estate magnate, Trammell Crow, and his wife, Margaret, had been collecting Asian art almost willy-nilly, simply because they liked it. With more than 7,000 pieces scattered among their homes, offices buildings, and hotels, they eventually decided to gather them in one place to share with the public.

ARTS AND LEISURE

The family touch shows in the intimacy and warmth of the museum's design. Highlights include about 120 of Trammell's beloved 1,200 jade pieces and a world-class grouping of 19th-century Chinese art.

ART GALLERIES

500X GALLERY

500 Exposition Ave., 214/828-1111, www.500x.org

HOURS: Sat.-Sun. noon–5 P.M.

Map 5

Existing for 30 years in the same spot—an Expo Park warehouse that dates back to 1916—hasn't made 500X complacent. Matter of fact, if anything, this nonprofit art co-op has grown even more dynamic every year, providing a professional exhibition space for up-and-coming local and regional artists.

BOOKER T. WASHINGTON HIGH SCHOOL: GRAMMY HIGH

Booker T. Washington School for the Performing and Visual Arts is kind of like the high school from the movie and TV show *Fame*, minus the '80s leotards and the spontaneous lunchroom dancing. Those who remember *Fame* most likely remember a scene from the opening credits, when the tough, steely dance instructor played by Debbie Allen warns her students, "You want fame, but fame costs. And here is where you start paying...in sweat."

OK, that may be a little overdramatic, but drama is appropriate, as is dance, music, and art: Booker T. Washington is simply one of the best arts schools in the country. The kids *do* sweat, spending hundreds of hours rehearsing and building exceptional skills. And it pays off – many of Booker T.'s alumni are household names, well-known actors, and even Grammy winners.

But Booker T. began not as proud bastion of arts education but as an emblem of a less proud chapter in Dallas' history: segregation. In 1892 Booker T. began as the Dallas Colored High School, the only school that allowed African-American students in the entire town. It remained the only one to do so, in fact, for decades, even as the black population of Dallas grew.

In 1922, the school moved to a new building at 2501 Flora Street, now the heart of Dallas'

Arts District, where it still stands today. The school continued to take on every African-American pupil in Dallas County, juggling schedules and enrollments to accommodate such a large number of students. Booker T. continued to expand and grow, morphing into a technical high school, until finally it became the Dallas school district's arts magnet school in 1976. From there, Booker T.'s destiny – and that of its talented students – blossomed.

Booker T.'s come a long way since 1892. Today, after a $55 million renovation and expansion, the school added 70,000 square feet to its original grounds. The original building, its classic schoolhouse brick still intact, now houses an art gallery, a theater, and a display area that shows off school history and student and alumni accomplishments. And while the school relies heavily on donations, it still part of the Dallas Independent School District, and as such stands as a public school success story.

NOTABLE BOOKER T. WASHINGTON SCHOOL ALUMNI

Erykah Badu: Badu, who still lives in Dallas, might be the school's most famous graduate. She went on to Grambling State for college, and then basically started working her tail off on her music career.

It paid off. Many of Badu's neo-soul re-

KETTLE ART

2714 Elm St., 214/573-7622,
www.kettleart.com
HOURS: Thurs.-Sat. 7-10 P.M.
Map 5

Owned by one of the pioneers of the Deep Ellum renaissance, Frank Campagna, Kettle Art is a scrappy neighborhood gallery that specializes in Texas artists and photographers. Not Texas *folk* art, mind you—

Campagna and gallery executive director Kirk Hopper's tastes run a little more intense and cutting-edge than that. Since it opened in 2005, the gallery has willed its way into the fabric of the underground Dallas community as an epicenter of music, film, and general artistic mayhem. But that mayhem has a purpose: Campagna and Hopper have brought Deep Ellum's rebellious spirit into the 21st century.

cordings have gone gold, platinum, and even triple-platinum, and she's won several Grammys. She's probably best known for her 1998 masterpiece, *Baduizm*.

Badu's concerts are, quite frankly, mind-blowingly good, and she often makes surprise appearances with touring bands, including popular hip-hop/jazz/soul band the Roots, when they come through Dallas. She also performs in a free-form experimental collaboration called the Cannabinoids with local musicians

Edie Brickell: For years, Brickell was an integral part of Deep Ellum's second heyday – the late '80s to mid-'90s, when the streets there teemed with people and new bands popped up seemingly every three minutes. Reportedly, Brickell actually attended Booker T. to study visual art, and had few musical aspirations until, on a bit of a whim, she jumped onstage one night to sing with a band called the New Bohemians. Coincidentally, a couple of the New Bohemians attended Booker T. as well, although they didn't know Brickell.

The rest is well-known history in Dallas. The band continued with Brickell taking the lead singing spot, was signed by Geffen Records, and released a hit record, *Shooting Rubberbands at the Stars*. The record's first single "What I Am" climbed to #4 on the Billboard chart.

While performing "What I Am" during an appearance on *Saturday Night Live* Brickell caught the eye of guest host Paul Simon. The two were married in 1992 and live in Connecticut.

Roy Hargrove: One of the best American jazz trumpeters of our time, Hargrove graduated from Booker T. and then went on to Berklee music college in Boston for a year before landing in New York City, where he began recording with several established jazz performers. His first album, *Diamond in the Rough* came out in 1989 on Novus Records, and he remained at the label until signing with legendary Verve Records. He's won two Grammy awards – one for his work on the album *Crisol* and one for *Habana*.

Norah Jones: The daughter of Ravi Shankar, Jones is another Booker T. Grammy-winner. Her 2002 debut album *Come Away With Me* won five Grammys, including Album of the Year.

Jones, who majored in jazz piano before dropping out of the University of North Texas' lauded music program to move to New York, transfixes audiences with an unlikely blend of throwback aesthetic and contemporary sounds. Her sultry, soulful vocals lilt over intricate but classic piano. It's a sound she didn't begin to explore until her time at Booker T.

ARTS AND LEISURE

THE PUBLIC TRUST

2919 Commerce St., 214/760-7171,
www.trustthepublic.com
HOURS: Weds.-Fri. 11 A.M.-6 P.M., Sat. noon-6 P.M.
`Map 5`

The Public Trust owner Brian Gibb has always shown a knack for pushing the artistic envelope with his *Art Prostitute* publication, but that doesn't mean said art is inaccessible. His Deep Ellum gallery (formerly also called Art Prostitute) provides a hodgepodge of edgy eclecticism, in an entirely inclusionary way. If you're lucky, you'll catch an opening here, and if so, be prepared to stay up late.

SPACE

2814 Main St., 214/334-4481, www.thisisspace.com
HOURS: Tues.-Fri. noon-8 P.M.
`Map 5`

Dallas photographer Hal Samples is a hidden treasure, and so is his work/live/gallery space called, appropriately enough, Space. Samples may be best known for his work with the indie choral band the Polyphonic Spree—when he produced one of their videos for the song "Running Away," he painstakingly collated 70,000 still photos to make an animated effect—but he's also an accomplished fashion and documentary photog. His talents are many, as are his achievements, but perhaps his best feature is his eye for fantastic, cutting-edge photography, which he often curates at Space. Go to the website to see if you're lucky enough to be in town during a show.

TEXAS ART GALLERY

5570 W. Lovers La., 214/350-8500,
www.txartgallery.com
HOURS: Mon.-Sat. 10 A.M.-6 P.M.
`Map 3`

Lovers of watercolors, landscapes, and Western art will enjoy strolling around this homey spot, which features Texas artists in addition to a number of nationally known painters.

PERFORMING ARTS

THE BATH HOUSE CULTURAL CENTER

521 E. Lather Dr., 214/670-8749,
www.bathhousecultural.com
HOURS: Tues.-Sat. noon-6 P.M.
(10 P.M. on performance nights)
`Map 11`

The odd name comes from its proximity to White Rock Lake: One of the first structures in the Southwest to incorporate art deco architecture, the Bath House once held the changing area and lockers for folks looking to take a dip to escape the Texas heat. It has long since been converted to a unique 120-seat cultural center that hosts dance performances, plays, and music, like the White Rock Rhythms Jazz series, and also serves as White Rock Lake's humble museum.

DALLAS BLACK DANCE THEATRE

2700 Flora St., 214/821-1500, www.dbdt.com
COST: $10-50
`Map 1`

The oldest continuously existing dance troupe in Dallas, the Dallas Black Dance Theatre consists of 12 full-time dancers who perform a mixed repertory throughout the year.

DALLAS OPERA

2100 Ross Ave., 214/443-1000, www.dallasopera.org
COST: $129-1,020
`Map 1`

In 1958, the Dallas Opera kicked off its inaugural season with a recital by internationally renowned singer Maria Callas, and it has continued its tradition of combining rising stars with famous ones

© DALLAS CVB

The Dallas Black Dance Theatre receives raves from critics and audiences alike.

ever since. The company's prestige should rise even further now that it's moving into the stunning Winspear Opera House, in the brand new Dallas Center for the Performing Arts.

◀ DALLAS SYMPHONY ORCHESTRA

2010 Flora St., 214/979-6430,
www.dallassymphony.com

`Map 1`

Under the direction of new conductor Jaap van Zweden, the DSO has stepped it up a notch. The orchestra has always been generally well received, but van Zweden's bold leadership, along with new digs at the fabulous new Dallas Center for the Performing Arts, has invigorated the institution. Each year, the DSO takes on a combination of traditional pieces along with more risky and commissioned works, which, in van Zweden's capable hands, appear less precarious than they actually are.

FORT WORTH SYMPHONY ORCHESTRA

Bass Hall, 525 Commerce St., 817/665-6100,
www.fwsymphony.org

`Map 8`

For 75 years, the Fort Worth Symphony Orchestra has exceeded expectations, delivering big-city quality to the 27th largest city in the nation. Unlike many around the country, the FWSO has shown a remarkable ability to adapt to the times, growing both its endowment and its attendance with creative programming. Especially popular, for instance, is the FWSO's Concerts in the Garden series, which take place in the beautiful confines of the Botanic Gardens near the Cultural District. Other than similar off-site excursions, the orchestra makes its home at Bass Hall.

GRAPEVINE OPRY

300 S. Main St., Grapevine, 817/481-8733,
www.gvopry.com

COST: $15 adult, $10 child

`Map 11`

Harkening back to the traditions of the Grand Ole Opry, this roots music hoedown has grown into one of the premier country music shows of its kind. Backed by a helluva house band, notable regional—and sometimes national—bluegrass and country performers get in on the act at the spontaneous shows, which are housed in the 70-year-old Palace Theater.

TEXAS BALLET THEATER

Bass Hall, 525 Commerce St., 817/763-0207

`Map 8`

If the recent addition of several new permanent dancers is any indication, the TBT seems to have righted its recently wobbly financial ship as it enters into its inaugural year as the house company for the brand-spankin'-new

ARTS AND LEISURE

Winspear Opera House in the Dallas Arts District. Assembled from a reorganization of the Fort Worth Ballet, the TBT is now the second-largest ballet company in Texas.

TURTLE CREEK CHORALE

2301 Flora St., 214/526-3214,
www.turtlecreek.org
Map 1

This 225-member men's chorus has been blowing audiences away since 1980 with its dramatic and well-honed take on many different types of music. Each year since its inception, the chorale has grown increasingly popular, and in doing so has transcended mere regional recognition and grown into the most recorded men's chorus in the world. The chorale performs mainly at the Morton H. Myerson Symphony Center on downtown's Flora Street, though special events are often scattered around town.

THEATERS AND THEATER COMPANIES

CASA MAÑANA

3101 W. Lancaster Ave., 817/332-2272,
www.casamanana.org
Map 10

For 50 years, Casa Mañana's signature aluminum geodesic dome has housed some of the most popular theater in the city. The unique location introduced permanent theater-in-the-round to the country, and over the years the stage has seen countless productions of family-friendly fare, Broadway musicals, local productions, and top-name touring comics such as Jerry Seinfeld. By the late 20th century, the once-cutting-edge dome had grown dated; in 2003, a circular addition surrounding the dome updated the venue, but somewhat diminished its dramatic effect.

CIRCLE THEATER

230 W. 4th St., 817/887-3536,
www.circletheater.com
Map 8

More adventurous than many of its local brethren, Circle Theater specializes in producing contemporary plays, often local ones, out of its historic home in Sundance Square.

◖ HIP POCKET THEATRE

1950 Silver Creek Rd., 214/246-9775,
www.hippocket.org
Map 11

A primarily outdoor theater, Hip Pocket's unusual setting reflects its unusual mission: to produce cutting-edge plays, musicals, and other forms of stagecraft such as puppet shows. Hip Pocket has long been known for its eclectic lineup and penchant for experimentation, often to exquisite results.

JUBILEE THEATRE

506 Main St., 817/338-4411,
www.jubileetheatre.org
Map 8

One of the best African-American theater troupes in the country, the Jubilee stages consistently high-quality musicals and plays, many of them originals.

MAJESTIC THEATER

1925 Elm St., 214/880-0137,
www.liveatthemajestic.com
Map 1

The last working theater standing in Dallas's old "Theater Row," the Majestic hosts an assortment of productions year-round. The Elm Street mainstay stands proudly restored, right down to the 23-karat gold-leafing and detailed molding, as host to local and national stage acts.

STAGE WEST

821 W. Vickery Blvd., 817/784-9378,
www.stagewest.org

Map 8

Stage West isn't just extremely popular in Fort Worth—it has developed into a major regional theatre. Since its inception in 1979, the company has bounced to several homes around town, producing about 200 plays ranging from Shakespeare to Edward Albee to P.G. Wodehouse, before finally settling down 25 years later in its original funky old building near downtown. With a permanent home, Stage West also brought back its popular dinner service in the Ol' Vic Café.

MOVIE HOUSES AND FILM

ANGELIKA THEATER

5321 E. Mockingbird La., 214/826-3300,
http://angelikafilmcenter.com
COST: $10 adult, $6.50 youth, $6.50 senior,
$8 matinee

Map 4

The Angelika combines the good parts of a mega-theater monolith with the chill aura of an arthouse. That is to say, there's plenty of comfy stadium seating, legroom, and amenities, but the lineup here lists toward indies and foreigns or, at the very worst, Oscar-nominated blockbusters. The lines at the lower-level bar and coffee shop tend to get long just before showtime; one of the several cash bars upstairs might be a better option.

INWOOD THEATER

5458 W. Lovers La., 214/764-9106,
www.landmarktheatres.com
COST: $10 adult, $7 youth, $7 senior, $7 matinee

Map 3

A DFW institution, the Inwood Theater once

Inwood Theater

© LANDMARK THEATRES

was the only place in Dallas to catch an art-house flick. Things have changed—for one thing, the once independently owned theater is now owned by the large Landmark company. But the Inwood's distinctive history, its art deco panache, its dark bar that specializes in martinis, and its unique seating (couches, bean bags, recliners) make it a favorite, even 60 years after it opened.

MAGNOLIA THEATER

3699 McKinney Ave., Ste. 100, 214/764-9106
COST: $10 adult, $7 youth, $7 senior, $7 matinee

Map 2

It's owned by the large theater conglomerate Landmark, but the Magnolia has the look and feel of an independent arthouse. Befitting its arty atmosphere, the warm, sophisticated lobby has a slow-paced, grown-up feel, with

ARTS AND LEISURE

a cozy bar (and, yes, you're allowed to bring your cocktail with you to watch the movie). As you might expect, the theater sticks primarily to indie and foreign films and arty first-runs, and is a major destination for a number of film festivals.

Festivals and Events

SPRING
AFI DALLAS INTERNATIONAL FILM FESTIVAL
3801 Parry Ave., 214/720-0555, www.afidallas.com
COST: Individual screenings: $5-8.50. 10-ticket vouchers: $50. Passes: $50-750.
Map 5

Even though it's a young festival, AFI Dallas has garnered lots of attention and celebrity attendance from the likes of Charlize Theron, Will Smith, and local boys the Wilson brothers. The fest focuses mainly on works from emerging directors, but also premieres the latest films from legendary ones.

DALLAS INTERNATIONAL GUITAR FESTIVAL
Dallas Market Hall, 2200 N. Stemmons Fwy., 972/240-2206, www.guitarshow.com
COST: $20-40 adult, $15 student
Map 11

Lovers of vintage gee-tars, banjos, mandolins, and just about every other string instrument you can pick flock to this yearly festival that has grown from humble, regional beginnings to the biggest and best festival of its ilk in the country. Hundreds of vendors, exhibitors, and fans mingle at the Dallas Market Building in search of the perfect Tele, or to catch one of the dozens of guitar-based bands who shred at the attendant MusicFest. Ticket packages include discounted multiday passes and pricier VIP selections.

DEEP ELLUM ARTS FESTIVAL
www.meifestivals.com/deepspr.html
Map 5

For three days in the spring, the Deep Ellum Arts Festival shuts down the streets around Deep Ellum and lets the neighborhood do what it does best: rock. The fest features four music stages, all going simultaneously, with a parade of Dallas favorite bands ranging from hip-hop to alt-country to indie rock. The tunes are often the center of attention, but they also provide a unique soundtrack for strolling the historic district and perusing the juried art shows, sipping a beer, or munching a treat from the many food vendors. Make sure to catch the pet parade.

HOOP IT UP
972/991-1110, www.hoopitup.com
Map 11

Given Dallas's penchant for sports, it should come as no surprise that the most popular amateur 3-on-3 hoops tourney started here. The venue and exact dates vary from year to year, but the popularity of this event never wavers, as ballers of both genders vie for the championship in various age and skill categories in what amounts to the world's largest pickup game. Hoop It Up has turned into much more than just the competition—bands, celebrities, and food now vie for spectators' attention, though the basketball is always the top draw.

JUNETEENTH

www.juneteenth.com/5texas.htm

While Abraham Lincoln's Emancipation Proclamation freeing slaves nationwide went into effect on the first day of 1863, it took a while for the news to get to Texas. The Proclamation had little effect on the lives of most African-Americans in the state, until June 19, 1865, when federal troops arrived in Galveston to enforce it.

Since then, a huge celebration has evolved around the middle of June, and June 19 itself is a Texas state holiday. This is one of the largest and most anticipated African-American celebrations of the year, with official cultural and artistic events around the city, as well as informal barbecues, parties, and get-togethers.

LOWER GREENVILLE ST. PATRICK'S DAY PARADE

Greenville Ave, www.greenvilleave.org

Map 4

Perhaps it's not the most authentic St. Patrick's Day parade as far as tradition goes, but when it comes to enthusiasm, Dallas's version ranks right up there. The parade began about 30 years ago as a loosey-goosey whim, but now comprises one of Dallas's major civic events, with 100 floats (more than the Cotton Bowl parade), thousands of participants, and parade-watchers numbering somewhere in the six-digit range.

MAIN STREET ARTS FESTIVAL

Main St., 817/336-2787, www.mainstreetartsfest.org

Map 8

Perhaps no other event of the year shows off Fort Worth's escalating cultural cachet more than this four-day downtown festival. Named the number three fine arts festival in the country by the *Art Fair SourceBook,* this festival stretches all the way down Main, from the courthouse to the Fort Worth Convention Center—a full mile of juried fine art, crafts, music, and food.

MAYFEST

Trinity Park, 2401 University Dr., 817/332-1055, www.mayfest.org

COST: $8 adult, $5 child ($1.50 if purchased online)

Map 10

Held every year for the past 40 years in a forested park nestled up to the Trinity River, Mayfest is intended as a celebration of the river as a civic resource. But really, it's just a hell of a lot of fun. For four days, a wide swath of shady land transforms into an enormous festival, with five different entertainment zones, including an excellent kids' area.

◖ VAN CLIBURN INTERNATIONAL PIANO COMPETITION

Bass Hall, 525 Commerce St., 817/738-6536, www.cliburn.org

Map 8

In April 1958, smack in the middle of the Cold War, a Texas-raised, classically trained young pianist shocked the world—most notably, the Soviets—by soundly defeating the competition at the prestigious first Tchaikovsky International Piano Competition in Moscow. The event was meant to display Russia's cultural superiority, especially when it came to piano; instead, Van Cliburn's drubbing of the competition was the concerto heard 'round the world. Inspired by his win, a group of Fort Worth schoolteachers established a competition in his honor, and the Van Cliburn International Piano Competition was born.

Today, the competition, held every four years (the year after each presidential election) is considered one of the most prestigious in the world—second only, perhaps, to the Tchaikovsky itself. Winners receive prize money, contracts, management, and touring opportunities. For Fort Worth, the competition is one of the highlights of the cultural calendar, as patrons fill Bass Hall by the thousands to witness the skill of familiar names as well as up-and-comers.

FALL

CEDAR SPRINGS HALLOWEEN PARADE

3900 block of Cedar Springs Rd.

Map 2

While the calendar for many gay communities revolves around Pride Week, in Dallas it centers on the Cedar Springs Halloween Parade. Each year, the festivities grow a little more outrageous (not exactly a kid-friendly event, this one), with floats, costumes, and drag queens galore entertaining thousands of spectators. Expect to go early and stay late—the traffic and parking get amazingly congested and stay that way. But given the wildness of the event and the good-time abandon in the air, you'll probably want to stay anyway.

DALLAS PRIDE PARADE
(ALAN ROSS FREEDOM PARADE)

Cedar Springs Rd. and Throckmorton St.,
www.dallasprideparade.com

Map 2

Some have argued that we live in a post-pride culture, that GLBT parades are unnecessary. Tell that to the roughly 40,000 people who crowd "the gayborhood," as the Oak Lawn area is known, every year to watch Dallas's version of the celebration. The parade is the highlight of Pride Week here (which mercifully takes place in relatively cool September, while most across the country occur in the summer), which sees charity events, dance parties, shopping specials,

variety shows, drag shows, and pretty much every gay thing under the sun, in one of the most gay-friendly cities in the nation.

FORT WORTH ALLIANCE AIR SHOW

Fort Worth Alliance Airport, 2221 Alliance Blvd.,
817/890-1000, www.allianceairshow.com

Map 11

Held at the Fort Worth Alliance Airport on the far north border of town, this exciting yearly event is a mind-blower, as the famous Blue Angels thunder through the air and the U.S. Army's parachute show, the Golden Knights, deftly maneuver through the sky. Even without the main attractions, a day here is chock full of aerial treats, be they in the air or, like the static display, on the ground. The latter attraction, featuring restored military planes from all eras, is one of the biggest in the nation—tour guides are available, or visitors can meander around the old-school fighters and giant cargo planes. A kids' zone and other activities round out the experience. The best part? Admission is free, though coolers and outside food and drink aren't allowed, so expect to shell out some dough for refreshments. And don't forget to bring your earplugs.

GREEK FOOD FESTIVAL
OF DALLAS

13555 Hillcrest Rd., 972/233-4880,
www.greekfestivalofdallas.com
COST: General admission: $5 adult, $3 youth,
free under 5.
Dinner plate: $15 adult, $11 youth.
Lunch plate: $10 adult, $7 youth

Map 11

Somehow, over the course of 52 years, this little gathering has blossomed into a massive city-wide affair, proving Greek food is so much more than just gyros and hummus. Each year, the asphalt corner of Hillcrest and Alpha Roads transforms into fertile ground, with Greek delicacies and traditional food as far as the eye can see. Besides the many food kiosks, you'll also find an *agora* (marketplace) and a *groceria,* with loads of imported Greek foods, plus authentic dancing, singing, and other entertainment.

RED RIVER SHOOTOUT

The Cotton Bowl, 3750 Midway Plaza, 214/634-7525

`Map 11`

There's no worse blood in college sports than that between the University of Oklahoma and University of Texas football teams, as evidenced by the hype surrounding their annual match-up. The last time the game was played in the legendary Cotton Bowl was in 2008; the battlefield has moved to Jerry Jones' new state-of-the-art stadium in Arlington, but that hasn't lessened the intensity of the game, nor has it dampened the area-wide festivities that fill the week surrounding the event.

WINTER

BIG D NYE

2500 Victory Ave., www.wfaa.com/bigdnye

`Map 1`

The Dallas version of the Times Square ball drop, Big D NYE takes place in Victory Park and features local bands, major sporting events, and a giant fireworks display at midnight.

◖ FORT WORTH STOCK SHOW AND RODEO

Will Rogers Memorial Center, 817/877-2400, www.fwssr.com

`Map 10`

Once a year, even the most cosmopolitan of Fort Worth's citizens dust off their Ropers and starch their Wranglers in anticipation

© FORT WORTH CVB

Fort Worth Stock Show and Rodeo

of one of the biggest events of the year: the Fort Worth Stock Show and Rodeo. It's a big enough deal in these parts that local school children receive an official day off of school to head down to the Will Rogers Memorial Center, where three weeks worth of attendant events are held during the end of January and beginning of February. During that time, every square inch of the Memorial Center—from the coliseum to the midway to the exposition centers—is filled with the bustle of commerce and competition.

The event is equal parts business and pleasure. For some, the stock show and exposition provides a venue for selling cattle and other hoofstock (in 2008, a record $4,322,000 was generated), for exhibiting different breeds, and for networking. But for many, the carnival, midway, and—especially—rodeo provide the best entertainment of the year. Hundreds of thousands of visitors descend upon the Will Rogers Coliseum to watch expert ropers and riders compete in what is truly a spectacle of the West.

Sports and Recreation

SPECTATOR SPORTS
COWTOWN SPEEDWAY
3925 New Hope Rd., Kennedale, 817/478-9952, www.cowtownspeedway.com

Map 11

Dubbed "the fastest lil dirt track in Texas, the Cowtown Speedway is an oval quarter-mile track that's been in operation since 1963. The Speedway hosts a variety of races for six classes of cars: Modified Class, Limited Modifieds, Street Stock, Sprints, Bombers, and Junior Mini Stock with go-kart nights and demolition derbies thrown in. It's a fast track indeed—some racers have been clocked up to 110 mph.

CROWNE PLAZA INVITATIONAL AT COLONIAL
Colonial Country Club, 3735 Country Club Cir., 817/927-4820, www.crowneplazainvitational.com

Map 9

One of only four invitationals on the PGA tour, this tourney has had many sponsors (and, hence, slight name changes) since its beginning in 1946, but it has always been steeped in history, and has always been held at Colonial Country Club on the west side of Fort Worth. The Colonial began with a legendary bang: One of the game's greats, Fort Worth's own Ben Hogan, won the first two tournaments. You'd think it'd be all downhill from there, but the Colonial has a knack for big-name wins—other victors include Sam Snead, Tommy Bolt, Arnold Palmer, Ben Crenshaw, Jack Nicklaus, Tom Watson, and Phil Mickelson (though Hogan won it the most: five times). One big name is missing from that list: Tiger Woods hasn't played the tour stop since 1997, and it's unclear if he ever will again. Still, Colonial always provides fireworks, such as in 2003 when Annika Sorenstam became the first woman to participate in a PGA tourney since Babe Zaharias.

Tickets can be hard to come by, and they can be expensive, but the Colonial is a dream experience for golf fans (except for the fact that Tiger Woods usually skips it). With the

© FORT WORTH CVB

Crowne Plaza Invitational at Colonial

summer heat usually beginning its annual boil, a large, sweaty, preppy crowd follows the stars of the links around like puppies. The cool green expanses and old-school country-club brick buildings provide an aura of history, and, as the excitement swells on the final Sunday, so do the crowds—come early to stake out a favorite spot.

DALLAS COWBOYS

Cowboys Stadium, 925 N. Collins, Arlington

www.dallascowboys.com

`Map 11`

One of the most storied franchise in sports, the Dallas Cowboys are not just a football team for Metroplex fans; they are a legendary collection of gods, worshiped in a brand-new cathedral—the $1.3 billion Cowboys Stadium—that rises dramatically out of the Arlington pavement and steals the show from nearby Rangers Ballpark.

This team has always been about spectacle, and Cowboys Stadium's ultra-modern glass and steel design, enormous HD television screens, and 63,000-square-foot retractable roof indeed provide a dramatic backdrop for the battle taking place on the field below.

And that's way below. With an 80,000-person regular capacity and the ability to expand to 100,000, Cowboys Stadium's may contain more nosebleed seats than fancy suites (though, to be sure, there are plenty of those too).

With an arena this size, hassles are to be expected. Cowboys officials claim the stadium is surrounded by 30,000 parking spaces—a big upgrade from the Cowboys' former home Texas Stadium, but expect to pay, and to walk.

Oddly, although North Texas is obsessed with its 'Boys, and fans follow the team rabidly, crowds at the games can be subdued compared to other franchises. Once they get ratcheted up, however, expect cacophony. Similarly, fans are reserved, but don't think that means you can sport the opposing team's colors without getting your fair share of razzing.

ARTS AND LEISURE

excited crowd at a Dallas Mavericks basketball game

DALLAS MAVERICKS

American Airlines Center, 2500 Victory Ave.,
214/757-MAVS, www.dallasmavericks.com

Map 1

The Mavericks began as an expansion team in 1980 under the leadership of their first owner, bowling alley "kingpin" Don Carter. For years, though they made the playoffs regularly with starters like Mark Aguirre, Rolando Blackmon, and Derek Harper, the Mavs were never much more than a blip on the NBA radar screen, save their seven-game series against the L.A. Lakers in the 1988 Western Conference finals. In fact, for the entire duration of the 1990s, they downright sucked, flirting several times with the NBA record for most losses in a single season. Even new ownership led by former presidential candidate H. Ross Perot didn't help.

But when the young, brash Internet honcho Mark Cuban bought the franchise in 2000, suddenly the Mavs were on the map. A series of trade and draft acquisitions brought stars like perennial all-star forward Dirk Nowitzki to the team, and that, combined with Cuban's intense desire to win and his even more intense desire to spend money in order to do so, helped the Mavs surge further along in the playoffs. Things looked bright.

Until the big fiasco. The Mavericks as a franchise had never made it to the NBA Finals until 2006, when they arrived after a grueling playoff season, with home court advantage to take on the Miami Heat. The Mavs kicked off the series with a pair of convincing wins. The city of Dallas began drawing up parade plans. The team traveled to Miami with visions of bringing a championship back to Big D. Then the wheels came off: Miami won the next four games, snatching the title away. For Dallas, it was an epic failure.

Dallas—the team and the city—doesn't seem to have gotten over the heartbreak. The Mavs went on the next two seasons to win a total of 118 games, yet both years were ousted from the playoffs in the first round. The sting of the disappointment still burns.

THE DALLAS COWBOYS

Where to begin?

Five Super Bowl victories. Eleven NFL Hall of Famers. A value of well over $1.6 billion dollars. A crazy owner. Constant drama. These are the Dallas Cowboys, America's Team. To say they are beloved by their city is like saying a mother loves her son – you don't even *know*.

The Cowboys have a singular, storied, spectacular history, the type found only among a handful of teams in any type of sports. Though it has struggled of late, the franchise has racked up an impressive string of credentials: 10 conference championships, 19 division championships, and 29 playoff appearances to go along with those Super Bowls.

It also has provided a list of legends: Clint Murchison, the team's first owner (who, some believe, helped engineer John F. Kennedy's assassination); Tom Landry, the fedora-sporting coach for the team's first 28 years, under whom they won two Super Bowls; Don Meredith, the boozy gunslinging quarterback; fierce defenders like Bob Lilly, Lee Roy Jordon, and Thomas "Hollywood" Henderson; Tony Dorsett and NFL all-time rushing leader Emmitt Smith; and, of course Super Bowl winning quarterbacks Roger Staubach and Troy Aikman, now revered as Big D gods.

Despite such luminaries, the Cowboys have never been far from controversy, and that's never been more true than during the reign of current owner Jerry Jones. Upon purchasing the team in 1989, Jones infuriated fans with a series of PR missteps, the most egregious being his unceremonious firing of Landry. The first several years of the Jones era were pure misery, including a 1-11 season, but the franchise regrouped after trading superstar Herschel Walker to the Minnesota Vikings for tons of draft picks. Jones' blunders were forgotten when the 'Boys turned around a miserable team and won three Super Bowls during the 1990s.

In 2009, amidst renewed fan anger against Jones for his indulgence in controversial players like Terrell Owens and an underachieving team, the owner unveiled the Cowboy's new stadium, located in Arlington. (The fate of Texas Stadium, the Cowboys' home since 1971, has yet to be determined.) The new stadium is a futuristic masterpiece, with a regular capacity of 80,000 (though that can be expanded to around 100,000), hybrid turf, and, as a continuation of the tradition of the "hole in the roof" at Texas Stadium, a retractable roof. Several big sporting events are already planned for the new stadium's inaugural years, including the 2010 NBA All-Star game, the NCAA Final Four tournament games, and the 2011 Super Bowl. Cowboy fans, of course, hope this last one proves to be home turf.

Still, the Mavs remain a hot ticket, especially in the beautiful confines of the American Airlines Center. Even though the specter of the Miami series hangs in the air, Mavs fans consistently post sellouts, and the team's recent acquisition of all-star point guard Jason Kidd, while controversial, provides crowd-pleasing offensive fireworks every night. Ever popular with fans, Cuban has initiated several fan-friendly promotions, including a limited amount of "cheap seats" and other specials—check the website for details.

DALLAS STARS

American Airlines Center, 2500 Victory Ave., 214/467-8277, www.stars.nhl.com

`Map 1`

Sun-drenched Dallas may not be the most hockey-centric locale, but Dallasites certainly have adopted their Stars, who were imported in 1993 when the Minnesota North Stars relocated here as native sons. And although there was much controversy when the NHL okayed the deal that sent a storied franchise into a heretofore hockey-ignorant town, the Stars have taken kindly to their Texas home. For those on either side who remained ambivalent, the team's 1999 Stanley Cup sealed the deal.

Of the original North Stars team, only two remain: right-winger Jeri Lehtinen and center Mike Modano. In 2007, Modano scored his 503rd goal, making him the only American-born NHL player to reach that mark. Fan still flock to watch Modano's magic on the ice, and most Stars games sell out; American Airlines Center always rocks to the rafters during home games (fans go so far as to yell "Stars!" during the part of the national anthem with the same word).

FC DALLAS

Pizza Hut Park, 9200 World Cup Way, 214/705-6700, http://fc.dallas.mlsnet.com

`Map 11`

A charter member of Major League Soccer, FC Dallas began as the Dallas Burn, a successful franchise that played home games at the famous Cotton Bowl in Fair Park before moving to Pizza Hut Park—built specifically for soccer—in the Dallas suburb of Frisco in 2005. Pizza Hut Park seats 20,000, though the FC Dallas crowd averages about half that. Tickets for FC Dallas games are cheap compared to many other Major League sports, and easy to come by.

The team is owned by Clark Hunt (son of National Football League legend Lamar Hunt), who also owns the Kansas City Chiefs, and has found great success since its inaugural 1996 season, having fought its way to the MLS championship three times and winning it once, in 1997.

Games at Pizza Hut Park are a fun, family-friendly affair, and the franchise churns out a constant stream of promotions and concerts to maintain interest. Be forewarned: The MLS season stretches from March to September, and in the summer months, the outdoor stadium can prove viciously hot.

FORT WORTH CATS

LaGrave Field, 301 NE 6th St., 817/226-2287, www.fwcats.com

COST: $4-15

`Map 8`

Even though they're part of a relatively small league, unaffiliated with Major League Baseball, the Fort Worth Cats of the American Association of Independent Professional Baseball might be more popular among Fort Worthers than their big-league brethren up the road, the Texas Rangers.

One reason for their popularity is their history. Unlike the Rangers, who moved to North Texas in 1972 and have done little since, the Cats date back to 1888 (when they were called the Panthers). They began that year as members of the Texas League, where they stayed until the mid-1950s. Along the way, the Cats played host to the likes of Ty Cobb, Babe Ruth, Lou Gehrig, and Rogers Hornsby, all of whom made their way to the Fort Worth home field to participate in exhibition games. Hornsby eventually ended up managing the club for a few years. For a while, the Cats were affiliated with the Brooklyn Dodgers and then the Chicago Cubs before branching off independently for good.

Besides their history, the Cats have another thing going for them: They've always been good. Back in the days when independent baseball was a hot ticket, the Cats consistently won Texas League championships. At one point, between 1919 and 1925, they rattled off seven straight championships in a row. During the 1930s, they won three more. The team also made a habit of winning the yearly Dixie Series, which pitted the Texas

League champion against the Southern League champion.

Yet even history couldn't save the Cats from the downslide in Minor League popularity, and in 1964 the team folded. In 2001, however, the Cats came back, 36 years after the last out at LaGrave field, which had since been torn down. The Cats' new owner, Carl Bell, decided to build a brand new LaGrave Field on top of the site of the last one. Bell even made sure the new home plate stood exactly where the last one had.

Bell built it, and the fans came. The new Cats have been a big hit ever since, picking up where they left off, making the playoffs a mere two years after their resurgence, and winning the league championship in 2005, 2006, and 2007. A number of Cats have gone on to play in the big leagues, most notably pitcher Luke Hochevar, the number one pick in MLB's 2006 draft.

FRISCO ROUGHRIDERS

Dr. Pepper Ballpark, 7300 RoughRiders Trail, 972/731-9200, www.ridersbaseball.com
Map 11

The RoughRiders haven't been around for too long, but they've certainly been burning it up since they got here. Formerly the Shreveport Captains, this AA squad, now a farm team for the Texas Rangers, arrived in 2003 and immediately made the playoffs as winners of the South Division of the Texas League. The 'Riders, led by a constant stream of sluggers, have in fact made the postseason almost every year since.

Frisco's home field is the awesome, $23 million Dr. Pepper Ballpark, a cool stadium built in 2003, which has consistently posted top attendance numbers for Minor League teams. The park has some fun touches—including a rentable swimming pool and seats

built around both bullpens—and it seats more than 10,000 fans.

GRAND PRAIRIE AIRHOGS

QuikTrip Park, 1600 Lone Star Pkwy., 972/504-9383, www.airhogsbaseball.com
Map 11

For years, independent professional baseball in the metroplex has been dominated by the legendary Fort Worth Cats, but a new squad on the scene, the Grand Prairie AirHogs, have already started to give the Cats a run for their money.

The Hogs (as well as the Cats) are part of the unaffiliated Southern League. In many ways, this is a last-ditch league, populated by young players who have gone unnoticed by Big League franchises and older players hoping for one last chance to be recognized by the majors. You'd think that would speak to poor-quality baseball, but quite the contrary: There's much at stake for all the players involved, and the spirit and intensity of the play make for excellent games. The Hogs made a fine choice in their first manager, former big-leaguer Pete Incaviglia (who once played for the Texas Rangers, among others), who guided the team to a Southern Division championship its inaugural year.

It helps, too, that the city of Grand Prairie spent $20 million on the AirHogs' home, QuikTrip Park. Seating only about 5,000, the intimate park features excellent views of the game from every seat. The park was built as part of a grander entertainment complex, complete with a bar and restaurant, cigar bar, playgrounds, and swimming pool. A day at the park is an exercise in attention-mongering. Inter-inning lulls are filled with giveaways, scoreboard games, and goofy on-field races. As is tradition in the smaller leagues,

The Grand Prairie AirHogs' new home is state-of-the-art.

promotional nights are wild and silly, and the Hogs have garnered quite a bit of national attention with their promo nights, especially "A-Rod and Madonna Night," and "Jessica Simpson Night."

HD BYRON NELSON CHAMPIONSHIP

Four Seasons Resort and Club,
4150 N. MacArthur Blvd., 972/717-0700,
www.hpbnc.org/byronnelson

Map 11

This PGA tour stop began as the Dallas Open in 1944 and has shared its name with various corporate sponsors since, but to golf lovers everywhere, it will always be called the Byron Nelson. Until his death in 2006, Nelson was a golden-boy legend around the world, and in Dallas he was a god. His name alone has lured the big boys from the PGA year after year—past winners include

Tiger Woods, Phil Mickelson, and Sergio Garcia.

The tourney, held in late April/early May, is played at the TPC Four Seasons club and features an unusual setup: The first two rounds are played on both of the Four Seasons' courses—the TPC Las Colinas and the Cottonwood Valley Country Club—with TPC Las Colinas hosting the final two rounds. If you plan on catching some of the action, consider avoiding parking hassles by using the shuttle that departs from Texas Stadium.

LONE STAR PARK

1000 Lone Star Pkwy., Grand Prairie, 972/263-7223,
www.lonestarpark.com
COST: $3-25

Map 11

Lone Star Park has only been around since 1994, but it has already built a name for itself as the premier thoroughbred track in Texas (and much of the Southwest, for that matter). The world-class facility hosts a 65-date meet that lasts from spring to mid-summer. The stands for the seven-furlong turf course and one-mile oval track usually hold about 8,000 people, though they were greatly expanded in 2004 for the Breeder's Cup. The grounds also include a simulcast center, sports book, concessions, and seating ranging from box seats to terrace level to general admission.

MESQUITE CHAMPIONSHIP RODEO

1818 Rodeo Dr., 972/285-8777,
www.mesquiterodeo.com
Map 11

If you only do one "Texas" thing during your time here, it should be the Mesquite Rodeo.

COLLEGE SPORTS

While college sports are huge in Texas, the scene is dominated primarily by the triumvirate of big universities, Texas Tech, Texas A&M, and the University of Texas. DFW has smaller fare, but there's still plenty of excellent competition to check out – and tickets are much more readily available. Just now recovering from the NCAA's death penalty enacted in 1987, Southern Methodist University's football team continues to improve, thanks to big-name coach June Jones. The University of Texas at Dallas is small, but their soccer program is one of the best in the nation. Texas Christian University's Horned Frogs football and basketball teams are always in the running, and always entertaining. The University of Texas at Arlington's hoops squad is the area's other basketball Mavericks – and they too can often be found at the top of the standings.

An evening here vibrates with excitement: If you've never seen bronc bustin' or bull riding, the spectacle at the 5,000-seat Resistol Arena will leave you breathless. The rodeo sticks to the traditional—calf-roping, barrel races, steer wrestling—along with a few new events, like "cowboy poker" and chuck wagon races.

STOCKYARDS CHAMPIONSHIP RODEO

Cowtown Coliseum, 121 E. Exchange Ave.,
817/625-1025, www.stockyardsrodeo.com
COST: General Admission: $15 adult, $10 youth, $12.50 senior. VIP Club Seating: $20 adult, $20 youth, $20 senior. Reserved Box Seating: $20 adult, $20 youth, $20 senior.
Map 7

This traditional, excellent indoor rodeo, held every Friday and Saturday at the Cowtown Coliseum in the Stockyards, is a thrilling way to spend an evening. The price of admission also includes Pawnee Bill's Wild West Show, which alone is worth the excursion. The show is a reenactment of a popular Old West troupe that performed trick riding, trick roping, trick shooting, and bullwhip acts. Keep in mind it's cash only at the box office; credit and ATM cards can be used online, for a $1-per-ticket fee.

TEXAS BLACK RODEO

Fair Park Coliseum, 1300 Robert B. Cullum Dr.
(main entrance) to 1438 Coliseum Dr., 214/565-9026
COST: $7-10
Map 5

A celebration of the historically overlooked African-American cowboys, the Texas Black Rodeo has been a mainstay since 1986. It also just happens to feature some of the most skilled bronc-busters, cattle-ropers, and horsemen—and horsewomen—around. Proceeds benefit the African-American Museum.

ARTS AND LEISURE

TEXAS BRAHMAS

NYTEX Sports Centre, 8851 Ice House Dr.,
North Richland Hills, 817/336-4423,
www.brahmas.com

COST: $12-30

Map 11

Texas may not be known for hockey of any sort, much less the minor-league variety, but the Brahmas have been a hot ticket ever since moving from their downtown digs to North Richland Hills, a suburb of Fort Worth. The proud purple and black have tasted the postseason a couple of times in their short existence since 1996, but the fans who sell out the 2,400-capacity NYTEX arena that serves as the Brahmas' home base show up even in the lean years. Tickets aren't as cheap as you'd expect, but the level of hockey is also better than one would imagine, and with plenty of promos and close-up action, the family-friendly atmosphere here is a definite draw.

TEXAS MOTOR SPEEDWAY (NASCAR)

3545 Lone Star Cir., 817/215-8500,
www.texasmotorspeedway.com

Map 11

Since it first opened in 1996, the 1.5-mile oval track Texas Motor Speedway has shifted from a sort of wannabe to a major player in the NASCAR world. Track improvements have played a major factor in the TMS's rise in popularity: For the first few years of its existence, TMS officials struggled with constant complaints about the track's safety, and also its odd "double bank" configuration. Those problems were slowly resolved, the track was refitted as a single bank, and the speedway is now one of the fastest in the nation.

The second factor in its popularity is the management. Upon taking over the reins at the track, longtime racing promoter Eddie Gossage introduced personal seat licenses and season tickets to patrons, a first for NASCAR, and

ARTS AND LEISURE

© FORT WORTH CVB

The Texas Motor Speedway is home to a NASCAR stop.

© ANDY RHODES

the Rangers Ballpark in Arlington

he also allowed fans to bring their own coolers into events, which endeared fans to the track. Crowds at TMS can top 212,000, and usually do, making TMS the second largest sports facility in the country.

Major events held at the speedway include two NASCAR Sprint races—the Dickies 500 and the Samsung 500; NASCAR Nationwide and Craftsman series events; and a single IndyCar race, the Bombardier LearJet 550.

◖ TEXAS RANGERS

Rangers Ballpark, 1000 Ballpark Way, Arlington, 972/726-4377, www.texasrangers.com

COST: $3-205

Map 11

In 1972, Major League Baseball's Washington Senators packed their bags and moved south, beginning a new era as the Texas Rangers. Since the move, the team primarily has been known for three things: trading away a then-rookie Sammy Sosa in 1989; the fact that former president George W. Bush once owned them (in fact, it was he who okayed the Sosa decision); and—a bright spot—as the place where pitching great Nolan Ryan had some of his most memorable moments. Ryan boasted two of his record-setting seven no-hitters during his years with the team, and also was wearing a Rangers uniform when he struck out his Major League record 5,714th batter. Ryan currently serves as the team's general manager.

Despite the Ryan years, for the most part the team generally holds mediocre—and some downright awful—ground in the American League's Western division. The last time the Rangers made it to the postseason was in 1999. Since the Rangers don't have much of a history or even some kind of interesting curse to explain their general ineptitude, sometimes the team's worst years end up the most storied, as

ARTS AND LEISURE

playing witness to the downward spiral often trumps the standings as the season's most interesting spectacle (if you want to read one of the best books ever written about one of the worst teams ever, check out Mike Shropshire's *Seasons in Hell,* about the "worst baseball team in history," the 1973–1975 Rangers).

Still, the Rangers provide plenty of reasons to head out to the Ballpark (no, really, the Rangers' stadium is called the Ballpark). The first one is the Ballpark itself. Gloriously rising from acres of Arlington asphalt, the stadium was built in 1991 with the cathedrals of the Great Game in mind. It's a fun place to watch a game, and because the Rangers aren't so great, tickets are plentiful and cheap, and crowds are often near capacity. Second, as GM, Ryan's emphasis on pitching and the farm system has provided hints of the unthinkable: the prospect that the Rangers might actually be good, soon. Finally, even if the pitching disappoints (and it always has in the past), this has always been a free-swinging club. Even the most pitiful teams Texas has ever assembled still manage to provide fireworks, with sluggers like Josh Hamilton spraying dingers all over the park, from the short right field line to the home run porch to straightaway center field 400 feet away.

PARKS AND RECREATION AREAS

BURGER'S LAKE

1200 Meandering Way, 817/737-3414,
www.burgerslake.com

Map 11

In a world full of expensive, high-tech, fancy water parks, many Fort Worth families prefer the chilled-out atmosphere of Burger's Lake, which essentially is a good old-fashioned swimming hole (accentuated solely by diving boards, a 20-foot slide, and a single trapeze). The lake—a one-acre, spring-fed pool—now serves as the centerpiece of a multi-acre park that has been privately owned since 1930. Sunbathers bask on the two sandy beaches that abut the lake, though most folks prefer the large swaths of shady picnic areas, and many people take advantage of the tennis and volleyball courts.

In 2008, the lake's reputation suffered a bit when dozens of visitors became ill after contracting a parasite there, but the owners have corrected the problem.

FOREST PARK

Martin Luther King, Jr. Blvd. and Gould St.

Map 10

Forest Park consists of a wide band of often thick packed greenery in the midst of the University area of town, near many of the city's sights (occasionally, you'll hear a lion's roar from the nearby zoo). Highlights include a duck pond at the abutting Trinity Park, plus surrounding soccer fields and the ever-popular miniature train ride that runs through the park.

◖ FORT WORTH NATURE CENTER AND REFUGE

9601 Fossil Ridge Rd., 817/262-4479,
www.fwnaturecenter.org

HOURS: Oct.-Apr. daily 8 A.M.-5 P.M.,
May-Sept. daily 8 A.M.-7 P.M.

COST: $4 adult, $2 child, $3 senior

Map 11

Just 10 miles from downtown Fort Worth, the Nature Center feels like what the DFW area must have been before it was settled. The 25 miles of trails on this 3,500-acre site meander through prairie, forest, and wetlands, all home to hundreds of species of flora and fauna, including a herd of buffalo (which, according to DNA testing, has no relation to domesticated cattle—a rarity for bison). The center offers programs, exhibits, tours, and canoeing for all ages.

GPX SKATE PARK

1002 Lone Star Pkwy., 972/262-4479,
www.allianceskateparks.com
HOURS: Sun.-Thurs. 10 A.M.-10 P.M., Fri.-Sat.
10 A.M.-midnight
Map 11

It didn't take long for this $1.2 million state-of-the-art skate park to get some attention—in 2001, just one year after it was built, GPX hosted ESPN's X-Games, and proceeded to do so the year after that as well. Every inch of this grand-scale facility is a skateboarder's dream, featuring courses for beginners, intermediates, and experts, including a 12-foot half pipe, bank ramps, handrails, inline hockey rink, and more.

KATY TRAIL

Trailhead at American Airlines Center, 2500
Victory Ave., Dallas
www.katytraildallas.org
Map 2

This 3.5-mile hiking/biking trail follows the original path of the now-abandoned Missouri-Kansas-Texas railway line. Originating at an elevated path near the American Airlines Center, the greenbelt winds around some of the most densely populated parts of Dallas, through lushly vegetated parts of the Uptown area.

Plans for the trail include construction of several new entry points and a soft-surface parallel trail made of recycled running shoes. Planners hope the Katy Trail eventually will be a leg of a comprehensive, countywide network of trails.

TRINITY TRAILS

600 Northside Dr., Fort Worth
http://trinitytrails.org
Map 7

Thirty miles of trails following the path of the Trinity River wind through some of the loveliest parts of the city. Although most parts of the trail are somewhat encumbered by reminders of the surrounding urban landscape, there are still plenty of river-cooled breezes, aviary life (especially red-tailed hawks, egrets, and ducks), and the occasional cow pasture to provide bucolic enhancement. The trails have numerous access points and are a popular spot for joggers, walkers, and bikers. The city also periodically stocks the river with trout, bringing out bands of fisherman, but the timing doesn't seem to follow any particular pattern or schedule; basically, if you see a bunch of fisherman, run back home and grab your gear.

WHITE ROCK LAKE

8300 East Lawther Drive, Dallas
www.dallasparks.org/parks/whiterock.aspx
Map 11

Initially created in 1910 as a reservoir to help alleviate a citywide water shortage, White Rock Lake is a popular recreation area in the middle of the city. The lake, more than nine miles around, attracts tons of recreationists, especially bikers, and is the site of a myriad cultural gatherings—although swimming and motor-operated boats are not allowed. It's also the site of the White Rock Marathon (www.runtherock.com), a unique event, held in December, that combines the main event with music, a fitness festival, and attendant social events. As a Boston Marathon qualifier, the race attracts many of the top runners in the country, and it's considered one of the nation's top marathons.

ARTS AND LEISURE

LEGENDARY WHITE ROCK LAKE

The lake's choppy brown waters hold a good deal of history and folklore. From 1933 to 1941, a troop of the New Deal-commissioned Civilian Conservation Corps established a camp at Winfrey Point. Combined with workers from the Works Progress Administration, the workers epitomized the function of the New Deal by building bridges, piers, and roads in and around the lake. Several of the lake's signature sites date back to the CCC and WPA projects.

At the onset of World War II, the former CCC barracks at Winfrey Point were converted into an Army Air Corps boot camp, until 1944, when it became a prison camp for captured German troops. These weren't just any German troops, either, but elite soldiers from Erwin Rommel's Afrika Korps.

The history of the lake, however, takes a back seat to its primary legend, that of the Lady of the Lake. The legend takes many forms, but the one connected to another Dallas legend, is perhaps most interesting. As author Frank X. Tolbert tells it in his book, *Neiman-Marcus, Texas: The Story of the Proud Dallas Store:*

> *One night about ten years ago a beautiful blonde girl ghost appeared on a road near Dallas' White Rock Lake. Mr. and Mrs. Guy Malloy, directors for display for the world-famous specialty store, Neiman-Marcus, saw the girl. Only they didn't recognize her, right off, for a ghost. She had walked up from the beach. And she stood there in the headlights of the slow-moving Malloy car. Mrs. Malloy said, "Stop, Guy. That girl seems in trouble. She must have fallen in the lake. Her dress is wet. Yet you can tell that it is a very fine dress. She certainly got it at the Store."*

> By "the Store," Mrs. Malloy meant the Neiman-Marcus Company of Dallas.

> *The girl spoke in a friendly, cultured contralto to the couple after the car had stopped. She said she'd like to be taken to an address on Gaston Avenue in the nearby Lakewood section. It was an emergency she said. She didn't explain what had happened to her, and the Malloys were too polite to ask. She had long hair, which was beginning to dry in the night breeze. And Mrs. Malloy was now sure that this girl was wearing a Neiman-Marcus dress. She was very gracious as she slipped by Mrs. Malloy and got in the back seat of the two-door sedan.*

> *When the car started, Mrs. Malloy turned to converse with the passenger in the Neiman-Marcus gown. The girl had vanished. There was a damp spot on the back seat.*

> *The Malloys went to the address on Gaston Avenue. A middle-aged man answered the door. Yes, he had a daughter with long blonde hair who wore nothing but Neiman-Marcus clothes. She had been drowned about two years before when she fell off a pier at White Rock Lake.*

GOLF

THE GOLF CLUB AT FOSSIL CREEK

3400 Western Center Blvd., 817/847-1900,
www.thegolfclubatfossilcreek.com
HOURS: Daily 7 A.M.-3 P.M.
`Map 11`

This gorgeous course stands as one of the last to be designed by Arnold Palmer, who messed with everyone's heads by bringing water into play on 13 of Fossil Creek's holes. Check online for specials or play discounted after 2 P.M. tee times, as the greens fees will cost you even more than all the balls you'll lose in the drink.

IRON HORSE GOLF COURSE

6200 Skylark Cir., Richland Hills, 817/485-0249,
www.ironhorsetx.com
HOURS: Daily 7 A.M.-3 P.M.
`Map 11`

Golf Digest digs this "thinkers" course a lot, having given it four stars in its "Places to Play" rankings. Even the lowest handicappers will find the variety of holes, pin placement, undulating fairways, and tricky greens provide constant challenges of both skill and brainpower. The course also has a slightly cutesy railroad theme, with copious rail ties and trestles flanking fairways and greens, and even railcar restrooms.

TENISON GOLF PARK

3501 Samuell Blvd., 214/670-1402,
www.tenisonpark.com
HOURS: Daily 7 A.M.-6 P.M.
`Map 11`

Tenison Golf Park consists of two different courses: Tenison Highlands and Tenison Glen. Don't play the Glen. Instead, brave the more crowded but infinitely higher quality Highlands course—the elevation changes, tougher greens, and 2001 renovation lures

players of all skill levels and proves a challenge to all. The moderately priced park's amenities—putting green, driving range, on-site grill—rival those of pricier course.

TOP GOLF

8787 Park La., 214/341-9600, www.topgolfusa.com
HOURS: Daily 9 A.M.-11 P.M.
`Map 11`

An excursion to Top Golf is guaranteed fun, even for those who don't particularly like the links. Why? Because there are no links at Top Golf. Rather, a double-decker row of weatherproof suites holds dozens of golfers who hit balls aimed at a number of pins on the driving range. The pins are surrounded by sensors in concentric circles around the target that pick up on a microchip in each ball. The microchips then report back to a computer—you get points for how close to the pin you get, and the computer screen at your station keeps track, so you can compete against your buddies. And trust us, with a chipper waitstaff delivering burgers and beer to your station, you'll need a computer to keep score for you. The facilities also include a fancy miniature golf course replete with a giant mountain and waterfalls, batting cages, and a pro shop. Plus, loaner clubs are available at no charge.

HORSEBACK RIDING

BENBROOK STABLES

10001 Benbrook Blvd., Benbrook, 817/249-1001,
www.benbrookstables.com
`Map 11`

The Benbrook stables make it easy for a beginner to get used to riding the range. The horses here are gentle; the trails, which wind a picturesque loop around Benbrook Lake, are navigable, even for the novice. In fact, fancy stuff—double riding, running, trotting—is

ARTS AND LEISURE

prohibited, so your day in the saddle will be a leisurely one. Arena riding is also available.

STOCKYARDS STABLES

128 E. Exchange Ave., #300,
817/624-3446

Map 7

Slap down your $40 and saddle up for a one-hour ride down the Trinity River, or, for the less adventurous, a mere 10-spot gets you 15 minutes in the corral. Either ride, surrounded by the history of the Stockyards, provides a glimpse into life in the Old West.

TOURS
DALLAS SEGWAY TOURS

972/821-9054, www.dallassegwaytours.com

HOURS: Daily 8:30 A.M.–5:30 P.M.

If you can swallow the geek factor, the Segway tours are an excellent way to get to know large swaths of the city in a short amount of time. Three tours are offered: the West End, which covers much of downtown's historical and tourist stops; the Katy Trail, which is a more laid-back glide through tree-shaded concrete trails, in a park-like setting; and the American Airlines Center tour, which covers Victory Park.

SHOPS

Perhaps nowhere else in the country does a city have such an intimate, particular relationship with shopping. In Dallas, shopping is not just a pastime or a way of gathering consumer goods; rather, it's interwoven with the social, cultural—even historical—fabric of the city.

Evidence of Dallas's relationship with shopping is most easily seen in the abundance of shopping centers in town, including the world's first planned shopping center, Highland Park Village. Heavily influenced by Highland Park Village's model, Dallas's shopping geography consists mainly of areas built specifically for shopping and containing a high concentration of stores—basically outdoor malls.

Fort Worth shoppers might not quite achieve the bloodlust found in Dallas, but there's still plenty to be had here, mainly in the paradoxical form of large malls and small, intimate boutiques. You'll find neither town fears a chain store, especially a high-end one, but the shopping destinations expand to many locally owned furniture, home decor, and gift stores. And while there's no shortage of stores sporting the latest in couture and brand new items, the city's resale, consignment, and vintage stores are also popular and continue to increase their presence.

To get your bearings, check out the *Dallas Morning News* website, which has an excellent

© JONANNA WIDNER

HIGHLIGHTS

LOOK FOR  TO FIND RECOMMENDED SHOPS.

Best Outdoor Mall: Is there any question? **Highland Park Village** is the world's first planned shopping center, and it's filled with couture (page 146).

Best Shopping Center: It's not really picturesque, but **La Gran Plaza**, which caters to Fort Worth's rapidly growing Hispanic population, features inexpensive Western shops and family wear, plus some fun treasures like *quinceñera* dresses (page 148).

Best Indoor Mall: Any mall that's made it onscreen as part of a Robert Altman movie has to be different. **NorthPark Center** , in whose fountain Farrah Fawcett frolicked in Altman's *Dr. T and the Women,* is indeed unusual, its upscale shops surrounded by world-renowned sculpture and lushly sculpted gardens (page 148).

Best Place to Find a Prom Dress: Don't consider the **J. Saunders** boutique's selection small, consider it well chosen. Fort Worth ladies have been coming here to find the perfect dress for years (page 152).

Best Outlet: The **Dickies Factory Outlet** store doesn't just have discounted work gear – it's got all the hipster gear, too, at low prices (page 155).

Best Splurge: If you need, say, an ornate, hand-stitched, custom-made saddle to give as a gift to some head of state or corporate bigwig, make your way to **M. L. Leddy's** (page 156).

Best Hidden Secret: **Wild Bill's Western Store** has a collection of new cowboy boots at used prices, around $100, which is unheard of in these parts (page 157).

Best Record Store: **Good Records** is what a record store should be: filled with discretely chosen vinyl and CDs, and chock full of funky atmosphere. Bonus points for the best in-store selection, by far (page 160).

Best Bookstore: The Northwest location **Half Price Books** is heaven for book-lovers. Seriously, the place is a grand palace of fiction, non fiction, art books, kids books, poetry...well, you get the idea. And we mean "palace" – the place is the size of the Taj Mahal (page 161).

Signature features of NorthPark Center are its tranquil fountains and beautiful floral displays.

shopping blog filled with the latest information on openings, closings, sales, and who has what (the paper's weird *F!D luxe* shopping supplement, by contrast, proves pretty useless). Fort Worth's glossy mag *Fort Worth, Texas* provides a good starting point in Cowtown. Finally, a frank word of warning: Amateur shoppers should pace themselves.

Shopping Districts

BISHOP ARTS

Bishop and Davis Sts.

Map 6

Bishop Arts, with its slower pace and tree-shaded red brick storefronts, often feels like a small Southern town within Dallas' big-city limits. A leisurely walk around the area, which is only a few square blocks, reveals hidden gems, quirky shops, and neighborhood restaurants.

CAMP BOWIE

Camp Bowie Blvd. at University Dr.

Map 10

The long main drag that stretches through the West Side of Fort Worth, Camp Bowie's offerings range from eclectic and offbeat to stately and classic. Along the long strips of shops on both sides of the street you'll find clothing boutiques, chain stores, houseware shops, tons of specialty shops, and jewelry stores. Sections of the boulevard are walkable, but keep in mind this is a long and busy street.

DEEP ELLUM

Between I-45 and Exposition Ave.

Map 5

Although Deep Ellum is better known nowadays as Dallas' music and art district, its neighborhood roots go back to a time when pawn shops and other stores anchored the street life, so why wouldn't it make for fine shopping? A stroll along Main and Elm Streets doesn't tender as many options as it used to, but it reveals a number of boutiques, jewelry stores, tattoo parlors, and head shops, along with a few non-seedy sex shops.

DOWNTOWN DALLAS

Map 1

The granddaddy, the big poppa, the old faithful, Neiman Marcus, got its start downtown and continues to hold down the fort to this day. While a visit to Neiman's alone is worth a trip downtown—hell, a glance in Neiman's windows alone is worth it—small, upscale, hip boutiques are cropping up in the once-abandoned buildings that are benefiting from the city's revitalization projects. Meantime, on the outer edge of downtown, Victory Park provides glitz and glam with several cream-of-the-crop stores, while the West End draws in tourists with a smattering of souvenir and Western shops.

GREENVILLE AVENUE

Greenville Ave., west of Lakewood

Map 4

Sometimes funky, sometimes ritzy, always busy, Lower Greenville Avenue is one of the best places in Dallas to stroll and not spend *too* much money. The strip from about Ross Avenue all the way up to Mockingbird features a mélange of thrift stores, antique shops, and unique gift stores interspersed among the many bars and restaurants.

(HIGHLAND PARK VILLAGE

47 Highland Park Village, Dallas

Map 3

Leave it to Dallas to have a shopping center that's a designated historical landmark. Opened in 1931 in the town's toniest neighborhood, Highland Park Village proudly claims its heritage as the nation's first shopping center. Many of the boutiques, storefronts, and restaurants have changed since then, but the center's unique Spanish/Mediterranean visual motif and its focus on the swankiest products have not. This is where the cream of the social crop in Dallas goes to shop; the only place that compares in both heritage and stature is Neiman Marcus.

7TH STREET

W. 7th between Main St. and University Dr.

Map 10

Just around the corner from the Cultural District in Fort Worth, the West 7th Street area has enjoyed a recent blossoming of specialty shops, vintage stores, and individually owned storefronts. The vibe here is laid-back and modern.

SNIDER PLAZA

Snider Plaza at Milton Ave.

Map 3

A slightly larger, slightly less stuffy version of Highland Park Village, Snider Plaza is a repository for some of the best boutique shopping in town. The walkable outdoor center is a perfect place to find unique items, especially stationery, gifts, housewares, children's wear, and even pet items. Snider Plaza also houses a wide variety of excellent eateries, ranging from hamburger joints to fine dining.

THE STOCKYARDS

131 E. Exchange Ave.

Map 7

If you're looking for a giant belt buckle,

A number of Stockyards stores stock cowboy hats.

© JONANNA WIDNER

checkered cowboy shirts, or a pair of custom-made boots, the Stockyards can't be beat for variety. There's no better way to shop for Western duds than by strolling down the creaky wooden sidewalks here and peering into the many stores. Beware, though, that with the touristy atmosphere often come touristy prices.

SUNDANCE SQUARE

333 Throckmorton St.

Map 8

The nostalgic buildings, unique civic additions (like shrubs cut in the shape of longhorn cattle), and fellow shoppers definitely get you in the mood to spend in this historic district downtown. Keep an eye peeled for hidden

HIGHLAND PARK VILLAGE

It should be no surprise, in a part of the world where shopping is often termed a contact sport, that there's a shopping center designated as a National Historic Landmark: Highland Park Village.

To fully understand Highland Park Village, it helps to know a little about Highland Park. The neighborhood is, technically, its own city – complete with its own schools, police department and fire departments, and parks. Originally intended as an elite enclave, Highland Park lived up to its destiny. In 1906, developer John S. Armstrong purchased a large tract of land just north of Dallas. Armstrong and his two sons-in-law, Hugh Prather and Edward Flippen, hired the same design team that planned Beverly Hills to lay out their new town. The team designed and envisioned a tony burg full of fine homes and greenery – they immediately set aside 20 percent of the land for parks. After that came the country club – Prather and Flippen built it, and indeed the wealthy came. In 1913, when Highland Park applied for annexation, Dallas refused. No doubt that proved a mistake – Dallas certainly would have benefited from Highland Park tax dollars over the years.

Nowadays, the town-within-the-city remains an exclusive, preppy place. Mercedes and BMWs fly down the tree-lined streets of Highland Park's 2.2-square mile area. Multi-story houses, many of them architecturally significant, nestle up to newly built McMansions, all homes to doctors, lawyers, oil tycoons, and football team owners (Dallas Cowboys owner Jerry Jones is a resident).

Catering to many of Dallas' richest residents, Highland Park's charming bistros, full- service stores, and fancy shops definitely list toward the high-end.

An exclusive township needs an exclusive shopping center, and that's where Highland Park Village comes in. It was Prather and Flippen's idea, and they envisioned an open-air town square created from scratch. The two traveled the world for design inspiration, studying the architecture in Spain, Mexico, and California. They settled upon an unconventional open-air design, with stores facing away from the street (an idea which many people assumed would lead to the center's doom), and off-street parking. The fruits of Prather and Flippen's world travels show clearly in the tiled fountains, stucco-colored walls, and Latin architectural style. The addition of the Highland Park Theater in 1935 was the capstone, cementing the Village as a landmark. Just as its creators envisioned, the shopping center became quite a happening place.

And it still is. Over the years as its changed hands, the center endured some down years, but when Henry S. Miller purchased it in 1975, he restored it to its original glory, refurbishing facades, revitalizing the lush landscaping, and even restoring the theater at great expense. Today shoppers flock from all over the country to indulge in retail that rivals New York's Fifth Avenue, with names as familiar as family members': Chanel, Escada, Carolina Herrera, Harry Winston, Jimmy Choo, Ralph Lauren. And, as always, the valet parking is free. You won't find *that* in Beverly Hills.

secrets like the gift shop of the Sid Richardson Museum, as well as large chain stores like Barnes & Noble books.

WEST VILLAGE
Map 2

Intersection of Lemmon and McKinney Aves.
Some people find this mixed residential/retail development to be a touch plastic; others find it to be a nexus of hipness. Either way, it's certainly got a lot of shops. The West Village is basically an inverted mall—branches of upper-echelon chains like Brooks Brothers and Ralph Lauren nestled elbow-to-elbow with a few locals, only they all are outside, facing sidewalks.

Shopping Centers

GALLERIA DALLAS
13350 Dallas Pkwy., 972/702-7100,
www.galleriadallas.com
HOURS: Mon.-Sat. 10 A.M.-9 P.M., Sun. 11 A.M.-7 P.M.
Map 11

This is the mother ship—four stories, 200 stores. There's an ice-skating rink, restaurants, and so many parking garages and levels, navigating them is like driving up the Matterhorn. For shoppers, the mix of high-end stores, popular chains, and more than a few surprises make the journey worth it.

◖ LA GRAN PLAZA
4200 South Fwy., 817/922-8888,
www.lagranplazamall.com
HOURS: Sun.-Fri. 9 A.M.-9 P.M., Sat. 10 A.M.-9 P.M.
Map 11

This giant mall, based on the Latin tradition of a city square of shops, caters to the needs of Fort Worth's ever-growing Hispanic population. It's in a kind of depressing part of town, but La Gran Plaza's mix of shops is colorful and unique, including a supermarket, several Western wear shops, and retail stores of all types and sizes.

MOCKINGBIRD STATION
5331 E. Mockingbird La., 214/421-5638,
www.mockingbirdstation.com
Map 4

A fairly new development, Mockingbird Station's hip, modern outdoor design comprises the bottom floor of a loft apartment building popular among SMU students. The shops here—American Apparel, West Elm, Urban Outfitters—cater to such a demographic. One end of the area is anchored by the lovely, arty Angelika theater and the hopping Irish pub Trinity Hall.

◖ NORTHPARK CENTER
8786 N. Central Expy., 214/361-6345,
www.northparkcenter.com
HOURS: Mon.-Sat. 10 A.M.-9 P.M., Sun. noon-6 P.M.
Map 3

You won't find any dingy head shops or discount stores at NorthPark Center, located just on the north cusp of the ritzy Southern Methodist University area, but you will find a colossal AMC movie theater, world-class art like sculpture by Mark di Suvero, a garden courtyard, and a library. Oh yeah—there are shops too, dozens of high-enders like Neiman's, Michael Kors, Bvlgari, and many others.

UNIVERSITY PARK VILLAGE

1612 S. University Dr., 817/654-0521,
www.universityparkvillage.com

Map 9

This outdoor mall has everything you need when it comes to the better franchise stores— Banana Republic, Ann Taylor, Talbot's, etc.— plus a few locals thrown in.

Boutiques

A. HOOPER'S & CO.

4601 West Fwy., 817/348-9911
HOURS: Mon.-Fri. 10 A.M.-6 P.M., Sat. 11 A.M.-5 P.M.

Map 10

This popular, enduring, modern spot brings a touch of New York couture, including Vince, Michael Stars, and Chloe, to Cowtown. Beware: As with any true house of fashion, you'll need good luck finding anything larger than a size 6 or 8, and bring your platinum card.

ALLIE-COOSH

6726 Snider Plaza, 214/363-8616
HOURS: Mon.-Sat. 10 A.M.-6 P.M.

Map 3

Owner/designer Paulette Martsolf creates one-of-a-kind, practical apparel that suits almost every body type. Her boutique, in one of the most exclusive shopping areas in Dallas, features her collection of ladies' wear that is cut and stitched in her own workshop in town. All of Martsolf's works utilize luxurious materials,

NEIMAN MARCUS FLAGSHIP

It all began here.

Dallas' reputation as a place where shopping is considered a contact sport began at the corner of Main and Ervay Streets, where Herbert Marcus, his sister Carrie M. Neiman, and her husband Al Neiman founded Neiman Marcus stores.

Today, the square footage of all of Neiman Marcus Group's retail holdings totals about five million square feet. In 1914, when the store opened its second "original" location (the first, built in 1907, was destroyed in a fire), it was merely a few floors.

Those floors, however, held something unique. When Marcus and the Neimans founded the store, they insisted from the beginning it was not a department store but rather something new: A specialty store catering to women who desired items that were both high quality *and* ready to wear. For years since, the hallowed ground here has acted as the cornerstone not just of fashionable aesthetic but of good taste and customer service.

Even for those less inclined to splurge on the latest bit of couture revel in the elegant and storied surroundings of the original store. Walking in off the downtown street is like walking out of a time capsule and into an era when shopping was an experience, not just a chore. Elevators open up to reveal glorious displays on every floor. The Zodiac restaurant beckons with old-school lunches like lobster salad and strawberry-butter popovers. Each floor is mod yet modern, with special touches of décor and service with a personal touch.

All that would be nothing if the product lacked, but fashion-philes still consider the place Mecca. For all of Dallas shopping destinations, none is as jam-packed with high quality names, goods from known designers and new phenoms, as Neiman Marcus. It is the epicenter.

like high-quality wools and silks, with subdued colors and a classic touch—perfect for traveling or for upper-crust dinner parties at home.

ANGIE AMADI

53 Highland Park Village, 214/559-4050

HOURS: Mon.-Sat. 10 A.M.-5 P.M.

Map 3

Small and choosy, this Highland Park Village boutique stocks high-end names, both trendy and classic.

ARMHOLE

1350 Manufacturing St., 214/760-7373, www.armhole.com

HOURS: By appointment.

Map 11

Sigh. Back in the day, Armhole was housed in an Uptown storefront, and the coolest of the cool could saunter in and choose their iron-on art and a T-shirt, and the Armhole folks would press it right there on the spot at the "T-shirt bar." The company has since moved to the more industrial (and aptly named) Manufacturing Street in the Dallas Market District, making walk-ins pretty much an impossibility. A good business move, perhaps, but sad for folks who want to make one-of-a-kind riffs on "I'm With Stupid." The good news is the Armhole peeps are still in the one-off business. Just give them a call and tell them what you're thinking, and they'll be happy to set up the T-shirt bar.

CARLA MARTINENGO BOUTIQUE

4528 McKinney Ave., 214/522-9284

HOURS: Mon.-Sat. 9:30 A.M.-6 P.M.

Map 3

Who knew this tiny, exclusive little boutique would end up such a power player in the Dallas fashion world? With an elite collection of designer pieces (Chloe, Blumarine, Gaultier) that are tough to find in the U.S., Martinengo's shop is like a bit of Milan transported to Dallas.

COWBOY COOL

3699 McKinney Ave., Ste. 407, 800/966-0122, www.cowboycool.com

HOURS: Mon.-Sat. 11 A.M.-7 P.M.

Map 2

When Kid Rock needs some skull cowboy boots or Billy Bob Thorton needs some skull...anything, they head straight for Cowboy Cool, a hip little store that features rock 'n' roll–laced casual clothes for men and women. The place may be best known for its unique cowboy boots that riff on heavy metal and goth influences, and the shirts, jeans, and dresses follow suit. Check the cool collection

Madonna and other stars pick up their hipster cowboy gear at Cowboy Cool.

© TEXAS TOURISM/KENNY BRAUN

of belt buckles if you're on a budget, and the small collection of rock memorabilia that's for sale if you're not.

CULLWELL & SON

6319 Hillcrest Ave., 214/522-7000

HOURS: Mon.-Sat. 9 A.M.-6 P.M.

Map 3

Housed in an enormous, beautiful store with dark gleaming wood and hardwood floors, Cullwell & Son has everything you need to smartly outfit several generations' worth of men: custom suits, shirts, tuxedos, shoes, and high-end casual wear for adults, adolescents, and boys, plus a tailoring department, "grooming room," and even a dry cleaners—all provided with excellent customer service.

DEAN-KINGSTON

821 Foch St., 817/689-8323

HOURS: Mon.-Fri. 10 A.M.-6 P.M., Sat. 10 A.M.-7 P.M.

Map 10

Both men's and women's fashion get playful at Dean-Kingston, a sunny storefront in Fort Worth's hopping West 7th Street area. The store celebrates classic upscale casualness (a pair of vintage Cadillac tailfins jut up from the roof, while the inside exudes a mid-century California cool), but is by no means low-rent—not with names like Ben Sherman, Custo Barcelona, and Nat Nast on the racks. While there definitely is plenty for the ladies here, Dean-Kingston pays attention to the metrosexual hidden in every man, featuring lots of dude-ish stuff like humidors and barwear.

EMERALDS TO COCONUTS

2730 Henderson Ave., 214/823-3620

HOURS: Mon.-Sat. 10 A.M.-7 P.M.

Map 2

Sure, Dallas has plenty of fancy-pants boutiques, but about the loony lady stores? You know, with incense, big clunky jewelry, and flowing skirts? The kind of place where you can pick up a sweater for your aunt's birthday and a cute bracelet for yourself? That place is Emeralds to Coconuts. Hemp and linen clothes aren't for everyone, to be sure, but those who lean toward the more bohemian look will adore the flowy outfits here, along with the concho belts, flip-flops, and other kooky bits.

EPIPHANY BOUTIQUE

412 N. Bishop Ave., 214/946-4411,

www.epiphanyboutique.com

HOURS: Mon.-Sat. 10 A.M.-5 P.M.

Map 6

Like the funky neighborhood that surrounds it, Epiphany is cool, laid-back, and eclectic. The collection of baby tees alone could easily provide a young Dallas woman with her summer wardrobe. Have one of the friendly staff help you match up one of those tees with some Chile Pepper jeans, and you're set for at least 85 percent of your social engagements. In all honesty, Epiphany is for the ladies, but men can pick up a snarky T-shirt or a pair of nicer jeans as well. Epiphany also stocks spa and bath items.

FORTY FIVE TEN

4510 McKinney Ave., 214/559-4510,

www.fortyfiveten.com

HOURS: Mon.-Sat. 10 A.M.-6 P.M.

Map 2

The word "boutique" usually conjures up the idea of a small, intimate storefront. Forty Five Ten basks in a luxurious 8,000 square feet, complete with courtyard fountain, café, and celebrity clientele, but it's a boutique nonetheless; that is, despite its breadth, the aesthetic of this housewares/

accessories/furniture store is governed by a unique sensibility.

HAUTE BABY

5350 W. Lovers La., 214/357-3068,
www.hautebaby.com

HOURS: Mon.-Sat. 10 A.M.-5 P.M.

Map 3

The infant and toddler clothes at Haute Baby are precious in all senses of the word: Indeed, they are simply adorable, but also expensive. Still, if you're willing to spend as much on a onesie as you are on dinner, your rugrat will be the best dressed person in the room.

HD'S CLOTHING COMPANY

3014-3018 Greenville Ave., 214/821-8900,
www.hdsclothing.com

HOURS: Mon.-Fri. 11 A.M.-7 P.M., Sat. 11 A.M.-6 P.M.,
Sun. noon-5 P.M.

Map 4

In a town full of clothiers of all kinds, there is no other shop like HD's Clothing Company. Simply put, even though the shop has been around since 1981, proprietors Harry and Vicki DeMarco are always two steps ahead of the curve, filling their cool industrial space with the latest and most unique casual men's and women's clothing before anyone can say "Diesel." There's definitely a Euro-flair thing going on here, as the DeMarcos import their goods from all the continental hot spots: Milan, Rome, Paris. But don't let that scare you off—there's no attitude here, just Texas charm and personalized service.

HOUSE OF DANG!

4219 Bryan St., 214/827-1146, www.houseofdang.com

HOURS: Tues.-Sat. 11 A.M.-7 P.M., Sun. 1-5 P.M.

Map 5

In 2004, when Dallas Art Institute graduates

Doug Voisin and Andrew Bayer tired of producing fashion shows that featured broom skirts and concho belts (and who wouldn't?), they figured they'd start shilling their own ready-to-wears. Setting up shop in an Old East Dallas storefront, they began House of Dang!, a store that definitely bears their unique mark. Though the House offers vintage finds, funky art, and a variety of designers, the centerpiece is definitely the HOD! label, instantly notable for its youthful flourish, bright colors, and cheeky patterns.

(J. SAUNDERS

4303 Camp Bowie Blvd., 817/732-8155

HOURS: Mon.-Sat. 10 A.M.-6 P.M.

Map 10

For years, this Camp Bowie institution has been *the* source for Westsiders in search of well-priced, unique formalwear, especially prom dresses. It's a touch tiny, but the personalized service and unique selection are worth it.

KACKY & CARL

2722 Routh St., 214/295-4486,
www.kackyandcarl.com

HOURS: Mon.-Fri. 11 A.M.-7 P.M., Sat. 11 A.M.-6 P.M.

Map 2

Conceived by a pair of Oklahoma transplants who both attended SMU, Kacky & Carl found a niche and then filled it with everything from zebra-striped couches to costume jewelry. The store, which takes up the bottom floor of an early 20th-century brick home off of McKinney Avenue, has been a hit from the get-go: Dallasites simply adore the unique designer clothes, knickknacks, and even high-end pet items that fill the space.

KEN'S MAN'S SHOP

309 Preston Royal Village, 214/369-5367,
www.kensmansshop.com

HOURS: Fri.-Weds. 10 A.M.-6 P.M., Thurs. 10 A.M.-8 P.M.
Map 11

No other men's clothing store in Dallas rivals Ken's for history and personality. Ken Helfman opened his store in 1964 and, through a bit of luck, found his natty threads had a following among many members of the (then-new and much more popular) Dallas Cowboys. In these parts, that's like God endorsing your wares, and since then, Helfman has successfully outfitted generations of Dallas men and their sons. Fortunately, Helfman doesn't just have Tom Landry's legend on his side—he carries upscale labels as well as his own sophisticated designs, and is known for the kind of stellar customer service you rarely encounter these days. If you buy a suit, take advantage of the on-site tailor and have it custom fitted, or simply stroll around and eye the gifts and antiques that are for sale.

KRIMSON & KLOVER

3111 Cole Ave., Ste. 101, 214/871-2334,
www.krimsonandklover.com
HOURS: Mon.-Fri. 11 A.M.-7 P.M., Sat. 11 A.M.-6 P.M.
Map 2

Fashionable threads for the youthful set (read: SMU students) fill this cutesy little store that has made a name for itself as an Uptown shopping staple. Customers regard K&K's stock of affordable designer tees, dresses, and accessories as a reliable source for everything from casual, everyday wear to that hard-to-find wedding outfit. The bright collection here lists more toward fun, West Coast, L.A. style versus New York-y runway seriousness.

MINE

4423 Lovers La., 214/522-4700, www.minedallas.com
HOURS: Mon.-Sat. 10 A.M.-6 P.M.

Map 3

This well-lit, high-ceilinged little shop (complete with exposed rafters and adorable chandeliers) houses a perfect collection for college women with credit cards or young professionals looking for an outfit for a casual night out on the town. Tom Ford, Yumi Kim, and Denim of Virtue are just some of the names you'll see sewn onto the labels of the high-end jeans, skirts, dresses, and accessories here.

RAGAN BURNS

5500 W. Lovers La., 214/369-1133
HOURS: Mon.-Sat. 10 A.M.-6 P.M.
Map 3

Simple and classy, the Ragan Burns men's clothing store stocks top names (like Robert Talbott, Burberry, and Ike Behar) in menswear and provides top service (like custom clothing and custom tailoring), to boot. In short, expect an old-school approach without the crustiness.

RICH HIPPIE

5350 W. Lovers La., Ste. 127, 214/358-1968,
www.richhippie.com
HOURS: Mon.-Sat. 10 A.M.-5:30 P.M.
Map 3

Rich Hippie owner Eric Kimmel recently created a line of clothing he calls "trashion," in which he takes name-brand items that are no longer usable to Sierra Leone, where Kimmel pays a collection of villagers to transform them with their own indigenous touches. There's no better name for the goods available at his boutique: funky, high-end, fashionable items that are utterly unique. From Park Cities society soccer moms to edgy fashionistas, everyone adores Kimmel's selection of jewelry, clothes, and groovy gewgaws.

SARTEL

4212 Oak Lawn Ave., 214/520-7176

HOURS: Mon.-Sat. 10 A.M.-6 P.M.

Map 2

Sartel owners Michael Eastman and Lily Hanbury cultivate their inventory with a brand of particularity resembling that of a museum curator. All that intensity pays off, as very select pieces from various designers are interspersed with Eastman's own runway collection. There's no filler at this boutique, just gorgeous, one-of-a-kind items.

SPOILED PINK

4824 Camp Bowie Blvd., 817/737-7465,

www.spoiledpink.com

HOURS: Mon. 11 A.M.-6 P.M., Tues.-Fri. 10 A.M.-6 P.M., Sat. 10 A.M.-5 P.M.

Map 10

Spoiled Pink keeps up with more youthful trends than a MySpace page. The look here is designer denim, ironic T-shirts, and Betsey Johnson, but at prices even a teenager can afford.

TEESIE'S ATTIC

4000 Arlington Highlands Blvd., Ste. 169, Arlington, 817/465-7200, www.teesiesattic.com

HOURS: Mon.-Sat. 10 A.M.-6 P.M.

Map 11

Jeans, jeans, jeans—Texans love them, and there's no better place to get them than Teesie's. We're not talking Wranglers and Rocky Mountains (see Western Wear for those); we're talking 7 for All Mankind, Joe's Jeans, Rick & Republic, and other premium brands, plus lots of shoes and tops to match, all at this little piece of L.A. in the middle of Arlington.

VOD BOUTIQUE

2418 Victory Park La., 214/754-0644

HOURS: Mon.-Sat. 11 A.M.-7 P.M., Sun. noon-5 P.M.

Map 1

Cool, breezy, and expensive, VOD Boutique doesn't fool around when it comes to high-end clothing. The one-of-kind inventory here covers a lot of the latest ground from designers such as Alexander Wang and Pauric Sweeny, but the real treats are the appointment-only shoe boutique-within-a-boutique and the collection of vintage wear curated by local store Archive Vintage. Oh, and you must check out Houston designer Diane Izzadin's line of jeans, available only at VOD.

Antiques and Vintage Clothing

CATTLE BARN FLEA MARKET

3401 W. Lancaster Ave., Barn 1, 817/473-0505

HOURS: Sat. 8 A.M.-5 P.M., Sun. 9 A.M.-4 P.M.

Map 10

Air-conditioned and jam-packed with antiques, collectibles, junk, and farm and ranch equipment, this is one of Fort Worth's most frequented flea markets. Besides the steals and deals, visitors enjoy the added benefit of the barn's genuine atmosphere—this is where real modern ranch folks do much of their buying, selling, wheeling, and dealing.

CLOTHES CIRCUIT

6105 Sherry La., 214/696-8634,

www.clothescircuit.com

HOURS: Mon.-Sat. 10 A.M.-7 P.M., Sun. noon-6 P.M.

Map 3

You know you're in Dallas when labels on even

used clothes read "Chanel" and "Prada." That's exactly what you'll find at Clothes Circuit: gently used couture and high-end ladies' wear, handbags, shoes, furs, and accessories. Don't go expecting bargain basement prices—you're not gonna find those Manolos at a thrift-store discount—but you'll find the inventory much more affordable than their brand new counterparts. Be sure to check the racks of designer suits and seasonal furs.

CURIOSITIES

2025 Abrams Rd., 214/828-1886

HOURS: Thurs.-Sat. 11 A.M.-8 P.M., Tues.-Weds. 11 A.M.-6 P.M.

Map 4

Curious, indeed—this Lakewood resale store is filled with wonderful gewgaws and awesome oddities that range from the kitschy to the glitzy. But don't figure on a granny's attic atmosphere:

The goods are curated with an eagle eye for quality, and the store is crisply run and organized. Curiosities also features a gallery showcasing out-of-the-box artists, many of whom utilize folk art and found objects in their work.

TRADER'S VILLAGE

2602 Mayfield Road, Grand Prairie, 972/647-8205, www.tradersvillage.com

HOURS: Sat.-Sun. 8 A.M.-dusk

Map 11

You'll literally find everything under the sun at this year-round, 106-acre outdoor flea market. Some of it's junk, some of it's secret finds—most of it's in between—but there's definitely something for everyone. Should you prefer other forms of entertainment besides browsing, Trader's Village is always hopping with kids' games, rides, festivals, and food.

Western and Work Wear

◖ DICKIES FACTORY OUTLET

521 W. Vickery Blvd., 817/877-0387, www.dickies.com

HOURS: Mon.-Sat. 10:30 A.M.-6:30 P.M.

Map 8

Dickies' colorful sideways horseshoe logo should be familiar to anyone who has paid attention to hipster clothing trends in recent years, but the work clothes supplier was cool in Fort Worth well before fashion developed its blue-collar fetish. That's because Dickies, which began in Fort Worth in 1922 as the Williamson-Dickie company, has long provided the town—and eventually the nation—with high-quality, low-cost work gear. Building on the brand's recent upswing in popularity, Dickies has been expanding its line

to cute, durable casual wear that only hints at its blue-collar legacy. The outlet is tucked away on an industrial street just south of I-30 where it meets downtown, and it's filled with cool attire for the whole family: men's cargo shorts, ladies' fitted logo tees, even kids' pajamas are available at a discount. Oh, and you can still find that perfect pair of work boots or a good pair of chef's pants, too, all at prices a working guy or gal can afford.

JUSTIN BOOT COMPANY FACTORY OUTLET

717 W. Vickery Blvd., 817/654-3103, www.justinboots.com

HOURS: Mon.-Sat. 9 A.M.-5 P.M.

Map 8

It's a little hard to find, but once you open the

door and the smell of leather hits you in the face, you know you've found the right place. Any cowboy worth his oats has at least one pair of Justins in his closet and another on his feet; the Fort Worth–based Western wear is a respected name in boot-making, a favorite brand among all types of cowpokes, because of the footwear's durability, style, and comfort. At the outlet store, you'll find a huge selection of "irregular" cowboy and work boots, most of which have slight defects that are hardly noticeable, at discounted prices.

LUSKEY'S/RYON'S WESTERN WEAR

2601 N. Main St., 817/625-2391,
www.luskeys.com
HOURS: Mon.-Sat. 9 A.M.-6 P.M., Sun. 1-5 P.M.
`Map 7`

Since 1919, the Luskeys and the Ryons have outfitted Fort Worth with both off-the-rack and custom-made Western clothes, work clothes, and tack and saddle (the Luskey family takes care of the garments, while the Ryons do the leatherwork). Nowadays, the well-stocked store features all sorts of Western wear from big names like Wrangler, Justin, and Carhartt. A good place to one-stop shop, from hats to boots.

MAVERICK FINE WESTERN WEAR

1000 E. Exchange Ave., 817/626-1129,
www.maverickwesternwear.com
HOURS: Mon.-Thurs. 10 A.M.-6 P.M.,
Fri.-Sat. 10 A.M.-10 P.M., Sun. 11 A.M.-6 P.M.
`Map 7`

Where else but Texas could you belly up to the bar, order a cold one, and then turn around and shop for Western gear? Yep, Maverick Western Wear sells two things that Texans love—booze and boots—all in the middle of the ambience of the Stockyards. Weirdly, along

© JONANNA WIDNER

Buy boots and booze at Maverick Fine Western Wear.

with their fine supply of cowboy clothes, the folks at Maverick also carry biker-style jewelry and clothing.

M. L. LEDDY'S

2455 N. Main St., 817/624-3149, www.leddys.com
HOURS: Mon.-Sat. 9 A.M.-6 P.M.
`Map 7`

This spacious store, appropriately situated in the same corner store in the Stockyards since before World War II, offers an excellent variety of Western clothes and accessories for men and women. But Leddy's is really known for its leatherwork—detailed, hand-tooled boots; custom saddles hand-worked from start to finish; beautifully crafted stirrups. Whether it's a yellow rose etched on an ostrich boot or an intricate design on a $5,000 saddle, if it's from Leddy's, it has been made with four generations of care behind it.

M. L. Leddy's craftsmen build their tack and saddlewear by hand.

PETER BROS. HATS

909 Houston St., 817/335-1715, www.peterbros.com

HOURS: Mon.-Sat. 10 A.M.-6 P.M.

Map 8

Any cowpoke worth his or her salt will tell you that when it comes to hats, there's more than just Stetsons. That's where Peter Brothers comes in. This store has been around for decades, and they've never made anything except hats—every make and model you can imagine. They also custom-make hats and can even re-create one from a photograph.

RETRO COWBOY

406 Houston St., 817/338-1194

HOURS: Mon.-Thurs. 10 A.M.-7 P.M., Fri.-Sat. 10 A.M.-10 P.M., Sun. noon-5 P.M.

Map 8

Tongue-in-cheek Texas goods are in abundance at Retro Cowboy. Make sure to order a Dublin Dr. Pepper when you step inside to check out all the Western-theme souvenirs (like the John Wayne lunchboxes), and sip on that sucker while you peruse the pearl snap–button shirts, cowgirl bags, and baby-size cowboy boots.

WESTERN WEAR EXCHANGE

2809 Alta Mere Dr., 817/738-4048, www.westernwearexchange.com

HOURS: Mon.-Sat. 10 A.M.-6 P.M.

Map 10

Western Wear Exchange is a pearl snap–button lover's dream. This consignment/resale store has racks and racks of vintage and used cowboy wear, including the hipster-favored pearl-snap shirts, plus all sorts of famous brand-name jeans, boots, hats, and belts. The store takes 50 percent off the asking price, which gets cut by another 25 percent after 60 days. The proprietors are sticklers for both condition and quality—much of the stock borders on new.

◀ WILD BILL'S WESTERN STORE

311 N. Market St., 214/262-4479, www.wildbillswestern.com

HOURS: Mon.-Fri. 10 A.M.-9 P.M., Sat. 10 A.M.-10 P.M., Sun. noon-6 P.M.

Map 1

For such a touristy locale, Wild Bill's certainly maintains some decent prices, especially on oft-marked-up Western wear like boots and belt buckles. Wild Bill's has those for as little as $100 and $12, respectively, which is unheard of in these parts. Steer clear of the overpriced menswear and hats, though. And while the lower-priced boots are there for a steal, Bill's also provides custom boots for a much heftier fee.

Bath, Beauty, and Spa

MARIE ANTOINETTE'S PARFUMERIE

101 W. 2nd St., 817/332-3888,
www.marieantoinettespa.com
HOURS: Mon.-Thurs. 10 A.M.-7 P.M., Fri.-Sat.
10 A.M.-9 P.M.
Map 8

Worthy of the indulgent attachments of its namesake, Marie Antoinette's Parfumerie is a one-of-its-kind for Fort Worth. Here you can choose from delicate bath items like soaps, essential oils, and lotions, but the coolest part is the parfumerie, in which the staff will help you create your own personal scent.

SHAMBHALA BODY GALLERY

320 W. 7th St., 214/943-7627,
www.shambalasoaps.com
HOURS: Tues.-Thurs. 11 A.M.-7 P.M., Fri.-Sat. 11 A.M.-9 P.M.,
Sun. 11 A.M.-5 P.M.
Map 6

Soothing and yummy-smelling, the soaps, scrubs, and lotions in this New Age–leaning store make for perfect gifts for those who eschew mass-produced products. The "lotion sticks" are especially popular.

VESSELS

301 Main St., 817/882-8743, www.giftvessels.com
HOURS: Mon.-Thurs. 10 A.M.-8 P.M., Fri.-Sat.
10 A.M.-10 P.M., Sun. noon-6 P.M.
Map 8

The folks at Vessels proudly proclaim they will help you find exactly what you're looking for, even if you don't know what that is. Embracing that state of ambiguousness is the most fun way to approach this store, and probably the best way to choose a gift. Browse around and sample the baskets of bath products and candles, or ask one of the friendly salespeople to pick out some chocolates and wine. Whatever you decide, the skilled hands here will wrap it beautifully, and to your specifications.

Gift and Home

NAMASTE

3418 W. 7th St., 817/989-0800, www.asia2africa.com
HOURS: Weds.-Sat. 10 A.M.-6 P.M.
Map 10

In the market for an African tribal headdress? How about a religious dance dress from Bhutan? A hand-woven basket with boar tusk handles? Namaste has the market cornered on exotic wares from far-off lands like Africa, Tibet, and the Far East. The store's far-flung variety sometimes resembles a museum, with rarities like Zulu spears and Tibetan scripture tables, but smaller-scale objects like clothing, toys, and even ostrich handbags abound.

NEST

6731 Snider Plaza, 214/373-4444, www.nestdallas.com
HOURS: Mon.-Sat. 10 A.M.-5:30 P.M.
Map 3

It's all about design at this home/stationery store. Nest is the kind of place you can find cute little items for the guest bathroom or

GET YOUR PINK ON

Alongside a busy highway in Addison, just north of Dallas, sits a large office building. Unlike many of the soulless glass-and-steel structures in this part of town, this one has character: It sprawls in a graceful half-moon arc around the entry grounds, the neatly trimmed grass cooling and welcome amidst Addison's miles of corporate concrete. A huge, handsome fountain bubbles before the impressively heavy glass doors. Inside, the lobby's polished floors, fantastically high ceiling, and glossy wood make it feel more like a swank hotel than the usual hive for worker bees. Smartly dressed women, all in skirts – nary a pantsuit in sight – dart around, the click of their sharp high heels echoing off the...pink granite walls? Welcome to **Mary Kay's** world headquarters.

In 1963, Mary Kay Ash from Hot Wells, Texas quit her job. She was in direct sales, and damn good at it, and the constant parade of men passing her by as they were promoted sickened her. So she quit, gathered up her $5,000 in savings, and started her own business.

Some would call it the business of selling make-up, but Mary Kay would call it the business of beauty. Her first headquarters on Exchange Park was as sparse as the current one is lavish, just one room, a shelf and a few bits of furniture. The one in Addison? Thirteen stories. Thirty-four acres. Six hundred thousand square feet. She came a long way, baby.

Before her death in 2001, Mary Kay had built a multi-billion-dollar company, famous for giving pink Cadillacs to its best salespeople, inspired an almost cult-like following, and became one of the most famous women in the world.

It's a feel good story, but a controversial one. Many people consider Mary Kay's company to be a pyramid scheme that preys on the insecurities of American women. Others claim it's an empowering organization, one that boosts its employees and salespeople's confidence while helping others bring out their own beauty.

Whichever you believe, Mary Kay's hold on people is crystal clear the minute you eyeball the giant pink monolith that juts into the sky above Addison. There's no way to fully grasp the company's influence and presence on American culture, and corporate culture, until you walk through those big glass doors.

Lest you feel odd about marching into a random office building, don't worry – Mary Kay aficionados flock to the **Mary Kay Headquarters and Museum** (16251 Dallas Pkwy., 972/687-5720, www.marykay.com, Tues.-Fri. 9 A.M.-4:30 P.M.) and it's encouraged (if you'd like a group tour, call three days in advance to book it). The museum is small, but impressive and fun, although the tributes to the "spirit of Mary Kay" can get a bit cloying. Definitely check out the displays about the much-coveted rewards given to salespeople, including the big mama of them all, the pink Caddy.

---

tasteful new takes on mid-century furniture. If you're on a budget and can't afford a $2,000 chair, check out their collection of gorgeous imported stationery, teapots, or tableware.

PS THE LETTER

5136 Camp Bowie Blvd., 817/731-2032,

www.pstheletter.com

HOURS: Mon.-Fri. 10 A.M.-6 P.M., Sat. 10 A.M.-5 P.M.

Map 10

Owner Linda Motley manages to pack a surprisingly large inventory of famous-name china, classic tableware, and fine crystal into this modestly sized store in the middle of one of Camp Bowie's shopping strips. Of course, as the name indicates, there's plenty of stationery here, too, especially that of the wedding ilk—the store is a favorite resource for wedding needs and registries.

Books and Music

BILL'S RECORDS

1313 S. Lamar St., 214/421-1500, www.billsrecords.com
HOURS: Mon.-Thurs. 10:30 A.M.-10 P.M., Fri.-Sat.
10:30 A.M.-midnight, Sun. noon-10 P.M.
Map 6

You never know what you're gonna get from Bill's—selection-wise, service-wise, and price-wise. Back when it was called Bill's Records and Tapes, this place was a music lover's mecca, the only place to find obscure Texas vinyl and that rare Smiths import you'd been searching for since 1986. But it always came with a touch of oddness—owner Bill Wisener, for instance, decides on each item's price based on, well, his own whim. That hasn't changed, nor has the haphazard organization or the cloud from Wisener's cigarettes. All the quirks are a turn-off to some, but to many, Bill's stands as one of the few record stores left with any character.

BRYSTONE'S CHILDREN'S BOOKS

6101 Watuga Rd., Ste. C, 817/656-9070,
www.brystone.booksense.com
HOURS: Mon.-Thurs. 10 A.M.-6 P.M., Fri.-Sat.
10 A.M.-5 P.M.
Map 11

Literary kids and parents alike dig this independently owned children's bookstore, an unexpected treat in the middle of Fort Worth's suburbs. The store specializes in high-quality books for the junior literary set, from picture books to kid lit to older kids' fare like Nancy Drew and the Hardy Boys. Although the prices are, in some cases, a touch higher than at the chain stores, you'll find the selection unbeatable, especially the stock of Newberry Award winners.

CD SOURCE

5500 Greenville Ave., 214/890-2900
HOURS: Mon.-Thurs. 10 A.M.-10 P.M.,
Fri.-Sat. 10 A.M.-10:30 P.M., Sun. noon-10 P.M.
Map 3

With the constant stream of patrons both selling and buying used CDs at this strip-mall store on Upper Greenville, it's amazing the hinges on the front door don't break. Fortunately, the high volume here doesn't translate to a dilution in quality. Quite the opposite: CD Source has a knack for always stocking the good stuff, including a surprisingly large supply of box sets and lots of new releases.

FOREVER YOUNG RECORDS

2955 S. Hwy. 380, 972/352-6299,
www.foreveryoungrecords.com
HOURS: Mon.-Sat. 10 A.M.-10 P.M., Sun. noon-6 P.M.
Map 11

Nowadays, any old place with three milk crates' worth of LPs is considered a record store; the family-owned and -operated Forever Young reminds us what a real record store should be. Walking through the giant fake jukebox facade that makes up the store's entry, vinyl-heads are treated to an old-school sight: 250,000 pieces of vinyl, cassettes, eight-tracks, music DVDs, and yeah, even CDs. There's something here for everybody, be they casual collector or serious music scholar, and the inventory spans decades (and about 11,000 square feet).

◖ GOOD RECORDS

1808 Greenville Ave., 214/752-4663,
www.goodrecords.com
HOURS: Mon.-Thurs. 10 A.M.-11 P.M., Fri.-Sat.

10 A.M.–midnight, Sun. 11 A.M.–9 P.M.

Map 4

It may be simply named, but Good Records has lots going on. This Greenville Avenue spot is a must-stop for Dallas lovers of independent and local music. The proprietors here know their stuff, as does all the staff; any choice from their rotating recommended selections is a guaranteed good listen. Here you'll find a high-quality selection of new and used CDs, vinyl, T-shirts, and other cool stuff, plus periodic in-store visits from indie and up-and-coming artists.

HALF PRICE BOOKS

5803 Northwest Hwy., 214/379-8000

HOURS: Daily 9 A.M.–11 P.M.

Map 11

Yes, it is a nationwide chain—heck, there are about six or seven Half Price outposts in the DFW area alone—but the sheer size of the Northwest Highway location makes it a must-visit for any reader. The sucker is as big

and cavernous as several airplane hangars put together, housing an equally enormous selection of used books. Special treats are the well-stocked art/photography selection, tons of used records, and the clearance section, where many a fine book can be picked up for a dollar.

PAPERBACKS PLUS

6115 La Vista Dr., 214/827-4860,
www.luckydogbooks.com

HOURS: Mon.–Sat. 9 A.M.–9 P.M., Sun. 11 A.M.–7 P.M.

Map 4

Paperbacks Plus is the best of the very few independently owned used bookstores in town. The two-story Lakewood location is a charmer, its strip-mall exterior belying the charisma of the interior's rambling rooms and staircases. Upstairs is the home of the Writer's Garret, a nonprofit group that holds classes, lectures, and readings. Often you'll find the sidewalk surrounding the store filled with books free for the taking.

Sports

BASS PRO SHOPS

2501 Bass Pro Dr., Grapevine, 972/724-2018,
www.basspro.com

HOURS: Mon.–Sat. 9 A.M.–10 P.M., Sun. 10 A.M.–7 P.M.

Map 11

Bass Pro Shops are, of course, an enormous nationwide chain, but their outposts are so massive and so well stocked with fishing, hunting, camping, and other outdoor goods that no sports enthusiast should bypass a visit. The word "store" doesn't do the DFW location justice: Here, thousands upon thousands of square feet of rods and reels, kayaks, guns,

tents, boats, golf gear, taxidermy, clothing, and orienteering gear abound, surrounded by dramatic artifice like a fish pond and waterfall. The store also offers tons of outdoor skills workshops and classes.

COLLECTOR'S COVEY

5550 W. Lovers La., 800/521-2403

HOURS: Mon.–Sat. 10 A.M.–6 P.M.

Map 3

Think of Collector's Covey as the antithesis of Bass Pro Shops. Whereas the latter is buzzing, democratic, and overstuffed with outdoor gear, the former is quiet, restrained, and bedecked with the accoutrements of the sporting life. The Covey's clubby feel manifests in its inventory of manly goodies, like expensive knives, hand-carved duck decoys, stamp prints, and watercolor paintings of mallards. This is the place to buy something for the man who not only owns his own duck blind, but the 1,000 acres it sits on as well.

LUKE'S LOCKER

3607 Oak Lawn Ave., 214/528-1290,
www.lukeslocker.com
HOURS: Mon.-Fri. 10 A.M.-7 P.M., Sat. 10 A.M.-6 P.M.,
Sun. noon-5 P.M.
Map 2

Those horrible souls in life we know as "people who exercise" will find themselves in heaven at Luke's Locker (while they're shopping there, feel free to pop next door to Lucky's and grab a cinnamon roll). Runners especially will swoon at the selection of Nike gear, tons of running shoes, and those little short shorts. Luke's has been around for years and is the go-to place when you need something in which to sweat. Best of all, the salespeople really know their stuff when it comes to running shoes.

Toys

FROGGIE'S 5&10

3211 Knox St., 214/522-5867, www.froggies5and10.com
HOURS: Mon.-Sat. 10 A.M.-9 P.M., Sun. noon-6 P.M.
Map 3

The parking sucks, the location is tough to get to, and it's a touch pricey. So why go to Froggie's? Two words: Sea Monkeys. Actually, that's not all they have. While Froggie's is one of those toy stores that secretly caters to adults, it's still a welcome respite from hyperactive video games and blingy Barbies. It's old-school here, and said Sea Monkeys have plenty of company amid the great kids' books, science games, and Rubik's cubes, which may be easier to solve than getting a parking spot.

Pets

LUCKY DOG BARKERY

8413 Preston Center Plaza, 214/368-6000,
www.theluckydogbarkery.com
HOURS: Mon.-Sat. 10 A.M.-6 P.M.
Map 3

Any dog who received something from this pet boutique would be a lucky one indeed. The Barkery has a giant collection of collars, leashes, pet clothes, beds, and toys for that special Fido, along with an assortment of organic, healthy food and treats.

HOTELS

The accommodations in Dallas, as in many large cities, lean heavily on chains, and there are plenty of those to choose from in any price range. For the most part, this section doesn't include those obvious choices, unless there's a particular quality—amenities, location, luxury—that makes it a notable choice.

As far as hotels in general, Dallas likes to go big, opulent, and amenity-laden, and "trendy" might be added to that list of late, as a number of nationwide name hotels have sprung up around town—the W Hotel and Hotel Zaza, to name but two (a Mandarin Hotel was beginning to take shape downtown on the edge of Victory Park, but in 2008 the economic downturn brought construction to a halt). There's no lack of high-end accommodations, from the staid and stately (such as the Mansion on Turtle Creek and the Adolphus) to the sleek and mod (such as the Palomar and the Hotel Lumen).

Although many of Dallas's hotels sprawl in a grand scale, in recent years a number of boutique—or at least boutique-*ish*—hotels have cropped up, but these also list toward the high end.

You won't find too many low-key hostels or B&Bs around these parts. Like the rest of Dallas, the hotel world here keeps it big and boisterous.

HIGHLIGHTS

LOOK FOR **[C** TO FIND RECOMMENDED HOTELS.

[C **Best Hotel Bar:** So many...so, so many. Try either of the two bars at **The Hotel Adolphus** . If you can't afford to stay there, at least you're able to bask in the opulence and people-watch people who can (page 165).

[C **Best Haunted Hotel:** Several ghosts supposedly haunt the 10th floor of the **Hotel Lawrence**, from which a woman reportedly jumped in the 1940s (page 167).

[C **Best Kept Secret:** Park Cities' **Hotel Lumen** is sleek and cool and in an excellent location (page 171).

[C **Best View:** The rooftop pool atop the **South Side on Lamar** offers beautiful panoramas of downtown and Fair Park (page 172).

[C **Best Atmosphere:** For authentic Western digs, you can't beat **Stockyards Hotel,** where ranchers, cattle barons, and meat-packing industry kings often cut deals in the lobby (page 173).

[C **Best Re-do:** The **Ashton Hotel** renovation involved refurbishing not one but two old buildings, and now the cozy lobby and restaurant host lovely teas within the historic confines (page 173).

[C **Best Kitsch:** The themed rooms at **Etta's Place** B&B are fun but not cloying, and the location can't be beat (page 173).

[C **Best B&B:** The friendly atmosphere at the **Texas White House Bed and Breakfast** coupled with its easy-to-navigate location make it a great place to stay (page 176).

© THE TEXAS WHITE HOUSE B&B

Texas White House Bed and Breakfast

For years, Fort Worth endured a dearth of hotel rooms that severely crippled its ability to lure large groups and conventions. Sure, the town could boast tourist attractions, a revamped convention center, and a lovely downtown, but even those features couldn't make up for a lack of lodging.

It's not that Cowtown's pre-existing accommodations weren't top-notch; upscale places like the Ashton Hotel and the Worthington provided luxury, while numerous B&Bs and Stockyards spots provided more casual digs for the temporary guest. There simply weren't enough beds.

Until at last, in 2009, the final brick was laid on the Omni hotel downtown. The addition provided the extra bit of oomph the hospitality industry needed, and has cemented Fort Worth's place in the pantheon of tourist destinations.

CHOOSING A HOTEL

Dallas is such a spread-out city that it can be difficult to figure out where to stay in relation to your destinations. A great bet is to stay downtown. While prices here can be a touch more expensive than other parts of town, the convenience of the central locale can be worth it. Moreover, many of Dallas's downtown hotels aren't as pricey as their counterparts in other cities. Take care, though, to book rooms as far in advance as possible: The city attracts its fair share of conventions, and downtown rooms book up quickly—and more expensively—when large groups are in town.

If downtown doesn't appeal, try uptown, where hipness prevails. You'll find yourself close to nightlife, shopping, and restaurants. Gay and lesbian travelers might try the Melrose, which sits at the very epicenter of the Gayborhood.

In all honesty, in Fort Worth, your hotel chooses you. Around TCU, the West Side, and most other residential areas, chain hotels are the most common—and often the only—choices. Downtown and the North Side's Stockyard areas provide a touch more variety. Although chain

PRICE KEY

💲 less than $150 per night

💲💲 $150-250 per night

💲💲💲 more than $250 per night

hotels show a presence downtown, some of the more unique lodging spots in that area cost about the same, so if you prefer a little character along with your turndown service, check for the best deals. For tourists, downtown and the North Side will be the most convenient locations.

HOTELS

Downtown Dallas

Map 1

◖ THE HOTEL ADOLPHUS 💲💲

1321 Commerce St., 214/742-8200,
www.hoteladolphus.com

Easily the grandest, most opulent hotel in downtown Dallas, this gorgeous old stalwart is a stately elm among saplings. While newer hotels often opt for sleek minimalism, the Adolphus, built in 1912 at the behest of beer baron Adolphus Busch, showers each guest in an atmosphere so unabashedly posh, even Marie Antoinette might blush. The outside of the multi-floor building is as ornate and lovingly detailed as a wedding cake, while the interior features antiques, grand staircases, and gilded frames. The crème de la crème here is the French Room restaurant. "Rococo," "baroque," and "Edwardian" are words often used to describe the atmosphere here, and the exquisite bas reliefs, polished marble floors, and lush murals on the 18-foot ceilings prove such words are not overstatements; the same goes for the meticulously crafted French cuisine. While such grandiosity easily could be overkill, with

the Adolphus it works, mainly because of the gorgeous details that transform old-fashioned camp into old-school lavishness.

It's not just window dressing—the Adolphus sets a high bar for service and amenities. Each of the 400-plus rooms is fit for royalty; in fact, a number of international royals have stayed here. Besides the opulent French Room, the Adolphus has a less formal bar and grill as well as a charming, casual bistro and two other bars. Of course, there are the usual perks—an exercise room, meeting areas, a business center—but how many hotels also offer afternoon tea?

HOTEL CRESCENT COURT 💲💲💲

400 Crescent Ct., 214/871-3200,
www.crescentcourt.com

For a hotel with such a giant footprint, it's a wonder that the Crescent manages such personal—and personable—service. At around $500–600 a night, one should expect nothing less, of course, but the Crescent always delivers, greeting guests across the elegant gymnasium-size, marble-floored lobby by name. The building itself takes up several Uptown blocks—all the more room to indulge in the Crescent's spa service, many shops, and glorious pool.

HOTEL INDIGO $$

1933 Main St., 800/972-2518

The Hotel Indigo can be had, if you're lucky,

for closer to the $100 side of things, and if you've booked it at that price, the place is a good bargain for a downtown stay. Even though it's owned by a chain, it's a boutique chain, so expect some character—in this case, manifested in hardwood floors and pastel, beach-y color schemes (which, admittedly, are a bit out of place in downtown Dallas). While

GHOSTLY OVERNIGHTS

If you're one of that strange breed who loves a case of the paranormal shivers, look no further than the **Hotel Lawrence** for accommodations in Dallas. The hotel was built in 1925 and, while it now serves as an affordable boutique hotel, it has a deliciously creepy pedigree.

For one thing, the basement once held a seedy underbelly of illegal gambling (many ghost hunters there today use poker chips to tempt the possible spirits to make themselves known). Hotel employees to this day report strange goings-on in the former casino – laundry baskets moving themselves, lights going on and off, electrical devices ceasing to work.

But the real spooky hijinks can be found on the tenth floor. Legend has it this is where a young woman fell – or jumped – to her death from the Presidential suite here some time during the 1940s. Alternate stories claim it was a man who fell – or jumped – and some say even that he was a congressman.

Well, no matter who fell or jumped, some odd stuff happens on the tenth floor. This is where staff have repeatedly report feeling "cold spots," and hotel patrons swear they've seen someone walking around who disappears into the night air. People also report hearing footsteps and a woman's voice at odd hours of the early morning. The most striking ghostly activity, however, has occurred when staff and guests have tried to open doors on the tenth floor, but to no avail. Folks who have encountered this phenomenon swear it feels as if someone is holding the knob from the other side.

A stuck doorknob proves a subtle haunting,

however, in comparison to the ghostly hubbub at the **Hotel Adolphus,** just a few blocks down the road from the Lawrence. The Adolphus is known as one of the most refined, fancy hotels in the country, and this was true in the early 20th century too, when the 19th floor ballroom hosted big band shows and parties. Descriptions of the ballroom sound similar to the hotel ballroom from the movie *The Shining*: It was glamorous, filled with champagne-swilling revelers in black-tie splendor, dancing the night away.

To this day, graveyard shift desk attendants at the Adolphus receive calls from 19th floor guests, complaining about hearing the music drifting in from the ballroom. Thing is, that ballroom has been abandoned for decades. Maybe the band plays to entertain the spirit of a longtime guest, who still is sighted taking her usual seat at the hotel's Bistro. Or maybe it's the jilted bride who has spooked more than one hotel guest.

While the stately Adolphus keeps the ghostly fuss to a minimum, a non-profit group called the DFW Ghost Hunters has been hot on the Hotel Lawrence case for some time now. The group even holds its annual conference on Halloween at the Lawrence, and the public is welcome to join in for a $25 fee (check www.dfwghosthunters.com for details). The conference begins in the evening, with speakers and lecturers, followed by the midnight ghost hunt. The kindly hotel even offers half-off lodging specials for conference participants, in case you want to spend the night. Not that you'll be getting any sleep, mind you.

the Indigo's little corner of downtown isn't the most convenient if you don't have a car, you can rely heavily on the hotel shuttle, which will take you almost anywhere. A friendly staff tops off the charm of the place. Free Wi-Fi.

◖ HOTEL LAWRENCE 💲💲

302 S. Houston St., 214/761-9090, www.hotellawrence.com

The rooms are a touch small and the hotel hasn't reached the level of its clear ambition to transform into a European-style boutique, but the Hotel Lawrence has little amenities such as bottled water, shuttle transport to downtown sights (including the Arts District and the Sixth Floor Depository), and Wi-Fi in each room—all free—making it a desirable place to stay. The faint of heart, however, should stay away: The Lawrence is famously haunted, and even offers spooky Halloween stay-overs for ghost hunters.

HOTEL ST. GERMAIN 💲💲💲

2516 Maple Ave., 214/871-2516, www.hotelstgermain.com

It's easy to surmise that there's no other hotel like this in the world, or at least definitely not in Dallas. The St. Germain transports guests back to the sleepy elegance of old New Orleans. French antiques, gilded mirrors, and ever-present ivy transform this turn-of-the-century house into a romantic inn. Canopied feather beds, 24-hour concierge service, and modern amenities transform it into pampering accommodations. The St. Germain is one of the best kept secrets in Dallas.

HOTEL ZAZA 💲💲💲

2332 Leonard St., 800/597-8399, www.hotelzaza.com

When it comes to the melding of opulence and stylishness, Hotel Zaza has no equal. The decadence in this case is in the details: Thick carpets cover every square inch of the rooms and suites, dense feather pillows await you on the bed, and heavy drapes block out the Texas sun. The general theme and decor is one of luxurious international exotica, with zebra stripes blending into Mideastern and Mediterranean patterns everywhere you turn. The hotel's signature motif, however, is its "concept" rooms and suites, which follow themes like "Rock Star" and "The Last Czar." The service can be cloying (turndown service involves retro candy; the free shuttle is called the Magic Carpet), but you'll be so blissed out from the spa, cocktails at the Dragonfly bar, and stellar service, you won't notice. Of course, the hotel features all the usual amenities such as a fitness center, a pool, room service, and a business center.

HYATT REGENCY DALLAS 💲💲

300 W. Reunion Blvd., 214/651-1234, www.dallasregency.hyatt.com

Normally, another cog in the corporate hotel chain might not be worth a mention, but when that cog just happens to be attached to a 55-story tower with a giant, revolving ball on top—well, it makes for memorable accommodations. The downtown Hyatt's proximity to Reunion Tower affords guests access to the landmark's amenities, such as the top-level (literally) rotating restaurant helmed by Wolfgang Puck. The hotel's other amenities are to be expected: several restaurants, a coffee shop, a fitness center, etc.

THE JOULE HOTEL 💲💲💲

1530 Main St., 214/261-4491

Much, much more than a place to rest your head, the Joule is a destination in and of itself.

HOTELS

"The Last Czar," one of the "concept" suites in Hotel Zaza

The downtown hotel, housed in a 10-story gothic building connected to the Neiman Marcus flagship store, has no equal when it comes to combining the warmth of a boutique hotel with the most modern aesthetics and amenities that luxury accommodations have to offer.

The building's remodel was custom designed by Adam Tiheny, and the results are astonishing. Tiheny incorporated two signature elements that make the Joule truly unique: The first is the cantilevered rooftop pool that juts out eight feet over the edge of the building; the second can be found in the lobby, where a pair of enormous gears loom over the exquisite combination of dark yet sleek ambience. Combined with the gothic architecture, the dramatic result feels like an industrial vision of the future, a la *Metropolis*. The aura extends to the much-praised gourmet restaurant Charlie Palmer at the Joule, which sits under the aegis of two industrial wind turbines.

If the atmosphere is grand, the service is understated and friendly, and amenities are plenty (the phones even have a direct line to a Neiman's personal shopper). Of course, expect to pay for it, as rooms vary from around $400 to $5,000 for the penthouse suite.

THE MAGNOLIA HOTEL 💲💲

1401 Commerce St., 214/915-6500,
www.magnoliahoteldallas.com

The Magnolia is hard to miss: It's the building with the giant red neon winged horse on top. Even without the iconic rooftop sign (a leftover from the building's days as the headquarters for an early incarnation of the Mobil oil company), the building itself would turn heads. Built in 1921, the 29-story neoclassical edifice was once the tallest building west of the Mississippi (and the first skyscraper in the country to have air-conditioning). Today, the refined, modern interior doesn't exclude the building's original detailed touches; instead, it incorporates them into a quietly chic aura. Boutique and unique, the Magnolia may not have the dramatic amenities of large chain hotels, but it does have an excellent continental breakfast and evening milk and cookies. And a Starbucks.

Uptown Dallas   Map 2

DAISY POLK INN 💲💲

2917 Reagan St., 214/522-4692

GLBT travelers will feel right at home in this super-cute little Arts and Crafts home that evokes a cozy European abode. In the mid-1990s, proprietor Wayne Falcone purchased the 1906 home from the family of Daisy Polk, who was a local opera star with quite a story, and the inn is a quick walk away from "The Strip," home to most of Dallas's GLBT hangouts. The inn is divided into three suites (all of which have private baths): The Daisy suite and the Reagan suite both house queen size beds, while the Dickason has a double bed.

ROSEWOOD MANSION ON TURTLE CREEK 💲💲💲

3411 Gillespie St., 214/559-2100,
www.mansiononturtlecreek.com

Once the magnificent estate of a cotton magnate and his family, the Mansion feels more like home than any other hotel in the city. Granted, 10,000 square feet of living space may not be the norm for most people, but the warmth and character of the Mansion, derived from the fact that a family once lived here, provides an extra touch of comfort. It's luxurious, too—the original opulence remains in the form of marble floors, exquisite staircases, stained glass windows, and intricately carved inlays. Although it's famous for its grandeur, favored by rock stars and heads of state alike

(Pakistan's President Musharraf stays here on visits to Dallas), the Mansion is even better known for its restaurant, which was begun by star chef Dean Fearing and his famous tortilla soup, and after a 2007 renovation, has moved brilliantly into the era of modern fine dining.

THE STONELEIGH 💲💲💲

1002 Lone Star Pkwy., 972/262-4479,
www.stoneleighhotel.com

Even though it recently underwent a multimillion-dollar renovation, the Stoneleigh still oozes history. The redo embraces the 1921 original's signature touches like marble columns, art deco details, and bold, glamorous lines, while adding some much-needed urbanity. Rooms start at well more than $200, but that's a bargain, considering the Stoneleigh's Uptown, centralized location close to the bars and shops of McKinney Avenue, the Gayborhood, and downtown. While the price is right and many amenities such as Wi-Fi, bathrobes, and shoeshines are free, keep an eye out for other cranked-up prices ($4 for a Coke; $14 for a coffeemaker). The hotel also takes pride in its signature spa, which is one of the best in town.

WARWICK MELROSE HOTEL 💲💲

3015 Oak Lawn Ave., 214/521-5151,
www.warwickdallas.com

Even though it was recently purchased by the

HOTELS

© WARWICK MELROSE HOTEL

Warwick Melrose Hotel

large Warwick corporation, the Melrose still retains its boutique feel. This 184-room hotel was built in 1924, and its classic aura shows in the charming red brick exterior, detailed interior, and handsome wood-paneled Library Bar. The old-school intermingles with the modern, however, especially in the sleek lines of the exquisite Landmark Restaurant—one of Dallas's best. Located right at the very epicenter of the Gayborhood—the nexus of Oak Lawn Avenue and Cedar Springs—the Melrose is popular among GLBT travelers, but is by no means exclusive to them, and caters ably to the business crowd with T1 lines, personalized voicemail, and large work desks.

Park Cities   Map 3

HILTON DALLAS PARK CITIES 💲💲
5954 Luther La., 214/368-0400,
www1.hilton.com/en_us/hi/hotel/dalpchf/index.do
Like everything else in Park Cities, the Hilton here goes a step above the usual luxury treatment. Here you'll find the usual amenities of an upper-end chain hotel, but the location and excellent service let you know you're in one of the most exclusive parts of town. The Park Cities Hilton is also close to all the major shopping areas and in a tree-lined, character-filled section of the area. Extra bonus: If you stay here, you'll be surrounded by hundreds of restaurants, but if you prefer to eat in, the Hilton houses OPIO, helmed by well-known Dallas chef Billy Webb.

© HOTEL LUMEN/DAVID PHELPS

Hotel Lumen

☾ HOTEL LUMEN 💲💲

6101 Hillcrest Ave., 214/219-2400,
www.hotellumen.com

Hotel Lumen is one of Dallas's little secrets. A four-story boutique hotel, the Lumen is situated just down the street from Southern Methodist University, making it a perfect place to rest your head during parents' weekend (if you plan on staying there during football season, make reservations well ahead of time). The accommodations here feel more like an L.A. hot spot than a stately hotel: Expect lots of mood lighting, mid-century decor, and luxury with a light touch.

Greenville
Map 4

HOTEL PALOMAR 💲💲💲

5300 E. Mockingbird La., 214/520-7969,
www.hotelpalomar-dallas.com

One of the newest modern luxury hotels in Dallas, the Palomar is housed in what was once a dodgy, drug-infested motel. It's completely renovated now, of course, in neons and pastels that evoke Hollywood cool. The Palomar is the first Texas foray of the high-end hotel brand from Klimpton and, as such, bears just about every amenity imaginable—including pampering for your pet. The chic downstairs restaurant, Central 214, and the old Polynesian stalwart Trader Vic's comprise the popular dining options, but the gorgeous bar is where the action really is.

East Dallas   Map 5

CORINTHIAN BED & BREAKFAST ⑤⑤⑤
4125 Junius St., 214/818-0400,
www.corinthianbandb.com

Folks like to apply the term "transition-ing" to the neighborhood surrounding the Corinthian, but really, the surrounding envi-rons are just plain bad. But adventurous souls are rewarded once they arrive on the wide swath of columned porch that wraps around

the B&B. There are five different suites, rang-ing from the Mayor's Suite to the Presidential Suite, all of which achieve a perfect balance between comfort and antique comeliness. The bright, airy rooms all feature king-size beds, TVs, and Wi-Fi. The Corinthian sits on Junius Street, one of the most historic in Dallas, just around the corner from magnifi-cent Swiss Avenue.

South Dallas   Map 6

◖ SOUTH SIDE ON LAMAR ⑤
1401 S. Lamar St., 214/428-4848,
www.southsideonlamar.com

Once a gargantuan Sears Roebuck distribution center that spanned several city blocks, the South Side on Lamar is now a stunning residential/re-tail building that also offers executive suites for those who avoid more sterile digs. Convenient

to downtown, the building houses a coffee shop, bar, fitness area, and rooftop pool with breathtaking views of downtown and Fair Park. Reflecting the interior of the many residential lofts, the suite's brick walls, exposed ductwork, and dramatically high ceilings provide more character than any four-star hotel could, with concierge service of equal or better quality.

Greater Dallas   Map 11

DALLAS IRVING BACKPACKERS ⑤
214 W. 6th St., Irving, 972/262-4479

Backpackers and low-budget travelers are hard-pressed to find hostel-type digs in the DFW area. The Dallas Irving Hostel is the best of the bunch. The hostel isn't conveniently located per se, situated as it is in Irving, a Dallas suburb, but it's pretty much equidistant between Dallas and Fort Worth, and is close to the TRE train that will take you to either town. The hostel's friendly, if somewhat disorganized, staff will put you up in a bunk bed (four to a room).

Wi-Fi, outdoor grills, and a large kitchen are also available.

WESTIN GALLERIA DALLAS ⑤⑤⑤
13340 Dallas Pkwy., 866/716-8137

Those with business in North Dallas often find themselves at the Westin, which is a good place to be. This is a world-class business hotel, fresh off a recent renovation and flush with ameni-ties. Excellent service, Wi-Fi, a gym, business center, and proximity to a number of highways are all well and good, of course, but really it's the fact that the Westin is literally connected to one of the largest (and swankiest) shopping malls in the world—the Dallas Galleria—that lifts these accommodations above the usual.

North Side Fort Worth   Map 7

◖ STOCKYARDS HOTEL ❸❸❸

109 E. Exchange Ave., 817/625-6427,
www.stockyardshotel.com

You'll practically hear the spurs a'janglin' when you enter this century-old bastion of Western-style luxury. With leather furniture, bordello-red paint, and longhorn-laden walls, the Stockyard Hotel plays up its history to the hilt—and when your former guests include everyone from Bonnie and Clyde to Michael Martin Murphy, why not? (Bonnie Parker's pistol, by the way, adorns the wall in the suite named after her.) Despite the historic flair, the service and amenities here definitely fall under the modern category.

Downtown Fort Worth   Map 8

◖ THE ASHTON HOTEL ❸❸

610 Main St., 817/332-0100, www.theashtonhotel.com

Modern luxury in a historic setting defines this boutique hotel, perfectly located a few steps away from both Bass Hall and Sundance Square. The hotel actually comprises two buildings, one built in 1890 and the other built in 1915. A 2001 renovation and restoration re-established the buildings' charm. With only 39 rooms, the Ashton's intimacy translates to personalized hospitality—in the dusk of evening, the glow of the warmly lit lobby of the Ashton practically begs passersby to drop in for a drink and a steak from the hotel's much-lauded 610 Grille. Amenities include free Wi-Fi in all rooms, babysitting service, and 24-hour room service.

AZALEA PLANTATION B&B ❸❸❸

1400 Robinwood Dr., 800/687-3529,
www.azaleaplantation.com

Decorated with more antiques than you'd find in your grandma's garage, this genteel B&B provides a relaxing haven for those who prefer books to 2 A.M. partying. Gardens and greenery buffer the Azalea's large spread from the surrounding neighborhood, which is not particularly picturesque. The B&B is a bit off of the beaten path, but particularly convenient to the Stockyards and the Texas Motor Speedway.

◖ ETTA'S PLACE ❸❸

200 W. 3rd St., 817/255-5760, www.ettas-place.com

It's fitting that Etta's Place can be found on Sundance Square, since the B&B's namesake was the Sundance Kid's sweetheart, and indeed, history and location make up a good deal of the appeal here. While it's billed as a bed and breakfast, Etta's can feel more like a historic hotel, with spa and business amenities and large, airy rooms—you won't find any of the musty Victorian frill that overtakes so many period-themed accommodations. What you

HOTELS

will find are tasteful, fun nods to Cowtown's Western heritage.

HOLIDAY INN EXPRESS DOWNTOWN $

1111 W. Lancaster Ave., 877/863-4780

If the words "Holiday Inn" conjure up images of dingy rooms and mustard-colored carpet, you'll change your thinking after visiting this inexpensively priced update on the old family-road-trip standby. This Holiday Inn is clean and sharp, with almost over-the-top mod furniture and appointments. The rooms, though perhaps a touch smaller than most, prove comfy and tidy. Since it cozies up to downtown, convenient to Sundance Square, the Cultural District, and TCU, the hotel might just have the best location in Fort Worth for the price. Ditto for the amenities, which include a shuttle bus, workout room, pool and hot tub, and breakfast buffet.

THE OMNI FORT WORTH $$

1300 Houston St., 817/353-6664, www.omnihotels.com

While the rooms are pretty much standard for an upscale hotel chain, it's the grandeur of the common areas that make this brand-new, city-initiated, downtown centerpiece such a thrill. Built specifically to lure conventioneers and other large groups to the city (which suffers a

dearth of hotel rooms), the Omni's thoughtful decor belies its scale (614 rooms, 25 suites, 29 meeting rooms, 777,000 square feet, four restaurants). Case in point: The striking $1 million limestone wall—a creative nod to Fort Worth's Western heritage with a 21st-century flair—that anchors the lobby. By the way, the luring strategy worked: Whichever AFC team is lucky enough to make it to the 2011 Super Bowl, which will be held at the nearby new Dallas Cowboys stadium, will be staying here.

RENAISSANCE WORTHINGTON HOTEL $$$

200 Main St., 800/433-5677, www.marriott.com/hotels/travel/dfwdt-renaissance-worthington-hotel-fort-worth

Once a favored spot for traveling oil execs and out-of-town businessmen, the Worthington's luxurious rep was matched only by its footprint on downtown. With the opening of the over-the-top new Omni Hotel, however, the Worthington might find its reputation as the best downtown hotel in jeopardy. Still, the instantly recognizable, pyramid-shaped building strikes a nostalgic chord, as well as a more tangible one. The service here has always been top-notch, the luxurious treatment devoid of frills, and the location unbeatable.

TCU and Vicinity

Map 9

HATTIE MAY INN $$

712 May St., 817/870-1931,
www.hattiemayinn.com

The serenity of this stunningly restored 1904 Queen Anne beauty belies a notorious history—in 1917, the house's owner, local gentleman James Liston, was shot and killed on the back porch as he returned home with the profits from his Hell's Half-Acre Saloon. His wife continued to live there for years afterward, and one of the six bullets shot at Liston is still visible today. Other than that, the wraparound porch, antiques, and charm of Hattie May's place inspires nothing but comfort, along with modern conveniences like cable TV, hair dryers, and an ironing board. Guests can choose from a number of tempting accommodations, from the Oriental Oasis room with its clawfoot tub to the Americana Room's sleeping porch. Inquire about special package pricing for adjoining rooms.

RESIDENCE INN UNIVERSITY $$

1701 S. University Dr., 817/870-1011

Empty-nester moms and pops who make the trip to TCU for a parents'-weekend glimpse into their kids' college life might struggle to find suitable digs. That's where the Residence Inn University comes in. While much of what this place offers sticks to the mid-level, large-chain paradigm, the inn is clean, easy, and convenient to the school and other Fort Worth sights. This branch also manages a touch of character, considering it once was an actual residence—many rooms even have fireplaces—but you can still expect free Internet and rooms with microwaves, mini-fridges, and a stove top.

HOTELS

© THE TEXAS WHITE HOUSE BED AND BREAKFAST

a Texas-style bathroom at the Texas White House Bed and Breakfast

◖ TEXAS WHITE HOUSE BED AND BREAKFAST ⑤⑤⑤

1417 8th Ave., 817/923-3597,
www.texaswhitehouse.com

You won't find Secret Service agents at this White House, but you will find the hospitable service of owners Grove and Jamie McMains, who are well versed in all things FW and happy to share their knowledge. Of course, considering the antiques, gardens, and gazebo, you might not want to leave the premises. If you do, however, the convenient location close to downtown Magnolia Street comes in handy.

Greater Fort Worth   Map 11

SANFORD HOUSE INN & SPA ⑤⑤⑤

506 N. Center St., Arlington, 877/205-4914,
www.thesanfordhouse.com

Although the Sanford House's charming Southern architecture evokes a B&B ambience, it really serves more as a freestanding hotel. If you're expecting a quiet, singular experience, you might be disappointed, but the lovely décor, gourmet food, and beautiful gardens definitely provide a luscious experience, even amid the mid-city concrete and large-scale tourist spots like the Texas Rangers ballpark just up the road. Guests choose between intimate cottages that surround the pool and rooms in the main house. Amenities are plentiful, including plasma TVs, Wi-Fi, breakfast, a bar, and a concierge.

© THE SANFORD HOUSE INN & SPA

Sanford House Inn & Spa

EXCURSIONS FROM DALLAS AND FORT WORTH

The sights, sounds, foods, and attractions of Dallas-Fort Worth are more than enough to keep you occupied, but should you feel the need to stretch your wings, the surrounding areas offer plenty of activity for anything from a day trip to a weekend excursion.

While DFW doesn't lay claim to a particular countryside lifestyle like, say, Amish country or even the Hill Country down near Austin, the outlying areas do maintain a certain thematic consistency. For miles around the metroplex, you'll find the stillness of low, quiet prairie land broken by farms and small ranches, some of which are nestled up to increasingly sprawled suburban development.

Along the way are small Texas towns, many of which ratchet up the charm factor with refurbished town squares surrounded by blocks of Craftsman and Victorian homes.

Three destinations in particular offer the perfect combination of fun sights and activities and laid-back nostalgia. South of DFW, the Glen Rose/Granbury area has a unique combination of old-fashioned Victorian charm and amazing natural history sites. Just north of the metroplex is "Texomaland," which borders Oklahoma and the Red River, where you'll find surprising roots of American political history abutting water recreation on Lake Texoma. The city of Grapevine, also to the north, provides

HIGHLIGHTS

LOOK FOR ◖ TO FIND RECOMMENDED EXCURSIONS.

◖ **Best Learning Experience:** Dinosaur Valley State Park has some of the best-preserved dinosaur tracks in the world. Kids and adults alike will enjoy this adventure (page 181).

◖ **Best Antique Stores:** Sherman's **Kelly Square** houses several antique shops under one quaint roof (page 185).

◖ **Best Designated Driver:** The Grapevine Vintage Railroad will take you from the Stockyards all the way out to the Grapevine wine country and back. If you're staying in the Stockyards, you can just stumble back to your hotel (page 187).

◖ **Best Place For Kids:** With its fantastically enormous indoor water park, on-line gaming lounge, and other kid-friendly attractions, the "lodge" part of Grapevine's **Great Wolf Lodge** is almost an afterthought (page 189).

© GRAPEVINE CVB

Grapevine is home to 10 winery tasting rooms.

a down-home take on wine country as well as modern destinations.

Speaking of wine, a quick note about booze: Many of the counties surrounding DFW are dry counties, meaning if you'd like to order a beer or cocktail at a restaurant, you'll have to sign up for a "membership," which basically means filling out an information card.

Occasionally, memberships come with a fee, but most places waive them. It's a rather silly piece of bureaucracy, but don't be surprised if your server brings it up.

PLANNING YOUR TIME

All of these spots are within an easy hour's drive of either city and can be done in a day,

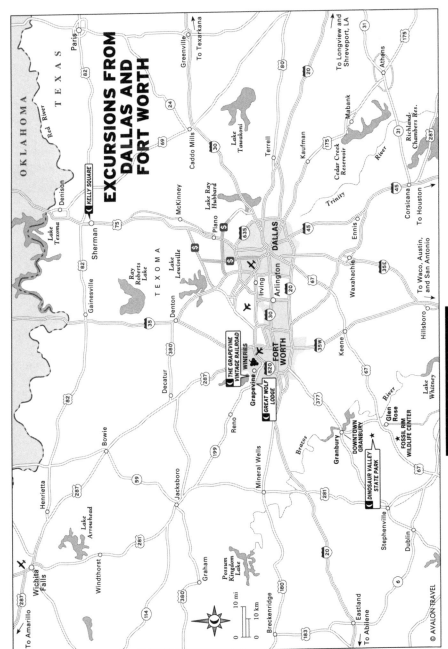

EXCURSIONS FROM DALLAS AND FORT WORTH

EXCURSIONS

should you choose your sites carefully, although a weekend would best do justice to their rich heritage, pretty scenery, and friendly folk. As is the way in this part of the country, there's not much in terms of public transportation, so a car is pretty much a must. You might consider, however, bringing bikes or ATVs along, as there's plenty of wide-open country to enjoy.

About equidistant between Fort Worth and Dallas, Grapevine is the closest to both cities. Glen Rose/Granbury is about a half hour south of Fort Worth, and nearly an hour from Dallas. Texomaland, the farthest away, can be found about an hour north of Dallas, two hours north of Fort Worth, though that increases if you end up spending time at Lake Texoma.

Glen Rose and Granbury

Glen Rose and Granbury offer two very different types of tourist sites, but seeing how they sit just down the road from each other, they're best taken as a package. In its earliest days, Granbury, as the seat of Hood County, saw a good bit of action, but it never blossomed into a large town (today, the population hovers around 5,000 to 6,000). Two events helped the small burg escape oblivion: In 1969, Lake Granbury was formed by the damming of the Brazos River, and in the mid-1970s, the town engaged in a massive

NOT BURIED IN GRANBURY?

Not one, not two, but three of American history's most nefarious figures faked their own deaths, then ended up spending time in Granbury. At least, that's what the locals say.

To start, Granbury folks are convinced that the man known as J. Frank Dalton, who lived in their midst until 1951, was actually none other than the outlaw **Jesse James.** Although the official story is that James was killed by Robert Ford in 1882, people in these parts insist that story is a ruse, and that James hid out under the Dalton alias in Granbury until his death at the age of 104. His Granbury headstone (found at **Granbury Cemetery,** at the corner of N. Crockett St. and Moore St., about eight blocks north of the town square) reads, "CSA – Jesse Woodson James. Sept. 5, 1847– Aug. 15, 1951. Supposedly killed in 1882."

Another supposedly dead gangster, **Billy the Kid,** also lived out a long, quiet life after his fake demise. The official story is that Sheriff Pat Garrett shot and killed Billy the Kid in 1881 in Fort Sumner, New Mexico, not too far from the Texas border, where the gunslinger

was then buried. The unofficial tale, however, insists that Garrett shot someone else and then covered it up, and Billy the Kid settled in Hico, Texas, but traveled to Jesse James 102nd birthday party – in Granbury, of course – in 1949. When the real Billy the Kid died of a mundane heart attack at age 90 in 1950, say the unofficial theorists, his gravestone in Fort Sumner went missing, only to turn up in 1976 – again in Granbury.

Finally, none other than Abraham Lincoln's assassin, **John Wilkes Booth,** reportedly ended up in Granbury after his pretend demise. Based on the 1907 book *Escape and Suicide of John Wilkes Booth* by Finis L. Bates, Booth went by the alias John St. Helen and tended bar at a Granbury establishment that is now a bakery called the **Nutshell** (137. E. Pearl St.). After St. Helen died, Bates had his body mummified and traveled the country displaying it as apart of a circus sideshows, until 1977. Attempts to exhume the body thought to be the "real" Booth have been rebuked by the courts.

refurbishing and revitalization of the town square. Both now draw thousands of day visitors, weekenders, and tourists. With its numerous bed-and-breakfasts, Granbury is a good home base for exploring nearby Glen Rose. Just a few miles south of Granbury down Highway 144, Glen Rose itself isn't much to write home about, but it's home to Dinosaur Valley State Park and a number of other destinations.

SIGHTS
◖ Dinosaur Valley State Park

Highway 205 west of Glen Rose leads straight to Dinosaur Valley State Park (1629 Park Road 59, Glen Rose, 254/897-4588, www.tpwd .state.tx.us/spdest/findadest/parks/dinosaur_ valley), which has some of the finest specimens of dinosaur tracks in the world. Turns out the limestone and sandstone bed of the Paluxy River, which runs through the park, was perfect for petrifying the giant prints

from about 100 million years ago. Today, several well-preserved tracks from sauropods and thereopods crisscross the western edge of the 1,524-acre park.

The park is also a beautiful place for hiking, biking, and camping. At this point in the local topography, some of the monotony of the plains begins to change to rockier, hillier, more picturesque ground, and here it serves as a home for many different types of wildlife. Check out the park's website for detailed information regarding camping permits, access, and hours.

Downtown Granbury

Filled with refurbished Victorian buildings, antique stores, and other points of interest, the entire charming "downtown" of Granbury is on the National Register of Historic Places. The fantastical stories of Jesse James and Billy the Kid's Granbury reappearance make more sense in the context of the back-in-time

© TODD SCHAEFER

Dinosaur Valley State Park

feeling of the town square. The old limestone **Hood County Courthouse** (1200 W. Pearl St.), with its original grand clock tower, was built in 1890 and still lords over the picturesque scene. Across the way you'll find the former **Hood County Jail** (208 N. Crockett St., 817/573-5135), now home to the chamber of commerce, with its former cell blocks and creepy hanging tower still intact and open for visitors' perusal. Finally, a stroll down the road apiece lands visitors at the **Granbury Opera House** (116 E. Pearl St., 817/573-9191, granburyoperahouse.net). The opera house, run by a nonprofit group that stages Broadway-type musicals and Branson-like events, is a popular stop.

Granbury Opera House

DENTON: THE BEST MUSIC SCENE IN THE COUNTRY

Music fans, take heed: A quick trip north from DFW, up Intestate 35, through suburban sprawl and country prairie, lands you smack in the middle of the best kept music scene in the country: Denton, TX.

At first, Denton might strike visitors as a mid-sized, quiet college town, home to the University of North Texas and not much else. There's a charming town square, B&Bs, plenty of grassy plains and Texas sky. But stay a few hours, do some exploring, and it grows more noticeable. Young, skinny guys with hipster facial hair stroll the streets, sporting trucker caps and beer coozies. Casual collegiate-types hide behind sunglasses. By nightfall, young ladies don their thrift-store best and begin to file in to one of the many DIY venues that can be found in unlikely places. Yep, the signs are there – there's music to be had.

Denton has always been fertile ground to creative types. The University of North Texas is one of the finest music schools in the country, a beacon for serious students (mainly of jazz) looking to take their craft to the next level. The school's output is prolific and a fine product, and even non-students from miles around are familiar with the Grammy Award-winning One O'Clock Lab Band, which consists of performers who must win a spot in the line-up, the most coveted on campus (the band is named for its place in UNT's class schedule). UNT also produced other stars, like Roy Orbison, Norah Jones, Don Henley, Meat Loaf, the members of Brave Combo, and even Pat Boone.

But there's an edgier side to Denton, one that extends way beyond the campus boundaries. It is in this scene you'll find synth-rock experimentalists and finely-honed pop creations, hard punk and smart alternative country, singer-songwriters, DJs, and revamped California rock. This is the scene that spawned names that are perhaps lesser known, but praised and worshiped by critics and indie fans. Artists like Doug Burr, Midlake, Shiny Around the Edges, Baboon, Slobberbone, and Centro-matic have all honed their chops in Denton.

You're sure to find a great band in one of the many laid-back venues that dot the Denton map. Although they all enjoy their own singular personalities, the club's independent spirit and communal philosophy reflects that of Denton itself, so a cross-genre aesthetic pervades.

Fossil Rim Wildlife Center

Fossil Rim Wildlife Park (2155 County Rd. 2008, 254/897-2960, www.fossilrim.org) feels like a safari in the middle of Texas. The 1,700-acre facility is first and foremost a refuge that specializes in captive-breeding programs for endangered species—we're talking giraffes, rhinos, zebras, and other exotics. But it's also a drive-through park, wherein $8 will buy you a bag of feed and the animals will walk straight up to your car. In addition to the drive, several viewing and pen areas allow up-close views of cheetah, ibex, and tons of other animals.

The park offers a variety of experiences. One cool option is to spend a night or two on-site, either at the lovely, comfortable lodge (around $200 a night, depending on season and occupancy) or at one of the more rustic cabins or bunkhouses (around $85, again depending on season and occupancy).

Entrance prices vary from season to season. Even if you're there for just an afternoon or a day, tours range from the self-guided drive (around $10 a person, depending on season and day) to the "behind-the-scenes" tour (around $50 a person, depending on season and day) to the adventure tour (about $300, depending on season and day). The pricing schedule is a bit confusing—best to check the website or, better yet, call to confirm prices.

EXCURSIONS

Hailey's (122 Mulberry St., 940/323-1160, www.haileysclub.com), for instance, provides a haven for cutting-edge dance music. We're not talking the generic brand of thud-thud-thud house that pervades most dance clubs; Hailey's sets expand the genre into all sorts of hybrid and experimental realms. The club also houses some of the best local and indie touring bands.

Dan's Silverleaf (103 Industrial St., 940/320-2000, www.danssilverleaf.com) leans toward a more roots music feel, with many local and mid-level acts sharing the stage, but still makes room for every genre (like nutty, profane soul man Blowfly). Try to catch Denton stalwart and musical genius Paul Slavens at his weekly Monday night gig here.

If you are the type whose musical taste often requires earplugs, try **Andy's Basement Bar and Grill** (122 N. Locust St., 940/565-5400), located right on the downtown square.

If there is an epicenter of Denton indie music, it's found in the former cement factory that is now **Rubber Gloves Rehearsal Studio** (411 E. Sycamore St., 940/387-7781, www.rubberglovesdentontx.com). A mecca for experimental and original bands, the stage at RGRS has held greats like Daniel Johnston, Jonathon Richman, and Modest Mouse.

The sheer number of high-quality Denton bands can be intimidating for a newcomer, and while your odds of discovering something you like – or at least something interesting – are good, a good rule of thumb for narrowing down your options is to explore the roster at two Denton production companies: **Spune** (www.spune.com) and **Gutterth** (www.gutterth.com). Both companies bring an almost obsessive drive and spirit to the scene, producing local showcases and festivals that feature the best Denton bands and a good deal of national acts. Look for a Spune- or Gutterth-produced show – there's one almost every night – or check out their web sites for just a taste of what Denton has to offer.

Of course, as any Dentonite will tell you, this is just the tip of the iceberg. The scene moves fast and is always spawning new bands, new movements, new ideas. The way to get to know Denton's music scene is to live there. But if you're just visiting, the best way might just be to take a chance. You definitely won't be bored.

ACCOMMODATIONS

It seems like every other house in this area serves as a B&B. Why not, since their gorgeous turn-of-the-century refinement is tailor-made for that type of thing? A favorite is Granbury's **Iron Horse Inn** (616 Thorp Springs Rd., 817/579-5535, www.theironhorseinn.com), which, at 7,000 square feet, is also one of the largest in town. Six rooms make up the accommodations in the century-old Craftsman-style house. Each room features wood floors, a double bed, and private bathroom. The full, hot breakfasts in the antique-laden dining room consists of gourmet-level vittles such as waffles, quiche, and fruit.

One of the better bargains of the Granbury B&B scene, **Alfonso's Loft** (137 E. Pearl St., 817/573-3308, www.alfonsosloft.com) is also one of the quirkier choices the town has to offer, as well as one of the most private: Unhosted, the B&B consists of one space, the top floor of one of the oldest buildings on the square.

The first floor, the bakery and lunch spot **The Nutshell,** is where you'll find your breakfast component, plus an odd bit of local lore. The former occupant of The Nutshell was the very bar where a certain John St. Helen slung drinks. Reportedly, on his deathbed, St. Helen confessed to his real identity—he claimed to be John Wilkes Booth, the assassin of Abraham Lincoln. Murals depicting Booth and the outlaw Jesse James (who it's said also faked his own death and settled in Granbury) adorn the walls of The Nutshell.

FOOD

Besides The Nutshell, another popular lunch place is the **Pearl Street Station** (120 W. Pearl St., Granbury, 817/579-7233, www.pearlststation.com), a Cajun/barbecue joint famous for its "granny" beans and turkey sandwiches on jalapeño cheese bread. For the full home-cookin' experience, try **Debbie's Restaurant** (1102 Hwy. 67, Glen Rose, 254/897-4399)—it's short on atmosphere, but the buffet is tasty and a great deal at about $8 a person.

Texoma

The area flanked by Interstates 35 and 75 north of DFW is known as Texoma—so named for its proximity to the Texas-Oklahoma border. Although dozens of small towns dot the Texoma map, activity centers around the region's twin towns, Sherman and Denison, which are about 10 minutes apart via Highway 89. The two towns are bitter rivals in some respects. The annual football game between the Denison and Sherman high schools, for instance, is called "The Battle of the Ax," and it's something straight out of *Friday Night Lights*. The Sherman natives also tease Denison citizens for living closer to Oklahoma.

For the most part, though, Texomaland is marked by "small-town values," bucolic expanses, and a "ya'll come back now" charm—it's a very Texas-y place. While its latest claim to fame is as the hometown of the Hudson Hero Captain Chesley B. Sullenberger III (who was born and raised in Denison), the area also spawned famous former Speaker of the House Sam Rayburn and former president Dwight D. Eisenhower.

Other Texoma attractions include the small

© AUSTIN COLLEGE PHOTO

Much of Texoma's cultural life revolves around Austin College.

liberal arts college Austin College and Kelly Square—both in Sherman—and the huge Lake Texoma, formed by the damming of the Red River (which also makes up the border between Texas and Oklahoma), to the north of Denison.

SIGHTS
Sherman

Sherman is a good introduction to the lay of the land. As the seat of Grayson County, this town of 37,000 proves a little more hopping than many of the smaller hamlets that surround it. Part of the energy is due to the presence of **Austin College** (900 N. Grand Ave., 903/813-2000), a small liberal arts school with about 1,200 students. The oldest college in the state still operating under its original charter, AC's campus is small and strollable. Make sure to check out the bookstore, where you can find

plenty of paraphernalia featuring the school's mascot, the kangaroo.

Kelly Square

Just down the road from downtown Sherman, you'll find Kelly Square (115 W. Travis St.), a collection of cafés and antique and knickknack shops that take up a block of downtown. An adorable, turn-of-the-century setting, Kelly Square is actually four old buildings refurbished and connected. Antique lovers will really like the **American Victorian Furniture Museum** (201 E. Lamar St.), while history buffs will enjoy the **Red River Historical Museum** (301 S. Walnut St., 903/983-7623, Tues.–Sat. 10 A.M.–4 P.M.), which displays everything from old farm equipment to antique china.

Dwight D. Eisenhower Birthplace State Historic Site

To find the Dwight D. Eisenhower Birthplace State Historic Site (609 S. Lamar Ave., Denison, 903/465-8908, Tues.–Sat. 9 A.M.–5 P.M., Sun. 1–5 P.M.), head north up Business 75 toward Denison's Main Street. From there, head south on Crockett Street to Nelson Street, then west to Lamar Avenue. The main feature of the site is the two-story house in which Eisenhower was born, coupled with a visitor center's small museum. The site also includes six acres of hiking ground.

Sam Rayburn Library and Museum

The other political figure from these parts was Sam Rayburn, perhaps the nation's most famous Speaker of the House, a title he held for 17 of the 49 years he spent as a representative from Texas. Although Rayburn wasn't

EXCURSIONS

born in Texas, as a youth his family moved to Bonham and settled into the 12-room home that now serves as The Sam Rayburn Library and Museum (800 W. Sam Rayburn Dr., 903/583-5558, Mon.–Fri. 9 A.M.–5 P.M., Sun. 1–5 P.M.). Rayburn established the library before his death as a gift to his beloved hometown. Besides its existence as a research library, the building houses a replica of the Speaker of the House's private Washington office, as well as memorabilia from his life.

Lake Texoma

You'll find Lake Texoma fairly accessible from just about any town in the area. One of the largest reservoirs in the country, Lake Texoma is an extremely popular place for recreation—in fact, on weekends it can be tough to find a secluded spot. Anglers, sailers, and other water recreationists find Texoma one of their favorite destinations.

ACCOMMODATIONS

Sprawled over 900 acres, **The Tanglewood Resort** (290 Tanglewood Cir., Pottsboro, 800/833-6569, www.tanglewoodresort.com) doesn't exactly meld with its forested lakeside environment—the place rather resembles a huge Embassy Suites plopped next to a lake—but it can't be beat for amenities. The resort's swimming pools, golf course, large rooms, outside tennis and basketball courts, and business facilities please pretty much all crowds. The place is flexible, too: Rooms start at around $100 and go up to $450, and accommodate parties of one to eight.

Moms and dads up for Austin College's Parents' Weekend might consider **Hart's Country Inn** (601 N. Grand Ave., Sherman, 903/892-2271), a beautifully restored Victorian divided into five different rooms, directly across the street from the school. If you prefer Denison, try the Inn of Many Faces (412 W. Morton St., Denison, 903/465-4639), a rambling, turreted Victorian with gorgeous rooms and fair prices ($110–140).

FOOD

You'll find the cute diner **Fried Pie** (202 W. Main St., Gainesville, 940/665-7641) in Gainesville, a little off your path, but close to Lake Texoma, and the fried namesakes are only $1.50 and worth a few extra miles. The best restaurant in the area, however, might be Sherman's **Blue Door Café** (219 N. Travis St., 903/893-5053), on the downtown square. This odd little bistro feels more New York than North Texas, and the constantly reinvented menu is full of surprises, with everything from Indian cuisine to Mediterranean treats.

Grapevine

As you approach Grapevine from Highway 114 (coming from either Fort Worth or Dallas), don't be disheartened by the vast expanses of freeways, strip malls, and Chili's restaurants; when you get to the heart of it, Grapevine is a hidden Texas treasure. Strangely, even though Grapevine is home to such modern entities as the ginormous Dallas-Fort Worth International Airport, the town is deeply dedicated to preserving its heritage, at least that of its historic downtown section—it's here, amid many of Grapevine's well-known sights, where this town of about 45,000 shows its pride in restored buildings, quaint restaurants, and year-round festivals.

SIGHTS
📻 Grapevine Vintage Railroad

If you're beginning in Fort Worth, a good way to get to town is by hopping aboard the Grapevine Vintage Railroad (817/410-3123, www.grapevinesteamrailroad.com, $20) in the Stockyards. The train will drop you at the depot in downtown Grapevine, where you'll also find the **Grapevine Heritage Center** (701 South Main St., 817/424-0516, www.grapevinehistory.org). The Center provides

a sculpture by Archie St. Clair in downtown Grapevine

EXCURSIONS

PUTTING THE "GRAPE" IN GRAPEVINE

The Mustang grapes that once grew wildly in the area gave Grapevine its name, but these days, it's other grapes that contribute to the town's unique identity: Grapevine has become a hotbed for wine culture. On pleasant weekends, hundreds of DFW wine lovers make their way to the small town, located almost equidistant between Dallas and Fort Worth, to sip new vintages and savor old favorites. Dozens of wineries have popped up here over the years, and much of the town's cultural life revolves around wine.

The following is a list of the popular wineries in the area. Note that vineyards and tasting rooms often host private parties and thus occasionally are closed during regular hours. In the case of public special events, they may offer extended regular hours. A good rule of thumb is to always call ahead.

DELANEY WINERY

While many of Grapevine's wineries are relatively small, Delaney is lush with roomy grounds and 10 acres of vines. The free half-hour tours that commence every hour cover everything from growing to bottling. Tastings begin every half-hour and cost $10 for a sampling of six different wines. Delaney Winery does things on a larger scale than most of the local tasting spots and is a popular locale for weddings, corporate events, and the popular harvest grape stomp. 2000 Champagne Blvd., 817/481-5668, www.delaneyvineyards.com.

HOMESTEAD WINERY AT GRAPEVINE

The winery's super-cute, single story Victorian home provides a great atmosphere to chill out and sip any number of the handful of reds and wide variety of whites offered at Homestead. Try the strong, full-bodied Merlot (but only if you have a designated driver – the sucker's alcohol content registers over 14 percent). 211 E. Worth St., 817/251-9463, www.homestead-winery.com, Mon.-Sat. 11 A.M.-5:30 P.M., Sun. noon-5:30 P.M.

LA BUENA VIDA VINEYARDS

The grapes for the wines offered at La Buena Vida actually are grown in nearby Springtown but served here by the taste, by the glass, by the bottle, and in bottles to go. Definitely stick around to sip it among the cool fountains, lush greenery and Spanish tile. The winery boasts three different labels: Buena Vida, Springtown, and Walnut Creek, all locally produced, and specializes in ports.

True to its commitment to the good life, Buena Vida also provides low-key live musical entertainment (often jazz) on Thursday evenings and on Saturday afternoons. 416 E. College St., 817/481-9463, www.labuenavida.com, Sun.-Tues. noon-5 P.M., Thurs. noon-8 P.M., Fri. noon-7 P.M., Sat. 10 A.M.-7 P.M.

SU VINO WINERY

Laid back and friendly, the Su Vino Winery and tasting room has all the usual reds and whites, made from their own varietals, but the site also features an interactive aspect: Visitors have the opportunity to bottle and cork their own wines, complete with custom made labels. Su Vino also stocks a number of epicurean items-such as condiments, cheeses, and chocolate sauces-made with their wine, along with gift baskets, cute kitchen items and Texas-themed gifts. 120 S. Main St., 817/424-0123, Tues.-Sat. noon-7 P.M., Sun. 1 P.M.-5 P.M.

WINE TRAILS

Organized wine trails, which involve a prepaid charge and stops at several different wineries, are also popular and a good deal. Here are some of the most trafficked offerings (keep in mind prices and dates vary, so go to www.grapevinetexasusa.org for up to date details):

Valentine Wine Trail (Feb. 14 and 15)
New Vintage Wine Trail (mid-April)
July the Fourth Wine Trail (July 4 and 5)
Halloween Wine Trail (Oct. 30)
Holiday Wine Trail (early December)

visitor information, maps, and itinerary suggestions, as well as housing a blacksmith, leather shop, and farmers market.

Grapevine is named after the mustang grapes that grow wild all across the region, and town denizens finally started putting those grapes to use; now, Grapevine is known as an up-and-coming vintner's region, and it seems every few feet yields a new vineyard, wine shop, or tasting room. Try **Homestead** (211 E. Worth St., 817/251-9463, www.homesteadwinery. com, $5), a tasting room dedicated to regional wines only.

C Great Wolf Lodge

Not all of Grapevine's highlights are quaint, however. Great Wolf Lodge (100 Great Wolf Lodge Rd., 817/722-3931, www.greatwolf. com), for instance, is a monstrous complex consisting of an indoor water park and other grand-scale diversions meant mainly for kids, to go along with hotel rooms. Kids love the place, though parents eye it warily with one hand on their wallet.

Grapevine Mills Mall

The Grapevine Mills Mall (3000 Grapevine Mills Pkwy., #214, 972/691-8559, www .grapevinemills.com) may not fall under the picturesque category, but it remains popular nonetheless as an outlet center. The *huge* (1.6 million square feet) mall has remained a consistent favorite, drawing shoppers from as far away as Oklahoma, mainly because of its high-quality discount stores: Neiman Marcus' Last Call, Nike, and Saks 5th Avenue's Off 5th, to name a few.

FOOD

Mmm…a bowl of chili at **Tolbert's** (423 S. Main St., 817/421-4888, www.tolbertsrestau-rant.com, Mon.–Thurs. 11 A.M.–9 P.M., Fri.–Sat. 11 A.M.–9:30 P.M., Sun. 11 A.M.–7 P.M.) simply can't be beat, especially in such charming historic surroundings as this tin-roofed, brick-walled café. **Bread Haus** (700 W. Dallas Rd., 817/488-5223) bakes luscious loaves daily, and its bars, cookies, and scones are delightfully sinful.

EXCURSIONS

BACKGROUND

The Land

GEOGRAPHY

The Dallas-Fort Worth metroplex is located in what is known simply as "North Texas," an area in the state just south of the Red River that separates Texas from Oklahoma. The term "North Texas" is a touch misleading, since the Panhandle is technically farther north, but DFW is indeed in the upper central part of the state, in what is known as the Blackland Prairie area of the Great Plains.

The Blackland Prairie stretches from the Red River down to San Antonio, about 6.1 million hectares in all, marked by a variety of clay soils and diverse tallgrasses, dominated by Indian grass and little bluestem. For centuries, the vegetation here was "disturbance maintained"—that is, growth of the grass was kept in check by grazing bison herds and periodic fires (which are still common today). The consistent maintenance also prevented a dense buildup of trees, and to this day the highest concentration of trees can be found around rivers, streams, and other bodies of water.

What all these dry facts add up to is this: While both cities camouflage their geographic attributes with loads of concrete and asphalt, a

short drive away from either city center reveals the area's Great Plains beauty. Gentle hills covered in prairie grass roll on for miles, and the wide-open sky unfurls.

In springtime, vibrant wildflowers like bluebonnets, Indian paintbrushes, and black-eyed Susans blanket meadows and highway dividers alike. And the vegetation attracts wildlife, both in rural and urban areas. It's not uncommon to see a hawk swooping amid downtown buildings or a possum in someone's backyard. Deer and bird hunting are popular in nearby locales.

Although Dallas and Fort Worth are almost identical in terms of vegetation, wildlife, geography, and climate, the two cites retain a few topographical differences. The edge of the Austin Chalk Formation escarpment runs north-south through Dallas, and its 200-foot rise is most noticeable in the Oak Cliff section of town, but does not affect Fort Worth. For the most part, however, the two cities are relatively flat, and low—elevation is well below 1,000 feet.

CLIMATE

DFW has four seasons—barely. Actually, maybe it's closer to three, with winter losing out.

Summertime is infernally hot, exacerbated by the intense humidity that couples the 90-plus-degree temperatures. The heat index (a gauge, based on temperature and humidity, of what the air feels like to the body) regularly climbs well into the 100s. Of course, so does the regular temp. Don't be surprised at heat waves with the mercury topping 100 several days in a row.

Fall, meantime, is pleasant, though not "fall-like" in the sense that, say, folks from the East Coast might relate to. While the summer heat drags well into September, the leaves and air begin to change in October and November.

A cold front, or "blue norther," might come through bringing chilly temperatures, but for the most part fall is mild, with nice days and jacket-necessitating nights. Fall is a time when many DFW denizens engage in outdoor activities.

Winter is dry and quite mild, often difficult to discern from fall. The mercury during the season hangs between the 55 and 70 degree marks, occasionally punctuated by a winter storm, during which the temp plummets to below freezing. When coupled with precipitation, usually in the form of freezing rain, these storms wreak havoc on North Texas drivers, who are unused to driving on slick roads. It rarely snows.

Spring is the area's most dynamic season. During this time of year, the warm, moist airflow from the Gulf of Mexico often collides with dry, cold air from the north, causing extraordinary volatility. Strong, often dangerous, storms are thus common during spring in North Texas, and tornados, high winds, lightning, and hail during the season are facts of life.

COURTESY OF THE DALLAS ARBORETUM

The vibrant colors of spring greet visitors at the Dallas Arboretum.

History

DALLAS

The history of Dallas is very much a history of Dallas business. Considering the player Dallas has become in the world economy, it's no surprise the city was founded by a man looking to trade (and, considering Dallas's one-of-a-kind character, it's no surprise the guy was half crazy).

In 1841, John Nealy Bryan, an Indian trader from Tennessee, parked himself on a bluff near where Dealey Plaza is today, overlooking the Trinity River. He planned to establish an outpost there to trade with the local Caddo Indians.

The problem was, after a treaty pushed the Native Americans out, Bryan didn't have much of a customer base. So, knowing an extension of the Preston trail was due to pass through the area, he decided to establish a permanent commercial settlement instead. Bryan staked his claim, scrabbling together a population with pioneers lured from nearby settlements. From the beginning, Bryan worked hard to ensure the survival of his outpost—he was the town ferryman, postmaster, and primary landholder. At the time, Texas was a free republic, having recently won its independence from Mexico. The Texas frontier was rapidly pushing west, and it didn't take long for Bryan's little town to start taking shape.

By 1846, Texans had voted overwhelmingly to join the United States. By 1850, Dallas counted 430 citizens. Dallas County had been organized, and the town of Dallas was designated as county seat.

Around 1855, a unique, colossal failure occurred that helped shape Dallas's cultural future. A few years before, a French socialist by the name of Victor Prosper Considérant had established a utopian colony in North Texas, near the site where Bryan had established his commercial one. The French colony, which went by the name La Réunion, was meant as a direct democracy, by which profits were dispersed to individuals in proportion to their labor and monetary investments. While about 2,000 people signed up to join the colony, only about 200 actually made it from France.

The members of La Réunion may have been idealists, but they weren't very good farmers. After about 18 months, the colony went bust, and by 1860, most of its members had dispersed—a good amount of them moving to Dallas.

The mini-Diaspora changed Dallas's future. While the La Réunion members may not have known how to work the land, they were thinkers, artists, and idealists. Their existence laid the cornerstone of Dallas's creative life today, a life manifest by the fertile music scene, the consistently sizzling art scene, and even the rapidly expanding downtown Arts District. For years, before the construction of the American Airlines Center, the main coliseum in Dallas was Reunion Arena, where Dallasites flocked by the thousands to see bands, shows, and other artistic endeavors. The word "Reunion" is still attached to many Dallas entities to this day.

At the time, however, the La Réunion influx meant little compared to the other changes that were occurring. A steady stream of settlers in search of good land continued to make their way to town. By the mid-1850s, the town had its first cotton gin, slaves, newspaper, and a covered toll bridge over the Trinity. In 1856, the Sixth Texas Legislature granted Dallas a city charter, and the town of around 700 adopted its first mayor, Dr. Samuel Pryor, along with a group of aldermen. By 1860, 2,000 people lived in Dallas, and the railroad, sure to attract even more business, visitors, and new citizens, was rapidly approaching.

Then came the Civil War. The townsfolk had voted 741-237 in favor of secession, and when the war began in 1861, Dallas was, for the most part, all for it. Far from the horrors of battle, the city actually benefited from the war. While many locals joined the Confederate Army, Dallas's primary role was as a transportation hub and supplier—yet another precursor to Dallas as a center of commerce. Specifically, the town served as a quartermaster and commissary post for the Trans-Mississippi Army of the Confederacy; built a munitions factory; and acted as a storage and transportation hub.

Dealey Plaza is perhaps Dallas's best-known locale.

Because Dallas suffered little, if any, damage due to the war, it boomed during Reconstruction. While the fate and economy of many Southern towns plunged due to destroyed infrastructure, Dallas's commercial strength and prairie soil held promise. Many Southerners—their plantations destroyed—flocked to the area to take advantage of the fine land, while others, including a good deal of freedmen, realized Dallas was one of the few places where jobs could be found.

The postwar boom coincided with another key factor: transportation. For years, after it turned out the Trinity River was unnavigable, Dallas had been held back as a major player by its isolation. Dallas needed rail lines. In the 1870s, it got them, first the Houston and Texas Central, then the Texas and Pacific, and then the Missouri-Kansas-Texas. Suddenly, Dallas enjoyed a huge regional presence as a transportation hub, specifically for cotton, grain,

leather, and buffalo products. Businessmen, merchants, and entrepreneurs set up shop along the rail lines. By 1880, the population had jumped to more than 10,000 people.

From there, Dallas's maturation as a business center—and thus as a full-blown city—began picking up steam. From the latter part of the 19th century through the early part of the 20th, Dallas grew into the world's biggest inland cotton market as well as the world's leading manufacturer of saddlery and cotton gin parts, in addition to leading the region in a myriad other markets—wholesale liquor, printing, and jewelry, to name a few. Banks and insurance companies led by men whose names now adorn city street signs (Gaston, Ross, Kessler) cropped up around the new industries. The industrial gains spawned social and cultural ones. Dallas now had two major newspapers, several schools, ready-to-wear

WHO THE HECK IS "DALLAS," ANYWAY?

The only surviving bit of information we have today about how **John Nealy Bryan** named his town is that he named his settlement "after my friend, Dallas."

Not super helpful there, Mr. Bryan – there are a lot of people that could be. To this day, nobody really knows the identity of the "Dallas" after whom the city is named.

The most popular candidate is George Mifflin Dallas, who was James Polk's vice president. Yet John Nealy Bryan's town was known as Dallas well before Polk became president, and, moreover, George Mifflin Dallas and Bryan prob-

ably never met, so chances are they were never friends. (To confuse matters, records state that Dallas *county*, established several years after the town, was officially named after the veep.)

A second candidate is George's brother, Commodore Alexander Dallas, who fought against piracy in the Gulf of Mexico. Then there's Walter Dallas, who fought against Mexico in the battle of San Jacinto, or possibly *his* brother, who was a Texas Ranger.

In all honesty, we'll probably never know. But that's OK – Dallasites tend to look forward, rather than look back.

department stores, a hospital, telephones, a state fair, a board of trade, electricity, and its first steel skyscraper, the 15-story Praetorian Building, built in 1907.

For the next couple of decades, Dallas continued to grow—by 1920, the population was 159,000—in a rather non-dynamic way. The federal government helped it along by designating it as a site for a Federal Reserve Bank, and on the north side of town, Southern Methodist University broke ground. A Ford Motor Company plant moved in, and the city expanded through the annexation of Oak Lawn and Oak Cliff. Perhaps most significantly, aviation became a factor during World War I, when Love Field was established as an aviation training ground, for which the already established Fair Park was also used.

But it was oil that knocked Dallas up a peg. In 1930, an enormous oil field was discovered in East Texas, not too far from Dallas, spawning a dramatic boom. Even as the Great Depression loomed, Dallas quickly became the business and financial center for the oil economy of the entire region, even Oklahoma, and continued its pace of rapid construction. The

money flowed, the building cornerstones were laid, until finally the force of the worldwide downtown, coupled with overproduction (a habit Dallas finds hard to break) overcame the upward momentum. The Depression hit Dallas as hard as any place: 18,000 people lost their jobs by mid-1931.

While the oil boom had helped slightly soften the blow, it took another bit of drama to not just pull Dallas out of the Depression's downward spiral, but also to lay the foundation for the 20th- and 21st-century powerhouse the city was to become. World War II yanked Dallas from its status a mid-level manufacturing center and into a role as a global leader. It began with war-related industries, such as aviation, that pushed industrial employment to 75,000. New attendant industries sprang up, at the rate of five new businesses a day and 13 new manufacturing plants a month by 1949. The modern presence in Dallas of huge, international private aeronautic and defense companies is but one legacy of the war.

Industrial money spawned entrepreneurship, a trend no more noticeable than in the case of Texas Instruments' Jack Kilby. One of the unsung heroes of technology pioneering, Kilby perfected a version of the integrated circuit in 1958. Although the Silicon Valley story overshadows his efforts, and those of other Dallas tech innovators, Kilby and his ilk helped kickstart the beginnings of Dallas leadership in technology and, later, telecom industries.

In 1974, the Dallas-Fort Worth International Airport opened, and again the business climate surged forward. This time, lured by the airport's convenience, plus Dallas's low cost of living, relatively cheap land, and generous perks, corporations by the dozens began moving their headquarters to the area. Today, more than 10,000 corporations make their homes here, including several Fortune 500 companies.

Today, Dallas is the ninth largest city in the country, home to 1,250,000 people, two airports, billions of dollars in commerce, major sports teams, and many legends. It's probably everything the old Arkansas tradesman Bryan could ever dream of. By the way, after shooting a man, years of battling the bottle, and a struggle with mental problems, Bryan died in the state insane asylum. His story is proof that, no matter how much business Dallas does, it will never lose its wild streak.

FORT WORTH

It never really was all that much of a fort.

In May 1849, Major Ripley S. Arnold arrived at the confluence of the Clear Fork and the West Fork of the Trinity River. He had been commissioned with establishing a fort at the far western edge of the boundary between the farthest settlements and Indian country. Sixty miles north of the closest fort, Arnold and his Company F of the U.S. Second Dragoons staked their claim.

Even though it nudged up against Indian country, the area Arnold had chosen had some

> ## DALLAS DEMOGRAPHICS
>
> About 1,300,000 people live in Dallas proper, up from 1,200,000 in 2000. The city contains 444,000 households, 37.2 percent of which are married couples. The median age of Dallasites is 32.1 years.
>
> The racial makeup of the city continues to diversify. While whites are still predominant at 57 percent of the population, the Hispanic population continues to skyrocket, and, at 42 percent of the population, is expected to surpass Caucasian as the majority. Twenty-three percent of Dallas is African-American, 2.7 percent Asian, with a smattering of other races filling out the demographics.

things going for it. The most important attribute was location: It stood atop a high bluff (where the county courthouse stands today), affording a 360-degree view for miles, which allowed the soldiers ample advance knowledge of raiding parties from local Comanche and Wichita tribes.

The real threat at the time, however, wasn't from a raid—it was cholera, which was ravaging tribes and settlers alike. The death rates from the disease had jumped considerably in 1849 as it raged across the West, regardless of age, sex, or status. Cholera, in fact, took the life of Mexican War hero General Jenkins Worth, and thus Arnold named his fort in Worth's honor.

The native tribes never amounted to much of a threat, and you can't battle cholera with guns, so the site proved more of an outpost than a fort. Arnold and his men built quarters, storage, and a few other structures, but as far as fanciful ramparts, turrets, or even fences were concerned, there were none. At the peak of its four-year run, the fort hosted a maximum of about 70 men, housed in neat, whitewashed

© FORT WORTH CVB

The history of the Old West can be re-lived at the Fort Worth Stockyards.

log and wooden houses, with nothing but a single six-pound howitzer and a rope fence to guard them.

The entrepreneurial spirit of North Texas is legendary, and it didn't take long for it to kick in among the pioneers Arnold was sent to protect. Two months after the erection of the fort, George Press Farmer became the area's first sutler, licensed by the government to sell goods to the dragoons.

The Western frontier eventually passed Fort Worth by, rendering it obsolete after a mere four years, at which point the fort was simply abandoned. The growing crop of families that lived nearby, many of whom had subsisted by trading with and selling wares to the company of dragoons, moved into the empty buildings rather quickly.

Slowly but surely, Fort Worth began to grow. By 1854, John Peter Smith had opened

a school with 12 students. Soon after, a flour mill, general store, and department stores cropped up. The town was a main stop for the Butterfield Overland Mail and Southern Pacific Stage Line, both of which extended all the way to California. In 1860, Fort Worth wrested the county seat designation away from neighboring Birdville (through a little ingenuity and a lot of, well, cheating). With close to 6,000 residents (850 of which were slaves), Fort Worth was on its way to becoming a bona fide city.

But, while the Civil War and Reconstruction helped Dallas in their own way, they almost wiped out Fort Worth. The war was hard on the newly established burg; food, money, and supplies grew scarce. The population dropped to below 200.

It was cattle that saved the town. After the war, the price of cattle in other parts of the country neared $30 a head, while in Texas, it was a mere $5. That got folks to move cattle pretty quickly, and, as part of the Chisholm Trail, Fort Worth became the gateway from Texas to the rest of the world as far as cattle were concerned.

The cattle industry equaled a classic boom. Between 1866 and the mid-1880s, Fort Worth saw about 10 million head of cattle herded through its streets, and the town exploded into a bustling burg of barter and commerce. Cattle were bought and sold, cowhands hired, suppliers haggled with, and general stores perused. Cowboys hitting the trail considered Fort Worth their last hurrah before facing weeks of dust and cow butts. Cowboys returning considered it the place to blow their just-acquired pay after months on the trail. Either way, it wasn't just cattle barons, suppliers, and ranch hands who made money here—it was also saloon keepers, gamblers, and ladies of the night. Actually, it was everybody with a hand in the game.

And there was more to be made right around the corner, if only Fort Worth could lure the railroads. And in the late 1870s, it did. The Texas and Pacific began using Fort Worth as its westbound terminus on July 19, 1876, and it could be argued there was no more important day in the history of the city. As other railroads followed—eight of them—they lifted Fort Worth's cattle industry and wholesale industries to the level of national distribution. Once a trailhead, Fort Worth was now a railhead.

The next few decades were a time of huge growth, and things were a-bustle. The town officially incorporated with a mayor and a city council. Weekly newspapers thrived, modern amenities arrived, and churches, schools, and hospitals were established. Fort Worthers lured two rivals—Swift and Company and Armor and Company—to anchor the burgeoning meatpacking industry. Combined with the stockyard and shipping facilities already in place on the north side of town, Fort Worth cemented its place as the center of all aspects of the cattle industry.

Three things changed all that. First, technological and ranching innovations slowly eroded the need for the type of centralized cattle processing/shipping Fort Worth had always thrived on. Second, World Wars I and II foisted great changes on Fort Worth, changes that transformed the city forever. With the wars came the aviation and defense industries, which have never left. American Airlines makes its home here, as does Lockheed Martin (formerly General Dynamics)—two enormous entities that play a great role in the local and regional economy.

The third change was oil. The big oil find in the late 1920s just east of the metroplex shifted the boom from cattle pens to oil rigs. Fort Worth was soaking in oil money.

Nowadays, cattle are still bought and sold in the old Stockyards Exchange Building—via satellite. True to form, Fort Worth has spawned new industries and brought new ones in, in addition to maintaining its deep roots in defense and aviation.

Government

DALLAS

Okay, okay, so former president George W. Bush lives in Dallas, but that doesn't make the entire town Republican, does it? Seriously, even though it exists in one of the reddest states in the Union, and sits at the nexus of the conservative Midwest and the conservative South, Dallas is not as politically right as one might think. In fact, as the city's demographics shift, Dallas proper is starting to head into downright blue.

The 2004 presidential election, 2006 midterm elections, and 2008 presidential election all signaled a potential sea change. In Dallas County in 2004, Democratic presidential candidate John Kerry lost to Republican George W. Bush by just 10,000 votes, or a little over one percentage point. Dallas as a city voted overwhelmingly for Kerry, with 57 percent of votes. The same year saw Hispanic and open lesbian Lupe Valdez elected sheriff.

The 2006 election, though reestablishing Republican holds on state and federal representation, saw huge Democratic gains in the city of Dallas, including the election of a Democrat district attorney and the ousting of scores of Republican judges—41 of 42 seats went to Democrats.

While Dallas mayoral races are officially nonpartisan, the political party leanings of the candidates are always well known, making the elections de facto partisan competitions. In 2006, Republican Tom Leppert defied the Democratic trend by defeating openly gay democrat Ed Oakley (had Oakley won, he would have been the first openly gay mayor of a major city in the U.S.). Leppert's victory was a bit of an anomaly: The past two mayors had been Dallas's first African-American mayor, Democrat Ron Kirk, and the rather liberal Democrat Laura Miller, former editor of the left-leaning alt-weekly the *Dallas Observer*.

In 2008, 57 percent of city voters in Dallas voted for Democrat Barack Obama for president. The margin was much closer in Dallas County as a whole, as it was in 2004, but in both cases the entire county still went for the Democratic candidate. The Dallas city/county dichotomy speaks to the dispersal of political parties in the area as a whole, as areas closer to the city center vote more Democratic, while the suburbs lean much more toward Republican.

FORT WORTH

Even though it's more laid-back and centered around arts and culture than Dallas, Fort Worth is way more conservative than the big city to the east. Folks here tend to vote to the right. In the past three presidential elections, Tarrant County voters have pulled the lever for the Republican candidate in overwhelming numbers. Fort Worth is also home to Congressman Pete Geren, a rare Fort Worth Democrat, who served as Secretary of the Army under George W. Bush and Barack Obama. Fort Worth's other famous Dem, Jim Wright, served as the 56th Speaker of the House during the 1980s.

ESSENTIALS

Getting There and Around

BY AIR

As the name implies, Dallas-Fort Worth International Airport, one of the biggest airports in the world, is the main air hub for both towns. DFW Airport is pretty much equidistant between the two towns. Put shortly, this is a major airport, the third busiest in the world, with almost every major carrier in service.

The airport is colossal: If you've never been there, give yourself plenty of time to do what you need to to do. There are five terminals, and while the walk from parking to terminal is minimal by design, getting from gate to gate,

much less terminal to terminal, can be a trek. Most of the terminals are designed in semi-circles, and there are no shortcuts in between, so walking from end to end is particularly time-consuming. The Skyline people mover, fortunately, links the terminals efficiently.

Public transportation options to and from the airport are few. The Trinity Railway Express train that runs between Dallas and Fort Worth provides service to and from both towns, but not late or on Sundays or holidays. Keep in mind that if you use the TRE, you will have to take the free shuttle bus from the

TRE airport station into your terminal, and this can take awhile, so, again, it's best to give yourself extra time. You might also try one of the many private shuttle companies that provide door-to-door service.

Dallas' Love Field is the second major airport in the area. Much smaller than DFW and servicing mainly Southwest Airlines' regional flights, the airport is easily navigable and quite convenient to many parts of central Dallas. There is no public transportation in and out of the airport.

BY TRAIN

Amtrak's Heartland Flyer and Texas Eagle lines service both Dallas and Fort Worth. Dallas' Amtrak station is downtown's Union Station (the main station for DART and the TRE as well), at 400 S. Houston St. The Fort Worth station is at 1001 Jones St., downtown Fort Worth.

BY CAR

Dallas and Fort Worth share Interstates 35 (north-south) and 30 (east-west), which run perpendicular to each other. It can get a bit confusing: I-35 splits north of the metroplex, in Denton, into East I-35 and West I-35. East I-35 goes through Dallas, West I-35 through Fort Worth, until the two rejoin south of town in Hillsboro, Texas. Interstate 30, which runs all the up through the Midwest to Minnesota, connects Dallas and Fort Worth (the area of I-30 between the two towns is called the Tom Landry Highway). Interstate 45 doesn't run through Fort Worth, but connects Dallas and Houston.

Dallas is surrounded by Loop 12, parts of which are also called Northwest Highway. Interstate 20 skirts to the south of each town, looping around Fort Worth in a segment called Loop 820. North Dallas is looped by Interstate 635, which ends at Highway 121. All of these highways are key access points into and out of the metroplex.

BY BUS

Dallas and Fort Worth both are serviced by the Greyhound bus system. Dallas' station is downtown (205 S. Lamar St., within walking distance of the public transportation/Amtrak hub Union Station. Fort Worth's station is at 1001 Jones St., downtown.

PUBLIC TRANSPORTATION

Though the light rail continues to expand and things continue to improve, don't expect much when it comes to public transportation. One of the few helpful modes of transport is the Trinity Rail Express that takes commuters between Dallas and Fort Worth, following more or less the route of Interstate 20. The trains are clean and quick, with free wi-fi and room for bikes. Despite several mid-city stops, the train ride only takes an hour, about the same it would take to drive. The end of the line in both towns, unfortunately, is downtown, although the Dallas Union Station terminal connects you with the Dallas Area Rapid Transit light rail and the final Fort Worth stop lands you at a city bus terminus.

Speaking of that light rail: The Dallas version, known as DART (Dallas Area Rapid Transit) doesn't cover the most expansive area in the world, but many expansions are scheduled. In the meantime, the light rail stops, both on the north-south line and the east-west line, are few and far between meant more for commuters than as a means to transport riders a few blocks one way or the other in the central part of the city.

Conduct and Customs

ALCOHOL

DFW likes to drink, to be sure, but of course the same liquor laws apply to the area as do the rest of the United States. Bars must stop serving alcohol at 2 a.m., and most close at the same time, though some of the more refined establishments close earlier-call ahead and find out if you're not sure. A few dance clubs will stop serving booze at that time and stay open and play music until 4 a.m. for those still wanting to boogie.

While Dallas and Fort Worth are in counties that allow the sale of booze, some of the surrounding counties still are technically "dry" counties, which means alcohol purchase there is restricted. This means you can't buy beer, wine, or alcohol within county lines unless it's at a restaurant or "club" (a bar, usually), where you have to buy a membership. Buying a membership entails filling out a card with your name and address and paying a minimal fee, though most places simply waive the fee or pay it for you. It's less of a hassle than it sounds.

Otherwise, if you need a six-pack of Lone Star or a bottle of whiskey, you have to cross the county line to find a liquor store, and there are often several just across the line.

SMOKING

Smoking isn't as frowned upon in DFW as in some other parts of the country, but both Dallas and Fort Worth-and many suburbs and mid-cities-have smoking laws banning smoking in restaurants, clubs, bars, and pretty much every public establishment. Many places have patios or close-by outdoor areas where smoking is allowed.

MANNERS

Texans are a strange mix of friendly and reserved. Strangers and service people will readily call you "hon" or some other term of endearment, but this is not the kind of culture where, say, sharing a table at a cafe with a stranger is common-communal tables at restaurants, for instance, often remain empty, even if the place is packed.

Tips for Travelers

BUSINESS TRAVELERS

Business travelers make up a large amount of the folks who visit the DFW area. Trade shows, meetings, and conventions take up pretty much every month of the year. For that reason, hotels are often booked well in advance, and when large conventions (such as the Mary Kay convention, held every summer) are in town, it can be difficult to find accommodations, especially

downtown. The city is currently planning a new convention center and giant hotel to go along with it, which will help ease the congestion, but even then, make sure you make reservations as early as possible—especially if you want the best available rates. The good news is, most hotels cater to business travelers, so on-site business centers with fax machines, computers, and internet access are common, and desk clerks and concierges are more familiar than usual with information about local outposts for FedEx, Kinkos, and other common companies used by businesspeople.

INTERNATIONAL TRAVELERS

Backpackers and those on a budget should know beforehand that there is a definite dearth of hostels and cheap lodging to be found in the metroplex. Word of mouth and Craigslist are perhaps the best way to locate a place to lay your head.

If that's not a concern, DFW is definitely a friendly place for international visitors, but perhaps not the most sophisticated in terms of other languages. Spanish is by far the most common second language spoken here (it's a pretty common first language as well), and the Latino population has filled the area with lots of culture that will feel like home to many Latinos. In addition, Dallas is home to the consulates of Peru and Mexico, as well as Thailand and Canada. Currency exchange is available at Dallas-Fort Worth Airport and at many places in the area —try the **American Express Center** (8317 Preston Center Plaza, 214/363-0214) or one of the many **Travelex Currency Services** (www.travelex.com). Fort Worth and the two cities' greater areas are more sparse, so if that's where you're headed, best to exchange at the airport.

WOMEN TRAVELING ALONE

While it's always advisable for a woman traveling by herself to keep an eye out for potentially dangerous situations, Dallas requires a little extra precaution. Dallas' rape statistics are higher than the national average, and it's not advisable to walk around most neighborhoods alone at night. While your chances of getting

CRIME IN DFW

An honest assessment of Dallas-Fort Worth's crime situation suggests a little extra caution is advisable. Dallas, especially, has a crime problem. While violent crimes such as rape and assault are more common here than elsewhere, you're more likely to suffer a property crime. Take special care to remove any valuables from your car and lock it, even if you are only going to be gone from it for a few minutes.

into a scrape are still low, it's best to stay on the safe side. Also, women who visit nightspots alone might find themselves consistently hit on, depending on the bar or club. Fort Worth is a little better, but rape averages here also exceed national rates. Erring on the side of caution is always recommended, especially in the area around the Stockyards.

SENIOR TRAVELERS

Day or night, the heat of North Texas summers (and even the months surrounding them) can be brutal, even dangerous—especially for seniors. If you are a senior visiting the area between May and September, make sure your accommodations have adequate air conditioning, and check to make sure any tours or activities you undertake involve plenty of shade.

The Dallas Area Rapid Transit offers senior discounts, but the catch is it requires a DART photo ID, which of course is not very expedient for travelers. If you have a Medicare card, it is also good for a discount.

TRAVELERS WITH DISABILITIES

Most of the DFW area is relatively easy to navigate for those with a special challenge.

However, some of the older parts of both towns can be difficult. The crowds combined with the old wooden sidewalks in Fort Worth's Stockyard area may present some difficulties, and similarly some of the sidewalk infrastructure is either narrow or crumbling (especially in Deep Ellum). You'll be hard-pressed in either town to find a hotel that is not ADA-compliant.

All Dallas Area Rapid Transit buses and light rail trains are required to comply with ADA standards, which they do. DART also offers a discount to non-paratransit riders with disabilities, and free fare for paratransit riders, but unfortunately, both require a DART reduced fare photo identification card—not very convenient for visitors. However, Medicare card holders also receive a discount, sans DART ID.

All wheelchairs must be secured on buses, as per ADA standards, and each DART bus has two securement locations. Service animals are allowed on all DART transportation.

TRAVELING WITH CHILDREN

With so many suburbs and families, you'll find the metroplex beyond kid-friendly, and just about every sight is kid-appropriate. Even usual adult fare like art museums and historical sites make children's outreach a priority (the Modern Art Museum in Fort Worth especially). Similarly, the sports teams here, both major- and minor-league, incorporate a number of family deals into their promotions (the all-you-can-eat seats and family pack seats at the Texas Rangers Ballpark in Arlington prove especially good deals). Still, the sprawl of the area can take its toll on the little ones—it's advisable to take travel time and legwork into account.

GAY AND LESBIAN TRAVELERS

Despite its rep as a stronghold of conservative values, Dallas-Fort Worth actually is a pretty comfortable place for GLBT travelers. Fort Worth has no designated "gayborhood" and few gay bars, but its culture, climate, and charm have attracted many gay and lesbian couples. The scene here is quieter, more family-oriented, and more woven into the fabric of the city. While Fort Worth may be a touch more conservative than Dallas, the town's pioneer roots promote a sort of "live and let live" mentality.

Dallas GLBT scene is more rowdy and visible. For decades, the scene here revolved around a row of bars, shops, and coffeehouses at the crossroads of Cedar Springs and Oak Lawn Avenues, known as "the strip" or "the gayborhood." Many GLBT-oriented businesses still stand there and are going strong, and the strip is still considered the epicenter of queer life in Dallas. This is where most folks head on out for happy hours, weekend revelry, the Pride parade (held in September here), and the (in)famous Halloween parade. For years, this also was the neighborhood with the highest concentration of GLBT homeowners and renters.

However, as in many cities, the need for a physical community has waned, as GLBT Dallasites have landed in increasing numbers in every neighborhood. Bishop Arts, Uptown, and Downtown are all popular destinations, for instance. Dallas has long been a destination for queer travelers, especially men, and the expansion of this already very visible community has only increased its cachet.

While all of North Texas continues to trend Democrat and more liberal, it is by no means a hotbed for the type of activism and radical (some would say) politics that abound in other places like San Francisco, Portland, New York, and Austin, so travelers who identify more on that side of things might be disappointed, although to be sure, the local community is friendly and welcoming.

It's also worth noting that you might find some of the smaller towns and rural areas surrounding DFW less welcoming toward queer travelers. In all honesty, a same-sex couple holding hands might get a stare or perhaps a muttered comment directed their way, though such behavior is the exception, not the rule.

Communications and Media

PHONES AND AREA CODES

Denizens of central Dallas use the city's original area code, 214. Further north it switches to 972 and other areas have switched to 469, though with the common use of cell phones, the geographical designations mean less and less. Fort Worth's original area code is 817, and the city just recently was forced to a second area code, 682.

INTERNET SERVICES

DFW and its environs, like any metropolitan locale, present multiple choices when it comes to internet service providers. Neither city leads the pack when it comes to providing free public wi-fi, though it's useful to know that all highway rest areas in Texas have free wi-fi. If you have a laptop, the Dallas Public Library also has free wireless connections that don't require a password, though use of the Library's communal computers requires a library card. Fort Worth Public libraries also provide computers with Internet access as well as wireless, but both require a library card.

MAIL SERVICES

There are around 40 USPS offices in Dallas, including a downtown office near City Hall. Most are open 8 or 8:30 a.m. to 5 p.m., weekdays, but the DFW turnpike location has extended hours, even on weekends. Fort Worth's downtown location is a gorgeous, imposing historic building on E. Lancaster Avenue. There are about 25 offices in the city.

NEWSPAPERS AND PERIODICALS

Dallas is a huge media market—the fifth largest in the country, to be exact. Surprisingly, the city is only served by one daily newspaper, the *Dallas Morning News*, owned by the A.H. Belo Corporation. A.H. Belo also owns the local Spanish-language daily, *Al Dia* and the free paper *Quick*, which provides abbreviated news and daily entertainment coverage geared at the younger set. The Morning News was once considered a top paper in the country, winning several Pulitzer Prizes, though the last one it received for reporting came in 1994 (the two most recent, in 2004 and 2006, were for photography). Though the entertainment section can be hit or miss, the sports section provides excellent coverage of the local professional, semi-pro, and even high school teams., as well as national sports news.

The alternative weekly *Dallas Observer* has been an institution since its inception, though it, like many weeklies across the country, has been brought into the fold of the Village Voice/New Times Media chain. Though many locals revel in criticizing the *Observer,* especially now that a large corporation owns it, it's still the go-to for cheeky sports, entertainment, and political news, and provides a lefty counterpunch to the *Morning News'* conservative bent (rare is the liberal who skips the *Observer*'s Jim Schutze's feisty, smart city politics column), and is still very much a player in local media. Former Observer editor Laura Miller, for instance, served as Dallas' mayor from 2002-2007.

The weekly *Dallas Voice* is Dallas' only GLBT paper, and it's a good one. The paper covers politics, culture, entertainment, and other issues with a queer slant, and it's been known to scoop both the *Morning News* and the *Observer,* despite fewer resources.

D Magazine's able writers deftly combine service-y type coverage with excellent investigative and culture pieces, all of which cover the city.

The weekday circulation of Fort Worth's only daily, the *Fort Worth Star Telegram,* tops 200,000. Founded by local legend Amon G. Carter and now owned by McClatchy, the "Startlegram," as some call it, caters mainly to the western half of the metroplex, including Fort Worth, Arlington, and even a bit of western Grand Prairie. The paper, like most nowadays, continues to endure financial struggles and recently announced it would be sharing some aspects of sports coverage with the *Dallas Morning News.* The Star-Telegram now takes the Texas Rangers coverage responsibilities, while the DMN takes on the Dallas Mavericks and Dallas Stars. Both papers cover the Dallas Cowboys individually.

RADIO AND TELEVISION

Two airwave media companies stand out in Dallas: The Belo Corporation is a spinoff of the A.H. Belo Corporation and owns the local ABC affiliate WFAA and the Texas-wide cable news channel TXCN, and manages a local independently-owned station, KFWD. The second is Univision Radio, a Spanish-language radio company—the eighth largest radio company in the country and the largest in the nation—owned by the Univision television corporation. Though the Univision mothership is in Los Angeles, the Univision Radio company is headquartered in Dallas.

Most television and radio stations provide service for both Dallas and Fort Worth. The major television affiliates for DFW are WFAA KDFW (FOX), KXAS (NBC), KTVT (CBS), KERA (PBS), KUVN (UNI).

Shared stations include:

- KMQX 88.5 FM and KVRK 98.7 FM The Power—Christian rock
- KZPS 92.5 FM Lone Star 92.5—classic rock
- KDBN 93.3 FM The Bone—classic rock
- KFWR 95.9 FM The Ranch—authentic country, Texas country, alt-country
- KSCS 96.3 FM—country
- KEGL 97.1 FM The Eagle—rock, Top 40
- KBFB 97.9 FM The Beat—hip-hop
- KLUV 98.7 FM K-Luv—oldies
- KPLX 99.5FM The Wolf—country
- KJKK 100.3 Jack FM—rock, classic rock, Top 40
- KWRD 100.Y FM The Word—Christian talk radio
- WRR 101.1 FM—classical
- KDGE 102.1 The Edge—alternative rock
- KDMX 102.9 FM Mix 102.9—Top 40
- KESN 103.3 FM ESPN radio—sports talk

- KVIL 103.7 FM Lite FM—adult contemporary
- KRNB 105.7 FM—contemporary R&B
- KHKS 106.1 FM Kiss FM—Top 40
- CASA 106.7 FM La Casa—Latin pop
- KOAI 107.5 FM The Oasis—smooth jazz
- KESS 107.8 FM—Latin
- KMKI 620 AM Radio Disney—children's radio
- WBAP 820 AM Newstalk 820—news/talk radio
- KRLD 1080 AM—news
- KFXR 1190 AM Fox Sports Radio—sports

Notable stations include:

- KNTU 88.1 FM—The University of North Texas' station delivers top-notch jazz.
- KNON 89.3 FM—Known as "the voice of the people," KNON is supported by listeners and sponsorships from small local business. The eclectic blend of talk and music programming is very popular.
- KERA 90.1—The local National Public Radio affiliate features a mix of local shows and favorites like "All Things Considered" and "This American Life."
- KTCK AM The Ticket—This irreverent local sports talk radio station is full of personality.

RESOURCES
Suggested Reading

TEXAS

Friedman, Kinky. *Kinky Friedman's Guide to Texas Etiquette.* Cliff Street Books, 2001. Written by the man whose Texas gubernatorial campaign slogan was "Why Not?," this guide will tell you everything you need to know about Texans and their ways. Friedman's famous for his mystery novels, humorous essays, and randy songs (his band is known as Kinky Friedman and the Texas Jewboys), and his unique humor runs throughout chapters like "Prisoner of War Camps in Texas," "Texas is the Only State," and "Big Hair For Jesus."

Selcer, Richard. *Legendary Watering Holes: The Saloons that Made Texas Famous.* Texas A&M Press 2004. Richard Selcer's final chapter in this book covers the legendary Fort Worth drinking spot, the White Elephant, which is still open today in the Stockyards. The excellent chapter doesn't just touch upon the lore and legends surrounding the saloon; it also provides a colorful and fascinating context, up to and including the history of the name "White Elephant," and the social and racial implications of Fort Worth's drinking culture back in the town's early days. A fascinating read.

DALLAS AND FORT WORTH

Hill, Patricia Everidge. *Dallas: The Making of a Modern City.* University of Texas Press 1996. Even though its title suggests yet another dry recounting that could have been written by the chamber of commerce, Everidge Hill's book is actually a fascinating alternative history of Dallas. Rejecting the common notion that Dallas has always been about commerce, Hill's well-researched thesis is that much of the city's history is on more communal, progressive, and sometimes even radical, grounds.

Roark, Carol. *Fort Worth: Then & Now.* TCU Press 2001; Contemporary photographs by Rodger Mallison and *Fort Worth's Legendary Landmarks.* TCU Press 1995; Photographs by Byrd Williams. Both of these books benefit from the extraordinary knowledge and resources of local expert Carol Roark, who provides succinct and educational context for all the photos. *Then & Now* is especially edifying, as photographer Roger Mallison reproduces the angles, vantage points, and perspectives of pre-existing old photographs of Fort Worth as best as possible, allowing the reader to study the details of their juxtaposition. *Fort Worth's Legendary Landmarks* is more text-heavy.

Internet Resources

Al Dia
www.aldiatx.com
The web version of Al Dia, DFW's main Spanish language newspaper, features the latest local news (along with national), as well as lots of sports stories-especially los Vaqueros de Dallas.

Art&Seek
www.kera.org/blogs/culture
The local PBS affiliate's arts blog stays on top of all sorts of arts and culture events, from underground art to huge opera extravaganzas.

Dallas Food
www.dallasfood.org
Less a Twitter-paced news blog and more a thoughtful look at dining, Dallas Food tends to follow along themes (a series of entries on Jefferson Avenue taquerias and tortas spots being a particularly good one). The blog also features close-up, large photos of meals, so you can see what looks delectable to you.

Dallas Morning News
www.dallasnews.com
It's got that annoying thing where you have to register to use the site (though it's free), but the Dallas Morning News blog will provide visitors with plenty of local news, sports, and entertainment info. The GuideLive section is notably useful, especially the food section, which contains top 20 lists for tons of different types of cuisine, price ranges, and locales, along with detailed reviews. The site also runs several blogs covering everything from

sports to shopping (check the latter often for updated info on sales and specials).

Dallas Observer
www.dallasobserver.com
The site for Dallas' weekly alternative newspaper is much improved over the past few years, and now is a great resource for the latest entertainment news and listings, along with music, food, and news blogs.

Dallas Voice
www.dallasvoice.com
The Dallas Voice is Dallas' only GLBT newspaper, and the web site provides plenty of updated info on local queer goings-on. Check the Instant Tea blog for the absolute latest.

D Magazine
www.dmagazine.com
Dallas' glossy mag lists toward the upscale/ high society side of things, although some of the younger members of the staff still have a finger on Big D's more fast-paced pulse. D's web site offers Best Of Dallas lists out the ying-yang. There are the usual helpful ones, such as Best Margaritas, Best Tacos, etc., but also the unexpected, such as Best Dentist and Best Contractor.

Downtown Fort Worth, Inc.
http://www.dfwi.org/home.aspx
Easy to use and well organized, the Downtown Fort Worth, Inc. web site contains basic info about living, working, and playing downtown. The handy lists of hotels,

restaurants, and entertainment options, and other services include phone numbers, street addresses, web addresses, and other vitals.

Find Your Way in Fort Worth
www.fortworthparking.com
Parking is much less of a hassle in Cowtown than it is in other places, mainly because the city provides a passel of free parking in popular areas like downtown and the Stockyards. This site provides interactive maps and directions that are easy to use and indispensably helpful.

FW Weekly
www.fwweekly.com
The Web version of Fort Worth's alternative paper provides listings and weekly picks with info on Cowtown arts and culture. If you're looking for a good band or the best place to find drink specials, the site is a good place to start.

FortWorthStockyards.org
www.fortworthstockyards.org
This site is a perfect resource for all things Stockyards.

Pegasus News
www.pegasusnews.com
One of the most comprehensive and easiest to use blogs ever, Pegasus News is an excellent way to get to know Dallas. The site utilizes its own staff to generate original local news, culture, and sports reports as well as compiling reports from other local sites and posting user-generated content. The result: hyperlocal, hyper-accurate, info about just about everything in the metroplex. Dallas newbies will especially benefit from the search mechanisms that allow users to pinpoint food, events, music, entertainment, and attractions according to location and genre. The entertainment listings might just be the most comprehensive and An absolutely vital tool for anyone in DFW, whether as a visitor or a local.

Visit Dallas
www.visitdallas.com
While it's a touch on the bland Chamber of Commerce-y side (you won't find tips about the latest underground dance club here), this site is super-helpful when it comes to providing tourist information about sites, hotels, neighborhoods, sports, recreation, and just about everything else. There's not much in the way of calendars or picks, but the general information is more than enough to get travelers-be they individuals or families-plenty of background and information.

West & Clear
http://westandclear.com
West and Clear is a discerning blog that covers everything Cowtown, from culture to politics. It's especially helpful for choosing arts and entertainment options.

We Shot JR
www.weshotjr.com
It's as snarky and insider-y as they come, but We Shot JR knows the ins and outs of the North Texas scene, especially that of the underground and Denton variety. If you're a fan of indie rock, or even quasi-indie rock, of the type that national music site Pitchfork covers, We Shot JR should be your portal into the best music this area has to offer.

What We're Doin'
www.whatweredoin.com

What We're Doin' is geared pretty specifically toward African-Americans who are past the bar-hopping stage but who still enjoy a vibrant social scene, but really it's got something for everybody (except, perhaps, the bar-hoppers). The site provides reviews, previews and information on all sorts of arts and culture and fetes about town, along with an informed "picks" section. Those with refined tastes will find WWD a helpful guide to Dallas' African-American social scene, from book signings to wine tastings.

Index

Restaurants Index

Nightlife Index

Shops Index

Hotels

MAP SYMBOLS

▦	Expressway	【	Highlight	✗	Airfield	♩	Golf Course
▦	Primary Road	○	City/Town	✈	Airport	P	Parking Area
▦	Secondary Road	◉	State Capital	▲	Mountain	▲	Archaeological Site
▪ ▪ ▪ ▪	Unpaved Road	⊛	National Capital	✛	Unique Natural Feature	⋏	Church
- - - -	Trail	★	Point of Interest			⛽	Gas Station
··········	Ferry	•	Accommodation	⟋	Waterfall	⬤	Glacier
▬ ▬ ▬	Railroad	▼	Restaurant/Bar	⚑	Park	▨	Mangrove
▦	Pedestrian Walkway	▪	Other Location	⊟	Trailhead	▨	Reef
▦	Stairs	⋏	Campground	⤢	Skiing Area	▨	Swamp

CONVERSION TABLES

°C = (°F – 32) / 1.8
°F = (°C x 1.8) + 32
1 inch = 2.54 centimeters (cm)
1 foot = 0.304 meters (m)
1 yard = 0.914 meters
1 mile = 1.6093 kilometers (km)
1 km = 0.6214 miles
1 fathom = 1.8288 m
1 chain = 20.1168 m
1 furlong = 201.168 m
1 acre = 0.4047 hectares
1 sq km = 100 hectares
1 sq mile = 2.59 square km
1 ounce = 28.35 grams
1 pound = 0.4536 kilograms
1 short ton = 0.90718 metric ton
1 short ton = 2,000 pounds
1 long ton = 1.016 metric tons
1 long ton = 2,240 pounds
1 metric ton = 1,000 kilograms
1 quart = 0.94635 liters
1 US gallon = 3.7854 liters
1 Imperial gallon = 4.5459 liters
1 nautical mile = 1.852 km

°FAHRENHEIT	°CELSIUS	
230	110	
220	100	WATER BOILS
210		
200	90	
190		
180	80	
170		
160	70	
150		
140	60	
130		
120	50	
110		
100	40	
90		
80	30	
70		
60	20	
50		
40	10	
30	0	WATER FREEZES
20		
10	-10	
0		
-10	-20	
-20	-30	
-30		
-40	-40	

INCH 0 1 2 3 4

CM 0 1 2 3 4 5 6 7 8 9 10